Teacher Education

and the

New Profession

of

Teaching

Martin Haberman

T.M. Stinnett

McCutchan Publishing Corporation
2526 Grove Street
Berkeley, California 94704

to Joseph Haberman

Contents

1

Elements
of the
New Profession

Beginning about 1950, the profiles of a new profession of teaching in the United States began to emerge. This presaged an eventual change in the format and processes of teacher education. As a matter of fact, until the mid-1960s teacher education and conditions of teaching in the public schools diverged so widely that there were charges that teacher education institutions no longer served the needs of teachers but were status hunting to improve their images with the prestigious universities and graduate schools. One of the great tasks of the 1970s is for teacher education to regain its former prestigious position as the predominant servant of the teaching profession.

This is not to say that the values, procedures, and standards of the liberal arts colleges and graduate schools are invalid. Valid as they are, however, they should not necessarily be binding on a professional school. The reason for this is quite simple. The physical and social science fields have as their primary objectives the discovery and teaching of new knowledge. There are certain well-defined standards of research as well as traditions of college teaching that are germane to these basic studies.

On the other hand, a professional school exists to take basic new knowledge and process and make it available for practical use by members of the profession. It does not follow that the procedures, rules, and standards used in the searching out of new knowledge will apply to the conversion of new knowledge for use in the profession. Thus, the professional school's client is the professional, not the student in the liberal arts college. The two populations intermingle at many points, and there is great danger that the institutions that should serve the profession will ignore this responsibility to the detriment of the practicing clientele. The teacher education institution's prime task is to process new knowledge in forms that practitioners can use in the field, not in forms that embellish the meritocratic

1

concepts of the liberal arts college. Those concepts may be of little use, in preparing teachers of the disadvantaged, for example, but their influence is easily gauged by considering how many programs have brought funds into universities with no carry-overs into practice.

The great task of teacher education in the 1970s is to draw closer to the newly emerging profession of teaching, to close the gap between standards of university performance per se and the performance of teacher education graduates in their subsequent teaching.

The Means of Change

Collective Negotiation

In 1946 the *Norwalk Teachers' Association* case heralded the development of a great schism between the teaching profession as it existed until about 1950 and the new profession that emerged in the 1950s and 1960s. This case was to introduce the principle of professional negotiation in relationships between the teaching staff and the school board. It began with a strike of the Norwalk Teachers Association in 1946 and was not decided by the courts until 1951. The issues involved were the rights of teachers to strike and to engage in collective negotiation with the school board regarding salaries and working conditions. The courts held that since teachers are public employees, the strike was illegal, but the school board did have the legal right to negotiate with the teachers. This decision became the basis for a procedure developed in Connecticut and designated "cooperative determination." This was the forerunner of what has come to be known as professional negotiation or, in union parlance, collective bargaining.

By 1971 more than half the classroom teachers of the nation were under professional negotiation agreements. Laws providing for collective negotiation for teachers existed in twenty-six states. And professional negotiation as a process existed in some form in all but a handful of states; with or without a specific grant of authority of state enactments, the principle has become almost universally accepted. This development forecast a new way of life for teachers, and in the future no teacher education program can ignore the process and fail to provide thorough instruction in it.

Prior to this development, teachers were expected to be passive and quiet. They were expected to accept whatever terms of employment school boards formulated and extended to them. With the adoption of the negotiation process, teachers' groups changed from passive compliance to somewhat aggressive action. The means used to enforce their demands were the application of professional sanctions and the strike. To date there have been more than 600 teacher strikes; in some years as many as 160 teacher strikes have occurred.

Only in recent years—since about 1965—has the majority of teachers in the United States been willing to embrace the strike as a bargaining weapon. A decade ago, in polls conducted by NEA a solid majority were opposed to the use of the strike. Recent polls indicate a reversal of this attitude. Generally, teachers answer "Yes, under certain circumstances," when asked if they would strike. This change of attitude was facing up to real forces and events in American life. The trend of some recent state legislation is toward removing absolute prohibitions against strikes by public employees but prescribing every possible recourse for avoiding strikes and authorizing walk outs only as a last resort.

A review of the conditions and events that led to the Norwalk strike will help to explain the origin of the new profession of teaching. Before the Norwalk strike, there had been about 20 teacher strikes in the 60-year period between 1880 and 1940. There were 110 such strikes between 1940 and 1962, and there have been over 600 teacher strikes in all. Before the strike there had been only three strikes in the 1940s, but after it there were 10 strikes in the remainder of the decade.

What happened? In 1946 there still were no states that sanctioned strikes by teachers. Since these strikes were illegal, there must have been extreme provocation for the teachers' actions. Generally, the provocation was the unbearable deterioration of teaching conditions during World War II.

During the war, there had been a staggering turnover in the teaching staff of the country. There were several reasons for this huge turnover. Military service was one, but the chief reason was migration from teaching into higher paying defense jobs. One estimate is that between 1939 and 1945 over 600,000 entered and left teaching. Pay scales in teaching were virtually frozen, because new taxes almost always went into the war effort. Despite this neglect, many devoted teachers stayed on the job in the hope that at the war's end the low salary situation would be corrected. But this did not happen. The demand for consumer goods after wartime shortages created an industrial boom; wages in industry skyrocketed, but teachers' salaries were still frozen. Again, thousands of teachers left their profession and sought increased pay in industry, but thousands of devoted teachers stayed on the job, feeling that their neglect was only a temporary result of the war. In Norwalk and a few other places, however, the teachers finally tired of the old rejoinder from the board that "we do not have the money to raise salaries" and sought to negotiate a settlement of their grievances against the board. The board responded that it had no legal authority to negotiate with the teachers. Desperate and with no other recourse, the teachers walked out and stayed on strike for nine days, during which an agreement was entered into with the board. This and a scattering of other teacher strikes shocked people everywhere, but it should have been clear that the Norwalk strike was a forerunner of a new ethic for teachers.

In 1951 when the state courts ruled that strikes were illegal but negotiation was not, the stage was set for more aggressive action. In Connecticut alone approximately 65 school districts entered into cooperative determination agreements with their teachers during the 1950s. The road to professional negotiations was finally open, and teachers' associations moved to secure specific legislation giving them the right to organize and negotiate salary and working conditions.

As early as 1947, the NEA Executive Committee had adopted a resolution calling attention to the emerging new posture of teachers. The resolution read,

Group action is essential today. The former practice where teachers individually bargained with the superintendent of schools or the board of education for salaries is largely past. For years there has been a steady movement in the direction of salary schedules applying to all teachers. In the present crisis it is especially important that there be professional negotiation on salary proposals. A salary committee composed of capable and trusted members of the group is necessary. This committee should be chosen by the entire teaching group and should have the authority to represent and act for the local educational association.[1]

This resolution was virtually ignored by boards and administrators. Either they did not believe that this was the wave of the future or they did not want to be bothered with its development. This was a perfectly natural and logical position; nobody cheerfully and willingly surrenders power. Thus, teachers had to take the initiative in bringing the concerted approach into being.

In 1957, after a series of "cooperative determination" agreements had been adopted in Connecticut, the secretaries of state education associations considered a resolution calling for the principles of professional negotiation, but the 1960 NEA Representative Assembly voted down a similar resolution. In 1962, however, the NEA Representative Assembly finally did enact such a resolution. Its essence was:

The National Education Association insists on the right of professional associations, through democratically selected representatives using professional channels, to participate with boards of education in the determination of policies of common concern, including salary and other conditions of professional service. . . . The seeking of consensus and mutual agreement on a professional basis should preclude the arbitrary exercise of unilateral authority by boards of education and the use of the strike by teachers. . . .

In that resolution, the NEA leaned over backwards to avoid the labor-management concept in negotiations with the board of education. It also advocated the seeking of legislation establishing the principles of professional negotiation.

In its 1962 convention the NEA adopted professional sanctions as the companion piece of professional negotiation, in effect eschewing the strike as a weapon of enforcement. Critics of this action quickly equated sanctions and strikes, although there were quite different approaches and implications. As was to be expected, both the American Association of School Administrators and the National School Board Association aggressively opposed both these resolutions.

In the beginning of the negotiation movement school boards were adamantly opposed to each new development. In 1963, at their first annual meeting after passage of the 1962 NEA resolution, NSBA adopted the following resolution:

The efforts of teacher unions to obtain collective bargaining rights and the activities and programs of professional teacher organizations calling for professional negotiations and sanctions will have significant effect upon the operation of our public schools in the years ahead. The National School Boards Association is opposed to sanctions, boycotts, strikes, or mandated mediation against school districts and does not consider them to be proper remedies for use in problem situations. The authority of the board of education is established by law and this authority may not be delegated to others. . . .[2]

The reaction of the school administrators' association to the professional negotiation proposal was much more conciliatory:

We believe there are common goals and interests among teachers, school boards, and administrators. We further believe that the development of school policies and programs and the solution of school problems can best be accomplished by these groups working in unison and with respect for the unique roles of each.

Efforts to superimpose a pattern of staff relations borrowed from another segment of society, whether through legislative fiat or staff election, will do major harm to the basic unity of our profession and should be resisted vigorously. We therefore support the concept that shared responsibility for policy development is a professional concept requiring a uniquely professional approach.[3]

But the growing turmoil in teaching, especially in the larger cities, forced revisions of both the NEA resolution and resolutions of the AASA and NSBA. In the meantime, successful strikes by members of the American Federation of Teachers in New York City forced new concepts. Teachers were securing passage of professional negotiation

laws in many states, making the question of the legal right to negotiate no longer a debatable question. By 1965, there could no longer
be a question about the direction of the movement.

The new attitudes of teachers was reflected in the following Associated Press article, published 10 September 1971:

Scattered strikes have forced the closing of schools in several cities across the
nation as teachers seek more money, smaller classes, and procedures for airing
their complaints.

Schools were shut down completely in communities in Michigan, Illinois,
Ohio, Pennsylvania, and Rhode Island, while others struggled to remain open
with nonstriking and substitute teachers.

In Levittown, N.Y., about 600 teachers defied a court order and stayed off
the job for the second day. Ten of the city's 16 public schools remained open
with 260 nonstriking teachers and 160 substitutes, but many of the 17,000
elementary and secondary pupils reported to classes, signed in, and left.

The Levittown Teachers Association, without a contract since June 30, demanded a 20 percent pay increase and voted to strike when the school board
offered a 6 percent increase.

Teachers' salaries under the old Levittown contract ranged from $8,000 to
$14,000.

No meetings were scheduled, and school officials said they didn't know what
their next step would be.

A 16-day strike in Decatur, Ill., has kept all 38 public schools closed, but the
school board says it will fire all first-year teachers who don't report to work
Monday. In addition, the board has asked the Circuit Court to void the contracts
of striking teachers with tenure and is advertising for replacements.

Two hundred of the 950 Decatur teachers did not join the strike, and the
school board sought to open three elementary schools but was stopped by a
court order. The court ruled all or none of the 38 schools must open, on the
grounds that opening only a few schools would discriminate against the pupils
who could not attend classes.

In Ann Arbor, Mich., striking teachers agreed Thursday to turn over the
salary and class size dispute to a fact-finding group. Classes were scheduled to
reopen Friday for the 21,000 pupils and 1,000 teachers.

Schools in three other Michigan cities remained closed by strikes. In Lansing,
32,000 pupils were out of school for the third straight day Thursday as their
1,000 teachers demanded more money and smaller classes.

In Waterford, Mich., the same issues canceled the scheduled Wednesday
school opening for 34,000 pupils and 660 teachers. The 1,400 teachers in War-
ren, Mich., struck Tuesday, the first day of classes, when the school board
refused to grant a temporary contract extension until a new contract agreement
was reached. The strike affected 34,000 pupils in elementary and secondary
schools.

In Dearborn Heights, Mich., 250 teachers in the city's School District No. 7
struck for lack of a contract extension while they negotiated for a new contract.
The strike was expected to postpone Friday's scheduled opening for the district's 5,500 pupils.

Pupils and bus drivers joined teachers on the picket line in Findlay, Ohio,
where the one public high school and all 10 public elementary schools are

closed. Both the teachers and drivers have failed to reach wage agreements with the board in the 10,000-pupil system.

In Rhode Island, contract disputes kept schools closed for all 4,800 public school pupils in North Providence, and for all 2,000 in North Smithfield for the second day.

The 230 teachers in North Providence and the 110 teachers in North Smithfield, negotiating separately, said they would withhold services until new contracts are signed.

In eastern Pennsylvania, strikes shut down classes for all 18,000 pupils in Allentown and for all 15,000 in Bristol Township. The Allentown School Board requested an injunction against the strike Thursday, and a hearing was set for Friday.

Teachers in both communities sought higher base salaries and across-the-board increases.

Teachers strikes extended into higher education in Michigan, where a strike by 216 professors at Oakland University in Rochester has halted classes for the 7,000 students. The strikers are seeking a 20 percent pay hike.

In the Chicago suburb of Glenrock, Ill., the school board said it would try to open the community's two high schools for all 4,500 pupils Friday, despite a strike by 280 of the 310 teachers. Classes for freshmen began Wednesday.

The teachers, on strike for a week, are seeking higher base pay, limits on class sizes, and binding arbitration on grievances.

In Logan, Ohio, a teachers association voted Thursday to return to work Friday, ending a three-day boycott of classes. Despite the boycott by 100 of the system's 142 teachers, all 3,000 pupils remained in classes, taught by nonstrikers and substitutes.

The teachers will continue to meet with school officials in efforts to reach an understanding on negotiation procedures.

In the San Francisco suburb of Daly City, 420 elementary teachers have voted to strike when classes open Monday. The strike would affect 10,000 pupils in 21 schools. The teachers want smaller classes, more teaching equipment and grievance procedures. But school administrators said they would hire substitute teachers and begin classes despite a strike.

Thus, professional negotiation has become an accepted process in the teaching profession, and teacher education institutions must deal with the process and prepare teachers, as well as administrators, to function in the process.[4]

Professional Sanctions

As a companion piece to professional negotiation, especially in the early days of that process, teacher education has been compelled to include information about professional sanctions in preparing teachers and administrators. Although the strike has grown in use since the early 1960s, professional sanctions are still used by NEA and its state and local affiliates, especially in the first steps of trying to reform conditions in school districts.

As has already been indicated, the same NEA convention that adopted the 1962 resolution on professional negotiation also adopted a resolution advocating the use of professional sanctions. The essence of that resolution was:

> The National Education Association believes that, as a means for preventing unethical or arbitrary policies or practices that have a deleterious effect on the welfare of the schools, professional sanctions should be invoked. These sanctions would provide for appropriate disciplinary action by the organized profession.

The immediate reaction of boards and administrators was that *sanctions* was just a softer word for *strike*.

Definition

While sanctions are generally viewed as a weapon, they are more a means of persuasion than a weapon. They are a moral force and are widely used by professions. They hold out a reward for correcting unsatisfactory conditions and the penalty of forbidding the services of members of the profession in extreme cases where moral persuasion fails to elicit remedial action. For example, the American Medical Association may warn a given hospital that its facilities are substandard, making satisfactory medical service impossible. If the conditions are not corrected by a certain date, the services of doctors may be withdrawn. Warning of inferior standards in education, as well as in health, is an obligation of the profession to the public. The public is not expected to be expert in matters pertaining to a given profession; it must rely on the standards of the profession to guide it to efficient and adequate services. In short, the application of professional sanctions to a school district for maintaining conditions of work and service to children depends in large measure on public opinion. A dictionary definition of sanctions might be "a means, often in the form of a declaration, that induces observance of a law or custom by impelling its object toward moral action through imposition of a detriment, loss, or reward or other intervention."

The teaching profession uses the following steps before it applies the ultimate one of withdrawal of services of its members.

1. It publicizes unsatisfactory conditions in the district that tend to prevent effective professional services. This is to warn the offending district that such conditions must be corrected and to alert the citizens of the district of conditions of which they may be unaware.

2. If the conditions are not corrected, the professional association requests its members not currently employed in the district not to seek or accept employment there until and unless the substandard conditions are corrected. Usually this edict is aimed at the succeeding school year.

3. If all else fails to produce remedial action, the profession requests all its members not to accept employment in the school district for the ensuing school year.

An important factor in the application of a boycott against a school district is an impartial study of conditions. Without the precise facts in a given case, great injustice could be done the school district by hastily drawn or biased conclusions about conditions in the district. The study is generally made by a special committee appointed by the National Commission on Professional Rights and Responsibilities. This committee is composed of members of the profession; a layman or two, usually school board members; and, generally, one or two members of the commission. Every effort is made to derive a factual, impartial report. The integrity of this report is all-important.

Uses

Several uses of professional sanctions have been suggested. They can:

1. Express the profession's concerned disapproval of unsatisfactory conditions
2. Attract the community's attention to specific problems that make adequate quality education difficult or impossible
3. Be used to withhold further professional service or support when such service and support would serve only to continue unacceptable conditions
4. Be a process through which the profession can protect its members from being forced to contract their services under conditions that are demeaning or intolerable
5. Be a process through which the profession can protect the public from unknowingly condoning and financing indefensible programs or unacceptable practices in education
6. Be a process for exerting the profession's influence in areas where it has expertise and should have autonomy
7. Be used to protect the public or children against incompetent or unethical practices by members of the profession.

Professional Standards

The Struggle for Autonomy

It should be observed that there remains a reluctance on the part of legislatures to concede to the teaching profession the same degree of autonomy in its affairs that is accorded other professions. Of course, the rationale for this reluctance is that teaching is a public profession. But that rationale is actually more an excuse than a valid position. Public school teaching is, of course, a public profession, but that fact cannot negate the principle that any profession should be in charge of the standards of selection, preparation, licensure, and performance of its members. Because of its lack of expertise in professional matters, the public generally must depend on each profession to determine the appropriate standards to be met. There should be, as there are in most instances, checks and balances developed to protect each segment of the profession against excesses of the other segments. Likewise, the public must be protected against monopolistic and selfish manipulations. For example, there are increasing demands that the American Medical Association exercise more controls over the obsolescent training of doctors.

Only by continued and aggressive insistence on the right to autonomy will the teaching profession bring about needed reforms and legislation. For example, when NEA and AFT proposed state legislation conferring on teachers the right to negotiate or bargain with school boards over economic and working conditions, those proposals were generally considered radical. But the idea is now generally accepted as sound. The same was true when it was first proposed that government employees should have the right to negotiate terms and conditions of employment. Kloss has expressed the urgency of autonomy:

> No profession can exist without this protection under the law. It alone must have the right to set conditions of admission. It alone must have the right to set codes of professional conduct. It alone must have the right to determine the values of professional competence. It follows from this that it alone must exercise discipline over its members and, with due regard to basic human rights, remove delinquents from the lists. Doctors are striken from the rolls, lawyers are disbarred, priests disfrocked.[5]

Organized labor long insisted on the right of public employees to bargain with their employers. The unions sensed that in an urban society activism, aggressiveness, and group action had to replace the passive individual bargaining for public employees that characterized earlier periods. In the states little headway was made toward the realization of this goal. The breakthrough came when labor persuaded President John F. Kennedy to issue Executive Order 10,988 in January 1962, authorizing collective negotiation for federal employees (but not the right to strike).

The task force that developed the report on which the order was based stressed the fundamental differences between public and private employment. Salient points in the task force report may be summarized as follows:

1. Collective bargaining as applied to private industry is inappropriate for public employees.

2. Federal employees do not have the right to strike.

3. The public interest must be paramount.

4. Professional and supervisory employees should have the right to establish organizations of their own.

5. The union shop and the closed shop are inappropriate for the government.

6. Labor arbitration as in private industry is not appropriate for federal government use.

7. Where Congress fixes salaries and other conditions of employment, these are not subject to negotiation.

8. All negotiations and agreements must conform to civil services regulations.

But this executive order was only an entering wedge. Since it was issued in 1962, almost all of the admonitions of the task force have been ignored or overcome. There have been strikes of federal government employees, including postal workers and flight supervisors, and although federal law still prescribes serious penalties for violation of the strike provision, they have not been enforced. In cities and states there have been countless strikes of policemen, firemen, and garbage collectors: all outside the law but effective. Moreover, among the twenty-six states with professional negotiation or collective bargaining laws for teachers, several of these recognize both collective bargaining and the right of teachers to strike. In 1962 not a single state endorsed the right to strike. Why the change? There are two reasons:

1. The flow of the times. Urbanization forced a new format to secure justice for employees

2. The aggressiveness and power of public employees banded together in a collective enterprise

Thus, those who scoff at the possibility of teachers attaining autonomy over their professional standards and affairs are ignoring recent history.

Professional Practices Acts

As a step toward professional autonomy, the National Commission on Teacher Education and Professional Standards has urged state education associations to seek the passage of professional practices acts, creating state professional practices commissions made up of members of the profession and vesting in these commissions the power to specify standards of practice. These commissions are also vested with the power to discipline members who do not observe the adopted standards of practice.

Excerpts from one of the state professional practices acts will indicate the purpose of the state commission:

Duties. It shall be the duty of the commission to develop and revise, consistent with state law, professional codes or standards relating to ethics, conduct, and professional performance and practices of persons engaged in the profession of teaching in the public schools. In the development of such professional codes and standards, the commission shall solicit the assistance of members of the teaching profession and representatives of school administrators, school board officers, and other interested citizens. The commission shall recommend such professional codes and standards as it may approve to the superintendent of public instruction, who after a hearing thereon may, consistent with state law, approve or revise such codes and standards as he deems proper and in the best interest of the public and the profession. . . .

Complaints against teachers. The commission shall accept and investigate complaints against any member of the teaching profession engaged in teaching in the public schools in regard to violation of regulations . . . or otherwise pertaining to his personal or professional conduct or performance, or such investigation may be made upon its own notion. Following such investigation, the commission may dismiss such complaint as unfounded, issue a written warning and reprimand, or following an opportunity for such teacher to informally appear before the commission, file a formal complaint with the superintendent of public instruction requesting the suspension for a period of time or revocation of the teachers certificate of the teacher involved and stating the reasons therefor.

Other Regulatory Processes

While efforts have been made to induce states to establish professional standards boards to recommend standards of selection, preparation, and certification of teachers, only two or three states have taken this step. The obvious reason is that other processes have been established, and states tend to resist setting up additional processes. For example, all states now have advisory councils on teacher education and certification, under that name or some other. These are legal (in 14 states) or extralegal bodies, consisting of members of the profession, that recommend to the state department or board of education standards for preparation and certification of teachers. Sixteen states have also established certification review committees made up of members of the profession. These review committees democratize the application of certification regulations by making exceptions that seem justified by substitution of courses or experience and other deviations that appear justified by the applicants' general and specific backgrounds.

Analysis of Advisory Councils on Teacher Education and Certification

As has been stated, every state now has a legal or a voluntary advisory council on teacher education and certification. These exist under a variety of names. The first was founded in 1933, in an effort to democratize the controls over teacher education and certification. In general these councils are, as their names imply, "advisory" to the state board or department of education. But they are quite powerful bodies whose recommendations are rarely vetoed by the state authority. In thirty-six states, the advisory body is a voluntary or extralegal one, usually created by the state board of education, with members appointed by the chief state school officer and approved by the board. Generally, the appointees are recommended by the professional associations in the state: the state education association, state federation of teachers, associations of administrators and supervisors, and associations of college professors.

In general, these advisory bodies make continuous studies of the needs of their states in the area of teacher education and certification. While their recommendations may be ignored, it is generally reported that their recommendations have great influence.

To cite one possibility, in 1970 there began a period of great teacher surpluses. A number of factors contributed to this situation, the first such oversupply since the depression years. All evidence points to mounting surpluses throughout the 1970s. Obviously, this is a period in which minimum preparation requirements for initial certification could be increased. There are still four states that do not require the bachelors degree for beginning elementary teachers; and only one state is enforcing the five-year requirement for high school

Table 1-1. Number of states enforcing degree requirements for elementary and secondary school teachers by decades 1900-1970[6]

Year	Number of States Enforcing	
	For Elementary School Teachers	For Secondary School Teachers
1900	0	2
1910	0	3
1920	0	10
1930	2	23
1940	11	40
1950	21	42
1960	39	51*
1970	48	52†

*District of Columbia and Puerto Rico are counted as "states in this calculation, making a total of 52.

†California, Arizona, and District of Columbia specify 5 years of preparation, but this requirement is fully operative in the District of Columbia.

teachers. The advisory councils are in strategic positions to increase quality requirements as well as to readjust the supply and demand for teachers. Requirements can be placed too high, of course. A good example is the lessened supply of doctors resulting, at least in part, from extremely long periods of preparation.

Table 1-2. Minimum preparation requirements by states for administrative certificates: 1970[7]

Number of College Years of Preparation or Degree Required	Number of States Requiring		
	Elementary School Principal	Secondary School Principal	Superintendent of Schools
7 years or doctors degree	0	0	1
6 years plus, but less than doctors degree	0	3	
6 years	4	1	25
Masters degree plus, less than 6 years	8	8	5
Masters degree	35	37	20
Bachelors degree plus, less than 5 years	4	0	1
Bachelors degree	1	3	
Less than bachelors degree	0	0	0
No certificate issued	*	*	*
	52	52	52

*Requirements are counted in above tabulation but District of Columbia, Michigan, and Virginia do not issue administrative certificates.

Other Factors

In addition to the right to participate in the determination of working conditions there are several other factors in the evolution of the new profession of teaching. One is the concerted defense of teachers against unfair dismissals from their positions without due process, i.e., without regard to the rights of the accused to know the charges against him, confront his accusers, have a public hearing, and summon witnesses in his behalf. Until about 1965 school boards could fire teachers almost at will for any reason they chose. During the late 1960s, however, the NEA Commission on Professional Rights and Responsibilities was empowered to intervene in such cases, and funds were made available for this purpose. The AFT, NAACP, and ACLU also intervened in many cases. Hundreds of firings have now been reversed by federal courts for lack of due process. In many such cases in recent years the charges have proved to be groundless, and the courts have ordered the teachers restored to their positions with back pay. The firing of a teacher is no longer a simple matter for boards exercising arbitrary and absolute power. This has given new dignity to the teaching profession.

Notes

1. NEA Executive Committee, "The Professional Way to Meet the Crisis," *NEA Journal* (February 1947): 47.

2. National School Boards Association. *Proceedings of the 1963 Convention* (Evanston, Ill., 1963), resolution 4, p. 327.

3. *Your AASA in 1963-64* (Washington, D.C.: American Association of School Administrators, 1964), resolution 21, p. 186.

4. For definitive histories of this movement as well as detailed explanations of the process see Myron Lieberman and Michael H. Moskow, *Collective Negotiation for Teachers* (Chicago: Rand McNally & Co., 1966); Edward B. Shils and Taylor C. Whittier, *Teachers, Administrators and Collective Bargaining* (New York: Thomas Y. Crowell Co., 1968); T. M. Stinnett, *Turmoil in Teaching* (New York: Macmillan Co., 1968); T. M. Stinnett, Jack H. Kleinman and Martha L. Ware, *Professional Negotiation in Public Education* (New York: Macmillan Co., 1966).

5. Alan A. Kloss, "What is a Profession," *The British Columbia Teacher* (January 1963): 1936-39.

6. T. M. Stinnett, *A Manual on Certification Requirements for School Personnel in the United States* (Washington, D.C.: National Education Association, National Commission on Teacher Education and Professional Standards, 1970), p. 23.

7. Ibid., table 6, p. 64.

2

Legal Requirements
for
Teaching

Need for Licensure

As is true of virtually all professions, licensure by the state is required to enter and continue in the practice of teaching. This is mandatory for all teachers in all public schools and for some teachers in some private schools (for explanation see below).

There are good reasons for such requirements. The public must be safeguarded against the unqualified, the charlatan, and the quack. There must be a guarantee of high quality service to the public; otherwise the public's taxes or fee payments will be wasted. Moreover, the practitioner himself, who has spent years of his life preparing for competent service in a given profession, requires protection against the unqualified.

History of Licensure

Licensure of teachers in the United States began in a rather haphazard manner. (Although licensure and certification are not precisely the same, the terms are used interchangeably here.) During the colonial period, schools sprang up in local communities with no state aid or control. They were subscription schools, and the licensing of teachers was left to the local community. Quite often, the minister of the dominant local church examined candidates and issued local certificates valid only in that community. The chief qualifications were not educational know-how but religious orthodoxy. Sometimes local boards issued the license. The standards for licensure were low or nonexistent, and the authority varied from community to community, sometimes being vested in towns, churches, royal commissioners, or even church authorities in Europe. There were no schools, as such, for preparing teachers. Under such conditions, standards were intolerably low and nepotism was prevalent. An examination of some sort was usually the requirement for a license, but it was elementary and often of little validity. In fact the local examination—usually administered by a county superintendent—actually continued in many states well into the twentieth century.

During the colonial period there were, of course, no state school systems; the first state school systems did not come into being until about 1820. Education was mentioned in the constitutions of only seven of the sixteen states comprising the union in 1800. Of course, the federal constitution made no mention of education, thus leaving the matter to the states. After 1820, state constitutions began referring to the need for education; later they began mandating the establishment of state systems.

The evolution of state certification structures began in 1825 when the Ohio legislature designated county officers to examine candidates and issue certificates for teaching. New York (in 1841) and Vermont (in 1845) provided for county superintendents of schools to perform these functions, among others. Between these dates and 1900, teacher certification authority was shared by state and county authorities and was almost completely based on the examination system. New York was the first state (1849) to accept credentials from its normal school as a basis of certification in lieu of the examination. As late as 1900 there were about 3,000 teacher licensing agencies in the United States, and in 1950 some states still certificated local teachers on the basis of examination.

All states now have centralized teacher certification in their state departments of education, except for a few minor exceptions, and the basis for certification is the completion of approved college or university programs.

Present Certification

Who Must Secure

All professional personnel in the public elementary and secondary schools of all states are required by law or regulation to hold certificates issued by the designated authority. The authority is usually the state board of education or the state department of education, and the personnel include teachers; administrators; supervisors; and professional nonteaching personnel, such as supervisors and counselors. In forty-nine states kindergarten teachers are also required to secure certificates, if the kindergarten is publicly supported. A total of nineteen states require nursery school teachers to hold state certificates, if the schools are publically supported. (However, only eight states now provide nursery schools as a part of the public school system.)

In addition, eight states require teachers and administrators in publicly supported junior colleges to hold certificates.

As for nonpublic schools, twenty-seven states (fourteen by law) require that teachers at some level or in some subjects hold state certificates. In addition, eleven states require certification of teachers in nonpublic schools, if the schools in which they teach are accredited by the state department of education. About twenty-three states have no provision for certifying teachers in nonpublic schools, but most will certify teachers who voluntarily request it.

The question of licensure for paraprofessionals and teacher aides is beginning to be debated. At the moment, only eight states have any provisions for regulating or licensing such personnel. But the probable increase in these types of personnel will doubtless lead to some kind of certification or control in the future.

Requirements

General Requirements

General requirements are those that every applicant, regardless of his field of teaching, must meet. For example: citizenship, license fee, good health, oath of allegiance, minimum age, and recommendation of his preparing college or last employer. Many of the general requirements have been dropped in recent years. The minimum age requirement is one example. Present college preparation requirements have made this requirement obsolete. Also, the number of states requiring loyalty oaths have diminished in recent years. A total of twenty-one states now require no certification fee; in the other states fees range from $1 to $20.

Preparation Requirements

In 1973 all states required that beginning elementary teachers have at least a bachelors degree, with the prescribed work in professional courses. See table 2-1. Thus, wherever one plans to teach, he should be prepared to meet the degree requirement.

For high school teachers, all states enforce the minimum of the bachelors degree including prescribed work in professional courses. The District of Columbia specifies the masters degree for senior and vocational high school certificates. Arizona and California specify the masters degree as a standard but are still certifying, temporarily at least, on the minimum of the bachelors degree. For administrators, the basic requirement is five years of preparation, with very few exceptions, and twenty-eight states require six years of preparation for superintendents. For teachers, a total of nineteen states now

Table 2-1. Minimum requirements for lowest regular teaching certificates in 1973

	Elementary School					Secondary School			
	Degree	General Education (s.h.)	Professional Education (s.h.) (total)	Student teaching *	Educational Philosophy Psychology Sociology *	Degree	General Education (s.h.)	Professional Education (s.h.) (total)	Student teaching *
Alabama	B	59	27	6	–	B	44	21	6
Alaska	B	AC	AC	AC	AC	B	AC	AC	AC
Arizona	B^a	40	24	6	3	B^a	40	22	6
Arkansas	B	48	18	6	3	B	48	18	6
California	B^b	AC	AC	AC	AC	B^b	AC	AC	AC
Colorado	B	AC	AC	AC	AC	B	AC	AC	AC
Connecticut	B^c	75	30	6	6	B^c	45	18	6
Delaware	B	60	30	6	6	B	60	18	6
Dist. of Col.	B^d	AC	AC	AC	AC	M^d	AC	AC	AC
Florida	B	45	20	6	6	B	45	20	6
Georgia	B^e	40	18	6	–	B^e	40	18	6
Hawaii	B	AC	18	AC^f	–	B	AC	18	AC^f
Idaho	B	42	24	6	6^g	B	–	20	6
Illinois	B	78	16	5	2	B	42	16	5
Indiana	B^h	97	27	8	10	B^h	50	18	6
Iowa	B	–	20	5	–	B	–	20	5
Kansas	B	50	24	5	12	B	50	20	5
Kentucky	B^i	45	24	8	–^{j}	B^i	45	17	8
Louisiana	B	46	24	4	9	B	46	18	4
Maine	B	–	30	6	3	B	–	18	6
Maryland	B	80	26	8	6	B	–	18	6
Massachusetts	B^k	–	18	2^l	–	B^k	–	12	2^l
Michigan	B^m	40	20	6	6^n	B^m	40	20	6
Minnesota	B	AC	AC	AC	AC	B	–	27°	6

State								
Mississippi	B	48	36	6	B	48	18	6
Missouri	B	AC	18	5	B	40	18	5
Montana	B	AC	AC	AC	B	AC	16	AC
Nebraska	B[p]	AC	AC	AC	B	AC	AC	AC
Nevada	B	—	18	6	B	—	20	6
New Hampshire	B[q]	AC	AC	AC	B[q]	AC	AC	AC
New Jersey	B	45	24	—[r]	B	45	15	—[r]
New Mexico	B[t]	48	24	6	B[t]	48	18	6
New York	B[u]	NS	24	NS[f]	B[u]	NS	12	NS[f]
North Carolina	B	35-40%	15-20%	—	B	35-40%	15-20%	—
North Dakota	B	NCATE	16	5	B	NCATE	16	5
Ohio	B[v]	60	29	6	B[v]	30	21	6
Oklahoma	B	50	21	9	B	50	21	9
Oregon	—	—	24	6	B[w]	—	20	6
Pennsylvania	B[x]	AC	AC	AC	B[x]	AC	AC	AC
Rhode Island	B[y]	—	30	6	B[y]	—	18	6
South Carolina	B	42-45	21	6	B	42-45	18	6
South Dakota	B[z]	30	26	6	B	—	20	6
Tennessee	B	40	24	4	B	40	24	4
Texas	B	60	18	6	B	60	18	6
Utah	B	AC	26	8	B	AC	21	8
Vermont	B	AC	18	9	B	AC	18	9
Virginia	B	60	18	6	B	48	15	6
Washington	B[aa]	70%bb	20%bb	—	B[aa]	70%bb	20%bb	—
West Virginia	B	40	20	6	B	40	20	6
Wisconsin	B	—	26	5	B	—	18	5
Wyoming	B	—	23	C	B	—	20	C

Key: s.h. means semester hours; — means not reported; AC means approved curriculum; B means completion of the bachelors degree; M means completion of the masters degree; C means a course; NS means not specified; NCATE means standards of the National Council for Accreditation of Teacher Education.

Footnotes for table on following page.

Footnotes for Table 2-1

a. For the temporary certificate, valid for five years only. Teachers must qualify for the standard certificate by completing a fifth year of preparation.

b. For the initial standard credential. Teachers must qualify for the permanent credential by completing a fifth year of preparation.

c. For the provisional certificate, valid for five years and renewable once for five years. Teachers must qualify for the standard certificate by completing a fifth year of preparation.

d. Bachelors degree for elementary and junior high schools; masters degree for senior and vocational high schools.

e. Effective July 1, 1974, the initial certificate, based on the bachelors degree, will be nonrenewable; completion of a fifth year of preparation will be required for continuing certification.

f. Not included in total professional education.

g. Three semester hours in educational psychology, three in principles of education.

h. For the provisional certificate, valid for five years only; teachers must qualify for the professional certificate by obtaining a masters degree.

i. For the provisional certificate, valid for ten years and extendable only on completion of a fifth year of preparation. A masters degree is required for the standard certificate.

j. Recommended but not required.

k. Or graduation from a four-year normal school approved by the state board of education.

l. The requirement is six semester hours for the bilingual education certificate.

m. For the provisional certificate, valid for six years and renewal for three; teachers must complete an additional eighteen semester hours for continuing certification.

n. Or equivalent.

o. Quarter hours.

p. Elementary teachers in accredited schools must hold certificates based on the degree. Nebraska does issue provisional rural elementary and commitment certificates on a minimum of sixty semester hours, valid only for specifically endorsed grades or subjects in designated classes of school districts for a limited time.

q. A provisional conversion license may be issued to the holder of a bachelors degree from a regionally accredited institution but not in a program approved by New Hampshire. A certificate will be issued on completion of the conversion program and recommendation of the superintendent attesting to competent performance and satisfactory professional growth.

r. College requirement; not included in total professional education column.

s. Educational psychology, included in total professional education.

t. For the provisional certificate, valid for four years and renewable once for four years. Teachers must complete a fifth year of preparation for continuing certification.

u. For the provisional certificate, valid for five years only. Teachers must qualify for permanent certification by completing a fifth year of preparation.

v. Total semester hours—124.

w. For the initial certificate, valid for three years and renewable once for three years. Secondary teachers must complete a fifth year of preparation for continuing certification.

x. For the provisional certificate, valid for three years and renewable once for three years. Teachers must qualify for the permanent certificate by completing 24 semester hours of postbaccalaureate work.

y. For the provisional certificate, valid for six years only. Teachers must qualify for the professional certificate by completing a fifth year of preparation (36 semester hours or a masters degree).

z. South Dakota still lists a nondegree elementary certificate, valid for teaching grades K-9, *except* in K-12 school systems. The 1970 edition noted that this certificate would be discontinued in 1972.

aa. For the provisional certificate, valid for three years and renewable once for three years. Teachers must qualify for the standard certificate by completing a fifth year of preparation.

bb. Ten percent electives.

* Included in total professional education, except as noted.

require the completion of a fifth year (or masters degree) in addition to a specified number of years of teaching on an initial certificate before issuing permanent certification.

Special Courses

About eight states require a special course that can usually only be secured within a given state: e.g., state constitution, state history, state and federal governments, and agriculture and conservation. About half of these states will accept prescribed scores on a proficiency examination, in lieu of the courses, to meet their special course requirements.

Types and Number of Certificates Issued

The usual practice is to issue separate elementary school and high school teaching certificates. The predominant practice for high school teachers is to issue certificates that specify the subjects or fields the holder is qualified to teach. For elementary school teachers, the predominant practice is to issue a certificate valid for grades one through six or one through eight. Certificates may be for terms of five-to-ten years, although five years is the predominant practice. A total of twenty-six states issue life or permanent certificates.

States still tend to issue too many separate name certificates. In 1970 the states issued a total of 539 separate certificates. This is about 11 separate certificates per state. This multiplicity of certificates tends to be confusing both to the profession and to the public. Most other professions issue only one legal certificate. The tendency to proliferate certificates is doubtless due in part to the constant development of new specialties in teaching; members of a newly emerging specialty frequently covet the status of a special certificate that sets them apart from other teachers.

Revocation of Certificates

The laws of each state spell out the conditions under which a teacher's certificate can be revoked. The most common are gross immorality, incompetence, insubordination (used decreasingly in recent years) and violation of the law (felony).

Some other causes mentioned in the laws of some states are abandonment of contract, unprofessional conduct, and negligence. A few states mention alcoholism, drug abuse, willful neglect of duty, falsification of credentials, and violation of rules of the board. Recent court cases, however, have tended to cluster the chief causes around the first three mentioned above: immorality, incompetence, and insubordination.

Reciprocity

One of the most persistent and vexing of teacher certification problems has been the lack of reciprocity among the states in issuing certificates to persons prepared in other states. A number of methods have been employed to overcome this weakness. One was the use of regional reciprocity compacts. But the mobility of teachers has long since outmoded this process.

Another method tried was national accreditation. The establishment of the National Council for the Accreditation of Teacher Education was intended to give states confidence in all credentials from any of the nationally accredited institutions. However, so few institutions preparing teachers were accredited by NCATE (515 out of 1,272) that its effectiveness was nullified to some degree. It should be pointed out, however, that these 515 accredited institutions prepare about 80 percent of the newly graduated teachers each year. About thirty states are now giving considerable weight in reciprocity to credentials from NCATE accredited institutions, and this number will probably grow.

A new process, developed in the last few years, is the interstate reciprocity compact, sponsored by the New York State Education Department. By enacting this model bill states would enter legally and formally into agreements to accept the certified graduates of the other cooperating states. About thirty-five states have now passed this law; it should extend reciprocity considerably.

Although the problem is not yet solved, enough progress has been made that a given teacher has a very good chance of having his credentials accepted for certification in a state other than the one where he prepared. If he is a graduate of a standard college approved for teacher education, and his college is accredited by NCATE or the appropriate regional accrediting association, there will be few instances in which he will have difficulty with certification.

Certification Examinations

In recent years states have increased the use of examinations in the certification process. These are not the crude kinds of examinations used in colonial days to award certificates. Comprehensive examinations are now being used to permit a given student to demonstrate mastery of a given subject without necessarily pursuing college courses for credit. The practice is similar to the honors programs in many prestigious colleges and universities, which permit students to "test out."

In their 1970 reports sixteen states indicated use of examinations in several different ways. For example, California uses the Modern Language Association Examination to demonstrate proficiency in a foreign language, trade and skill examinations for advanced vocational credentials, and the reading specialist part of the National Teachers Examination. Colorado uses proficiency examinations in typewriting and shorthand to qualify for teaching the subjects in high school and the MLAE for senior students preparing to teach modern languages. California, Connecticut, and Delaware also use the MLAE. Hawaii uses the Miller Analogy (MAT) and the National Teachers Examination (NTE) to validate preparation in unaccredited colleges. Maine allows up to six semester hours in education on the basis of the NTE examination, for renewal of certificates in lieu of course credit. New Jersey allows foreign students to validate work in institutions in their own countries through examinations. The New York State Education Department probably makes the most extensive use of examinations for certification in cooperation with its colleges and universities. College graduates who lack certain courses required for certification may demonstrate proficiency in these courses via an examination.[1]

All states have now established advisory councils on teacher education and certification. These councils are made up of members of the teaching profession and have been established to assist state departments of education in developing sound practices in keeping with the needs of the schools in each area. About sixteen states have established certification review committees to review decisions made by the legal authorities about whether credentials in given cases meet the substance and spirit of state laws and regulations. Both of these processes tend to offset arbitrary, unilateral decision making, give the profession more authority in decision making, and further democratize the administration of teacher education programs and the issuance of certificates.

Future Requirements

While no one can know for sure, it appears from the evidence at hand that minimum state requirements for initial certification will be stepped up rapidly toward the requirement of five years of preparation (the masters degree). We are now producing a vast surplus of teachers who will not find employment. Some estimates for the school year 1971-72 ran as high as 200,000 fully qualified teachers who could not find jobs. After the extreme teacher shortages that have plagued our schools for almost half a century, this is a new and startling development. Part of the problem is economic: when financial pinches come, schools tend to increase the size of classes or the number of pupils per teacher, rather than the size of the faculty.

Moreover, since 1957 the birth rate has shown a surprising and persistent decline. This means that fewer teachers are needed each year to service the total school enrollment. The decreasing enrollment has temporarily hit elementary schools hardest, but it will eventually include high schools.

Two ways a profession can reduce the supply of qualified practitioners is to inaugurate more rigorous and selective admission practices or so lengthen the period of preparation that fewer fully qualified candidates are produced each year. Better guidance and counseling of prospective teachers and higher standards for admission and graduation are also helpful.

We cannot expect the suggested lengthening of the preparation period to come overnight. It will probably come gradually, not by adding a full additional year all at once, but by adding portions of years. Students already in preparation or teachers in service need not worry about increased requirements since new requirements would not be retroactive.

New Vistas

There are now in progress certain experimental approaches that may be accepted for use in the future. In the first place, the profession in the public schools is seeking greater control over the certification process (in emulation of other professions). NEA has adopted a resolution that states: "The Association believes that, for maximum improvement in these areas [of uniformity and reciprocity of professional certification and accreditation standards and practices of educational institutions], broad and intensified participation of the teaching profession is essential."[2] The resolution then calls on the National Commission on Teacher Education and Certification to (a) study the feasibility of creating an office of certification and accreditation within the structures of NEA; (b) establish standards for professional certification and standards for accreditation of teacher training; (c) maintain a teacher placement service; and (d) coordinate all activities of the NEA toward the development and application of educational standards for programs, facilities, and performance.

Another development is the universal adoption of the approved programs approach, by which institutions design their own programs of preparation, in accordance with their philosophies, faculties, facilities, and clientele, and then submit the proposed programs to their state educational agency for approval. Once approved, each graduate's certification is based on his institution's recommendation rather than his transcript and course credits.

A third proposed innovation is for institutions to develop performance criteria for each position for which they are preparing teachers. Qualification would then depend on demonstrating the achievement of stated objectives rather than on completing a specific conglomerate of courses.

These innovations will take time to be accepted and developed, but they are in process and will eventually give the profession more control over certification. They should also make the public more confident about the competence of teachers.

Notes

1. See *College Proficiency Examinations* (Albany, N.Y.: State Education Department, n.d.), p. 752.

2. T. M. Stinnett, *A Manual on Certification Requirements for School Personnel in the United States* (Washington, D.C.: National Education Association, Commission on Teacher Education and Professional Standards, 1970), p. 6.

3

Emergence
of the
Normal School

The Need

Massachusetts established what has often been referred to as the first public school in the United States by the Satan Deluder Law of 1647. A similar law, based on the English Poor Law of 1601, was enacted in 1642 to provide some education for the indigent. Although neither of these laws established public schools as we now understand the term, we may consider the 1647 law a forerunner of the public schools that were to develop later.

Between 1647 and 1849 no institution was founded for the express purpose of preparing teachers for the common schools. True, there were a number of colleges and universities, but they had been established largely to prepare ministers. Some of their graduates did consent to teach in the common schools, but not many and then only when there were no positions open in their chosen profession.

The quality of the common schools deteriorated steadily, simply because the quality of teaching was poor. Jencks and Reisman have described the dilemma of how to get enough teachers for the common schools:

This haphazard pattern of recruitment into teaching continued down to the 1830's. By that time educational reformers like Horace Mann were convinced that if universal schooling of reasonable quality was to become an American reality, a larger and more dependable flow of teachers was necessary. The established liberal arts colleges did not seem the appropriate vehicle for providing this flow. In the first place they were still open only to men, and it seemed clear that an adequate supply of cheap teachers would have to depend mainly on women. In the second place, most of the colleges of the time were sectarian establishments, for which public subsidies were increasingly hard to raise. In the third place the better colleges of the time insisted on more than elementary education from their applicants, and even the worst ones pretended to do so. To require such lengthy preparation of prospective "school marms" seemed wasteful and would have excluded many whose services were badly wanted. The need was rather to develop a publicly financed training institution that would recruit women at the end of eight years of elementary school, give them semiprofessional training, and send them back to the elementary schools as teachers.[1]

The state normal school movement was a response to the popular dissatisfaction with the quality of education offered children and youth. More than 25 percent of the nation's children were enrolled in the common schools and taught by teachers who themselves had come from common schools. In other words, the teachers offered the same amount of education as they had had. The schools were kept open only three or four months a year and were poorly attended. They had to recruit teachers wherever and whenever they could find them. The situation was so chaotic that there was much talk of abandoning the common schools.

American Beginnings

A number of Americans became convinced that the United States had to borrow the idea of the normal schools from Europe. The first recorded teacher training class was conducted by Father De'Mia in France in 1672. The first normal school, as such, was established by De Lasalle in Rheims, France, in 1685. But the Prussian normal schools most impressed visitors from the United States, although the German system was a means of social stratification that would have been rejected by the Americans had they recognized it. Teachers of the *Volksschulen* in Prussia were recruited from the common people; they were not permitted to attend the secondary schools or the universities. Therefore, special institutions were necessary in Prussia to prepare elementary teachers. No such restrictions were imported to the United States when we emulated the normal school idea.

The first realization of the normal school idea was a private academy for the preparation of teachers opened at Concord, Vermont, in 1823. It was similar to most other academies of the time, except that its founder Reverend Hall gave a series of lectures on "School Keeping" to those preparing to teach. This series of lectures was later published, became the first textbook on teacher education, and was widely used in normal schools across the country. He also added a class of elementary children for demonstration or student teaching.

One of the leading American exponents of the normal school idea was Governor DeWitt Clinton of New York, who believed in it so strongly that he was willing to subsidize private academies to educate teachers. Thomas H. Gallandit wrote a *Plan for the Education of the Instructors of Youth,* which attracted a great deal of attention and proved to be very effective in the move to establish normal schools.

Articles by James G. Carter appeared in a Boston paper in 1825. Because of his intensive campaign for state normal schools, he was to become known as "Father of American Normal Schools." He believed that institutions for the preparation of teachers were a public obligation, not a private one. Part of his argument was the notion that the state would set a uniform standard for the preparation of all teachers. Carter was a member of the Massachusetts legislature and was in a political position to influence legislation. In 1837 he was able to secure passage of a bill creating the Massachusetts state board of education; Horace Mann became the first secretary of this state board.

Another early leader in the normal school movement was the Reverend Charles Brooks, who became acquainted with the idea from conversations with friends who had visited the normal schools of France, Holland, and Prussia. He was especially intrigued by the methods of Pestalozzi. He lectured extensively in Massachusetts and before state legislatures in New Jersey, New Hampshire, and Pennsylvania. He organized a series of conventions with the normal school as the focus of attention.

Perhaps Horace Mann was the single greatest influence in the movement, owing to his eloquence and his utter devotion to the idea. His most famous words on the subject were,

I believe normal schools to be a new instrument in the advancement of the race. I believe that, without them, free schools themselves would be shorn of their strength and their healing power and would at length become mere charity schools and thus die out in fact and form. Neither the art of printing, nor the trial by jury, nor a free press, nor free suffrages, can long exist, to any beneficial and solutary purpose, without schools for the training of teachers; for if the character and qualifications of teachers be allowed to degenerate, the free schools will become pauper schools and the pauper schools will produce pauper souls, and the free press will become a false and licentious press, and ignorant voters will become venal voters and through the guise of republican forms, an oligarchy of profligate and flagitious men will govern the land; nay the universal diffusion and ultimate triumph of all-glorious Christianity itself must await the time when knowledge shall be diffused among men through the instrumentality of good schools. Coiled up in this institution, as in a spring, there is a vigor whose uncoiling may wheel the spheres.[2]

Development in the Eastern States

In 1838, the year after the Massachusetts State Board of Education was created, Edmund Dwight, a member of the board and a friend of Horace Mann, offered $10,000 to the state for teacher education, if the state would appropriate a like sum for the same purpose. The appropriation was forthcoming, and on April 19, 1838, the governor signed a bill that provided for the establishment of three normal schools. The first was located at Lexington, another at Barre, and the third at Bridgewater. The whole venture was to be experimental and restricted to a three-year trial. This was a traumatic period for the three schools, but in 1842 the legislature appropriated $6,000 to continue them. In 1845, friends in Boston contributed $5,000 for normal school buildings on the condition that the state would match the funds. This was done, and a building was erected at the Bridgewater site. The Lexington school opened on July 3, 1839, with Cyrus Pierce as principal and three young ladies as students. The second opened at Barre on September 4, 1839; the third at Bridgewater on September 9, 1840; and a fourth at Salem on September 13, 1854.

The curriculums of these schools consisted of the usual subjects to be taught in the district schools: reading, writing, arithmetic, geography, grammar, spelling, composition, vocal music, drawing, physiology, algebra, geometry, philosophy, methods of teaching, and reading of the scriptures. Almost from the first day, a model school was organized to provide real experience for the normal school students.

Troubles beset the new normal schools from the start. Often students remained only a few weeks and left to take jobs offered them as teachers. The Lexington school course was for one year; not until 1860 was it able to extend the course to two years. In the meantime, there was an abortive effort by a legislative commission to abolish the normal schools and the state board of education. The opponents' principal objection was the cost to the public in taxes; they preferred private schools.

New York, which had led in so many innovations in education, did not establish a state normal school (in Albany) until December 18, 1844. Curiously enough, however, agitation for the normal school idea in New York antedated the intense campaign in Massachusetts. Had there been an able, driving force such as James Carter or Horace Mann, New York probably would have been the first to establish a state normal school. But the educational leadership of the state, rather than establishing a new kind of school at public expense, elected to make use of the private academies in the state and to subsidize them by legislative appropriations. A report by the Board of Regents in 1832 revealed their preference for using the private academies for training teachers for the district schools. They opposed the central controls in France and Prussia and pointed to the glories of American industrialism and the doctrine of *laissez-faire*. They also stressed that some private academies were already offering normal school work.

Thus, the New York legislature passed a law on May 2, 1834, to subsidize the work of the academies in teacher preparation. Authority to administer the act was vested in the Board of Regents of the State University of New York. The board selected eight academies to subsidize in the first year. This was later increased to sixteen. The funds disbursed amounted to $400 per academy, plus $191 to increase library materials. The money was, of course, to be spent only on preparing teachers for the common schools. Unfortunately, there were no enrollees in the normal classes in four of the academies, probably due to the low status of teaching and the contempt in which the usual academy student held the course. In general, the plan simply did not work well, and was far short of what the state needed.

In 1842, the state superintendent called a meeting of deputy superintendents and other school leaders. At the meeting proponents of the state normal school convinced the group that they should work toward the state normal school plan. In 1844 a bill was finally passed that established a state normal school at Albany and appropriated $9,600 to begin with and $10,000 per year for the next five years. The Albany school opened with an enrollment of 25 students, and 106 students enrolled during the first year.

Although subsidies in one form or another came to be common in other states, New York (1850) was the first state to subsidize normal school students in recognition of their pledged service to the state. The subsidy amounted to three cents a mile from the county seat of the student's county to Albany. In addition, that proportion of the appropriation not used for this purpose was divided equally among the students.

In 1866 New York took over the Oswego training school for teachers, which had been organized as a municipal institution in 1853. The use of Pestalozzian methodology attracted great attention to this school under the direction of Edward A. Sheldon. In the same year, New York established four new normal schools at Albany, Brockport, Fredonia, and Potsdam, and in 1867 the legislature established two more at Buffalo and Genesseo.

In Connecticut the leading proponent of the normal school movement was Henry Barnard. He established the *Journal of Education* and used its pages not only for general treatment of education information but also to argue the need for a teacher's seminary. As a young lawyer and member of the legislature, he introduced a bill to provide better supervision of the common schools, which he hoped would determine the condition of the schools, increase interest in them, and promote their usefulness. He became the first secretary of this board. In his first report to the legislature in 1839, he pleaded for at least one strong seminary for teachers. While he was waiting for sentiment to crystallize on the normal school, he organized a short normal institute. This solution to the teacher education problem spread to many states and in some of them was for a long time the only organized method of training teachers for the common schools.

The political climate in Connecticut had changed, however, and the law creating the commission was repealed. Barnard migrated to Rhode Island, where he was able to accomplish many of the things he had advocated for Connecticut. After ten years of agitation, the Connecticut legislature appropriated $2,500 a year to found a normal school at New Britain. Since the money was not to be used for buildings or fixtures, the citizens of New Britain formed an association to raise the money for the school building, and it opened on May 15, 1850, with Henry Barnard as its first principal. New Britain was one of the first normal schools to set fairly high standards for admission. Some of these were purity and strength of moral and religious character, good health, good manners, a competent share of talent and information, a native talent for teaching, and some experience in teaching.

While Barnard was in Rhode Island, he wrote and spoke extensively on the subject of state normal schools, and he got the state to make one district school in each town or county a model school that inexperienced teachers could visit to observe demonstrations of good teaching. He proposed a plan for two state normal schools, one of which was to be located in Providence and connected both with a public school for observation purposes and with Brown University. In 1854 Providence made an appropriation for a city normal school, but this was abandoned when the legislature established the Rhode Island Normal School at Providence. This institution was one of the few that did not maintain a model school.

The New Jersey legislature established the ninth state normal school in the nation by establishing the New Jersey State Normal and Model School. A total of $10,000 was appropriated annually for expenses, but nothing was appropriated for buildings. Trenton, the town where the school was to be located, was to raise the funds for a building. The school opened on October 1, 1855; the new building was ready for occupancy early in 1856; and the following year a model school building was completed. A local citizen donated funds for a practice school. This public support was a good illustration of the growing public confidence in the normal school idea. The model school at Trenton was the center of the school. Its first principal believed that the normal school should reflect what the public schools were trying to do, i.e., raise a generation of patriotic, responsible citizens. At the time there were two schools of thought on the model school. One group (especially in Massachusetts) felt that the normal school students themselves should act as students of district schools and serve as guinea pigs on which the normal school students could practice. Others felt that there must be an experimental school with real students. The Trenton school was something of a turning point toward the latter view, because it placed great emphasis on the experimental phases of the model school.

Pennsylvania's plan for sponsoring normal schools followed the lines of the New York experiment with subsidizing academies. A law passed in 1857 divided the state into twelve districts, each of which might have a normal school; but the schools were to be erected and controlled by private corporations in charge of the state board of directors. The course of study was to be set by the principal of each school and approved by the state superintendent of schools. The state specified certain conditions for establishing a normal school:

1. There must be at least ten acres of ground, a model school having 100 pupils, and a faculty of at least six persons.

2. The state superintendent of schools would be in charge of the examinations given for the awarding of diplomas, which would confer the right to teach in the public schools.

3. State subsidies would be based on the number of students enrolled. (This system made for low admission requirements.)

4. Each normal was to admit at least one student each year from each school district in its area.

5. Tuition would be fifteen dollars per term, to be paid by the local school board, and each student must agree to teach in his own school district for a period of three years, presumably to reimburse the district for money spent on his tuition.

The first state normal to be founded under the new law was the Lancaster County Normal Institute at Millersville, and it quickly became the largest in the East in terms of enrollment. Other schools were established in Edinboro (1861), Mansfield (1862), and Kutztown (1866). In the early 1900s the Pennsylvania law was amended to permit the state to purchase the private corporations and make them into state normals. Pennsylvania also followed the New York plan of encouraging private academies to convert to normal schools.

The proposition of the state normal schools in the eastern states was to take the students as they were and attempt to make teachers of them. This often resulted in even lower standards than those of the existing high schools and academies. As time went on and conditions improved, however, the normal schools began to raise standards of admission toward the college level, which, in time, they reached.

Westward Expansion

With the founding of Michigan State Normal in 1853, the normal schools really became a national movement. Until then all existing normals had been founded in the East. But the great expansion was yet to come. According to Charles Harper,

The Michigan State Normal was the sixth to be established in the United States. By 1875, there were 70 normal schools receiving state support and another 25 receiving support from counties and cities. In 1839, there were three students enrolled in normal schools. By 1875, this number exceeded 23,000. By 1875, normals existed in 25 states. Maine, Minnesota, and Vermont each had three, Wisconsin four, Missouri five, Massachusetts and West Virginia six, New York eight, and Pennsylvania ten.[3]

This development was to be expected in view of the growing popular sentiment in favor of the public school movement; the increase of compulsory school laws; the organization of graded schools; and increasing legislative appropriations for the schools, including provisions for local tax support. The expansion of public high schools, which was just beginning, was another factor. Furthermore, while the East was still the stronghold of private education, there was a new spirit in the West. The state school systems were just getting established, and the state normal schools took a leading part in planning these systems and their development. In addition, the system of higher education and high schools was not so far advanced that it restricted the normal schools, to preparing only elementary school teachers, for example.

To finance the new state normal school, the Michigan legislature appropriated ten sections of salt spring lands for buildings and fifteen sections for an endowment. Fortunately, in the west the normal schools generally had equal claims with the universities for lands granted to the states by the federal government.

After spirited competition, Ypsilanti was chosen as the site of Michigan's first normal school. Its first term opened on March 29, 1853, and from the first it was clear that this school would be the head of the system of common schools. Enrollment for the first year was 220. In the beginning, the course was made up largely of ancient and modern languages, with pupils as young as fourteen admitted with no pledge to become teachers. Four years later the admission ages for men and women were raised to eighteen and sixteen respectively, and all students were required to take the pledge to teach. The language requirement was reorganized to distinguish between those planning to teach in the elementary grades and those planning to teach at higher levels.

Illinois was the next Western state to establish a normal school. It was the acknowledged head of the public school system, since there was no state university at that time. From the beginning, the normal school was intended to prepare teachers for all branches of the common schools, including the high schools. It was called the Illinois State Normal University, indicating that it was to be of collegiate caliber from the start. The original appropriation was an endowment providing an annual interest of more than $10,000. In 1861 the legislature appropriated $65,000 to clear up indebtedness and provide expenses, and in 1865 an additional $31,000 was appropriated. These figures show the comparative liberality of the western states in relation to the funding of early normal schools in the East. The Illinois State Normal University was placed by competitive bidding, and Bloomington won out with a subscription of $141,000. The University began with a course of three years, and within ten years the enrollment reached 500 with almost as many in the model schools.

The late 1850s and early 1860s were prosperous times in the Midwest. Railroads were being built across and down the Mississippi Valley, and agriculture was booming. The heightened economic prospects had their impact on schools in general and on normal schools in particular. The first state normal west of the Mississippi was established at Winona only three months after Minnesota became a state. The law establishing the normal created a board consisting of one member from each of the six judicial districts of the state. The board was empowered to establish the first normal school within five years of the act's passage, a second within ten years, and a third within fifteen years. The Winona school was of college caliber from the beginning, and its center was a model or practice school, detached from the local school system. In 1869 Minnesota established a second normal school at St. Cloud. Kansas was the next state west of the Mississippi to found a normal school. The school was located at Emporia and opened on February 15, 1865.

While Iowa was still a territory in 1849, a law was enacted providing for three normal schools at Andrew, Oskaloosa, and Mount Pleasant. The first two did not last long since the state failed to provide sufficient funds. However, Iowa also made the normal department an integral part of the University of Iowa in 1855. This department flourished for a number of years, but the practice school was abolished in 1866 and the normal department languished. Not until 1876 did the state again establish a normal school. This was located at Cedar Falls, and in time became the only one supported by the state. It had a distinguished record and became well known throughout the midwest. Three curricula were established: the first prepared teachers for the elementary schools and was two years in length; the second was an advanced course designed to qualify teachers for the best high schools; and the third was a scientific course designed to prepare superintendents and elementary and secondary school principals. Cedar Falls was destined to become one of the largest and most highly regarded normal schools in the country.

Wisconsin had somewhat the same philosophy about normal schools as New York. The state depended on partial support from state funds of private and public colleges and universities. A board of regents of normal schools was established with authority to distribute the income of the normal fund (derived from the sale of swamp land) to colleges, universities (except the state university), and academies, based on the holding of normal institutes and the number of students enrolled in these institutes. The plan was a failure. Thus, a department of normal instruction was established at the state university, but, as was the case at the University of Iowa, the plan did not work. Henry Barnard, who was brought into the state as chancellor and professor of normal instruction at the university, organized a series of teachers institutes. His work aroused great interest in the normal institute idea throughout the state, so much so that by 1865 Wisconsin created a Board of Regents of Normal Schools. The normal school fund was authorized to build and establish state normal schools. The first was opened at Plattsville in October 1866. Others were later established at Whitewater, Oshkosh, and River Falls.

Thus the 1860s were years of a great westward expansion of normal schools. In addition to the ones described above, the decade witnessed the opening of normal schools in California, Indiana, Nebraska, West Virginia, and Maryland. In the South the pace was much slower. Although Louisiana and South Carolina started normal schools before the Civil War, the other southern states established schools much later. Harper lists schools established in the 1870s as follows: Kirksville, Missouri (1875); Warrensburg, Missouri (1871); Florence, Alabama (1872); Athens, West Virginia (1872); Shepherdstown, West Virginia (1872); Cape Girardeau, Missouri (1873); Glenville, West Virginia (1873); and Nashville, Tennessee (1875).[4]

By 1875, the normal schools had established themselves as the main source of teachers for the common schools. The enthusiastic acceptance of the normal schools in the West helped to enhance their general acceptance in the East. Of course, great differences existed within states and from state to state. But their great importance in building a real system of public schools for all peoples was now established.

Because of the lack of a systematic means for gathering statistics on the American public school system, it is difficult to give precise information on the number of normal schools existing at the height of their expansion. We do know that they expanded rapidly after the Civil War. In 1886 a committee of the normal department of the NEA reported that there were 103 state normal schools, 22 city normals, 2 county normals and more than 100 private normal schools.[5] According to a report of the Commission of Education in 1898 there were a total of 166 public normal schools with 44,808 students and 165 private normal schools with 23,572 students. In addition, Wesley reports that about 25,000 potential teachers were enrolled in universities, colleges, and high schools, bringing the total of those preparing to teach to 93,687.[6]

Notes

1. D. Reisman and C. Jencks, *The Academic Revolution* (Garden City, N.Y.: Doubleday, 1968), p. 79.

2. As quoted in Charles A. Harper, *A Century of Public Teacher Education* (Washington, D.C.: National Education Association, 1839), pp. 21-22.

3. Harper, op. cit., pp. 72-73.

4. Ibid., p. 94.

5. Edgar B. Wesley, *NEA: The First Hundred Years* (New York: Harper, 1957), p. 17.

6. Ibid., p. 31.

4

Teachers Colleges
Supplant
Normal Schools

Influences on Transition

The state teachers colleges began to replace the normal schools about 1900. This was the result, not of weaknesses or failures of the normal schools, but of new developments in education. The transition to the teachers colleges was a normal, evolutionary step in the educational development of the country.

Proliferation of High Schools

One of the chief factors in the transition was the rapid development of public high schools after 1860. Wherever they existed, high schools had been considered part of the system of common schools. Some taxpayers fought this idea. The *Kalamazoo* case settled the question in 1874. A taxpayer sued, claiming that high schools were not part of the common school system and that he was therefore being taxed illegally for the support of such schools. The court held that high schools were part of the common schools and taxes could be levied for their support.

Although it was not the only factor involved, the *Kalamazoo* decision gave great impetus to the proliferation of public high schools. The public high school was really a product of new demands on education brought about by the increasing complexity of life in general and the rapid expansion of industry and agriculture. A good illustration can be found in the rising standards for teacher certification. In 1911 only one state had made high school graduation a prerequisite for the lowest grade certificate; by 1919 eleven states had this requirement; by 1928 it had been adopted in thirty-three states; and in the following decade, all states adopted this minimum standard.[1]

With the growth of high schools, there developed a trend toward

41

requiring the teachers in these schools to be college graduates. Some of the normal schools were of collegiate caliber, but not many. Thus, there soon developed demands that normal schools be made into degree-granting colleges. There was some pressure to discontinue the normal schools and transfer their functions to existing colleges and universities, but this was resisted because many felt that the teacher education function would be slighted in the transfer.

Regional Accreditation

Regional accrediting associations had begun developing in 1882, and by 1900 there were four: the New England Association, the Middle States Association, the Southern Association, and the North Central Association. These associations began setting standards for colleges and high schools. In 1902, for example, the North Central Association of Colleges and Secondary Schools ruled that faculty members of its member high schools must be graduates of institutions accredited by itself or a comparable association. This increased the pressure on normal schools to qualify as collegiate institutions. Many could not qualify, and the pressure grew to replace them with degree-granting teachers colleges. Naturally, the normal schools fought back.

A statement at the NEA convention in 1908 reflected the thinking of normal school leaders about normal school standards:

1. That the normal schools make high school graduation, or equivalent, a basis for admission to the standard normal course;

2. That the normal school prepare teachers for the entire public service—elementary and secondary;

3. That the preparation of elementary teachers be two years, and of the secondary, four years;

4. That the normal school establish well-organized departments of research work leading to the solution of problems affecting education and life;

5. That while the normal school is not the only agent for the training of teachers, it is the state's chief agent, and as such, it should set up standards of teaching, determine ideals, and train men and women whose call is to educational leadership;

6. That the colleges and universities should not dominate the courses of study of the high schools to the ends of making them preparatory schools, thereby preventing these schools from being the best expression of the whole people;

7. That the curriculum of the normal school should be broad enough in scope to touch all phases of special preparation demanded by the broadening curriculum of the public schools.[2]

Effects of Transition on Normal Schools

The rapidity of the trend toward the bachelors degree as a minimum requirement for beginning teachers is shown by table 1-1.

According to Hughes, the state normal school at Livingston, Alabama, was the first to convert to a state teachers college (1882).[3] By decades, the following chart gives the transitions from normal schools to teachers colleges:

1881–1890	1
1891–1900	0
1901–1910	4
1911–1920	19
1921–1930	69
1931–1940	34
1941–1950	12
Total	139

By 1951, the transitions were as shown in table 4-1. Because of the shifting nature of the designations, it is almost impossible to be precise about the number of normal schools that made the transition to teachers colleges. To begin with, as minimum state requirements increased, a great number of private normal schools simply went out of the business of preparing teachers or reverted to their former status of academies or private high schools. Quite a number of former normal schools and teachers colleges simply changed their names to state colleges of education. This happened in New York State, for example. This was a transitional step from specific teacher education institutions to general state colleges.

The following is a listing from the certification manuals of the number of single-purpose teacher education institutions (normal schools, state teachers colleges, and state colleges of education) remaining in selected years, both public and private:[4]

1951	143
1957	126
1959	99
1961	55
1964	47
1967	19*
1970	16**

*Eight public, 11 private
**Five public, 11 private

The supplanting of normal schools by teachers colleges was a natural evolutionary process rather than a revolution. Times and conditions had changed, and a new institution was needed. It was a

Table 4-1; Normal schools and teachers colleges existing in 1951[5]

State	Normals	Teachers Colleges or State Colleges of Education	Total
Alabama		3	3
Arkansas	1	2	3
Colorado		1	1
Connecticut		6	6
District of Columbia		2	2
Georgia		2	2
Illinois	1[b]	4	5
Indiana	1	2	3
Iowa		1	1
Kansas		2	2
Maine		2	2
Maryland		5	5
Massachusetts	1	8	9
Michigan	1	3	4
Minnesota		5	5
Mississippi	1	1	2
Missouri		3[a]	3
Montana		3	3
Nebraska		5[a]	5
New Hampshire		3[a]	3
New Jersey		6	6
New York		11	11
North Carolina		6	6
North Dakota	1	4	5
Ohio		2	2
Oregon		3	3
Pennsylvania		13	13
Rhode Island		1	1
South Carolina	1		1
South Dakota		4	4
Tennessee		1[a]	1
Texas		4	4
Vermont		3	3
Wisconsin	7[a]	8	15
	15	129	144

[a]County (two year) normals   [b]State Normal University

perfectly natural development, in view of the expanding system of education. The normal schools had served their purpose and served it well; they had contributed greatly to the development of a profession of teaching. With the growth of high schools it was only natural that normals hoped to continue to serve this need, but they soon realized that nothing less than degree-granting colleges would suffice. For the most part, the normal schools simply adapted to the new circumstances and made the inevitable effort to become state teachers colleges.

In changing to degree-granting teachers colleges, the normals sought to maintain their status as the main source of teachers for the public schools. They were not seeking new status or a new kind of institution but trying to defend the field they had preempted. There was, of course, apprehension that the growing power of state universities and other growing colleges and universities would preempt the function of the normal schools.

Problems

Harper designates basic problems normal schools found in the shift as follows:

1. Enrichment of the curriculum and extension of the length of their courses by one to two years.

2. Securing the necessary means of popular support for the institutions.

3. Securing the legal right to grant degrees.

4. Finding ways of preventing colleges and universities from preempting the responsibility of preparing high school teachers.

5. Facing up to the problems of meeting new standards and full fledged accreditation as standard colleges.

6. Preserving their identities and functions as single purpose teacher education institutions.[6]

The natural temptation was to ape the standard colleges and forget their basic functions: to give in to the popular and prestigious appeal of stressing academic excellence and forget to place children in the center of the learning process. The normal schools actually had fulfilled both roles; they had not concentrated on "methods" to the exclusion of academic attainments. Many of them, of course, had started this way, but generally they grew steadily toward full college status. By 1900 there were only a handful of normals with degree-granting status; by 1940 there were almost 150 degree-granting teachers colleges.

The normal schools began discussing the possibility of becoming degree-granting institutions in the late 1870s. At that time the emphasis was on professional degrees apart from the usual liberal arts degrees. For example, medicine awarded the M.D. degree; divinity the Bachelor or Doctor of Divinity degrees, and law insisted on Bachelor of Law or Doctor of Jurisprudence. The arguments favoring the teaching degrees were based on the assumptions that a teaching degree would give teachers the status of a learned group, encourage the professionalization of teaching, and enhance the development of educational philosophy and practice.

Geographic Pattern

The first normals to confer degrees based on four years of college work were at Albany, New York, and Ypsilanti, Michigan. In 1890, the Albany Normal School was changed to the Albany Normal College, and the official board was authorized to award the degree of Bachelor of Pedagogy, Master of Pedagogy, and Doctor of Pedagogy, as conditions developed justifying these degrees. When the college abandoned the preparation of elementary school teachers in 1905, the degrees changed to the Bachelor of Arts and the Bachelor of Pedagogy Degree (based on five years of college work).

The Michigan legislature called its normal school the Michigan State Normal College and began awarding the Bachelor of Arts degree in 1905. In 1907 the legislature granted the degree-awarding privilege to four other normals and authorized the degree of Bachelor of Education.

This trend quickly spread to the South and West. But in the East, the normal school had virtually surrendered the preparation of secondary school teachers to universities and colleges and restricted themselves to the preparation of elementary school teachers, perhaps feeling more secure in this capacity. Not until 1937, for example, was the Trenton Normal College name changed to the New Jersey State Teachers College at Trenton.

NEA Policy

In 1908 the NEA Department of Normal Schools developed a "statement of policy" for the normal schools that was really a program for making the transition from normal schools to teachers colleges. The statement urged the dropping of the term *normal school* in favor of *teachers college*. Moreover, the statement proposed that (1) high school graduation should be a basis for admission to the standard normal school course; (2) the normal schools should prepare both elementary and secondary school teachers; (3) preparation requirements for elementary teachers should be two years, and four years for secondary school teachers; (4) normal schools should establish departments of research; (5) while the normal schools were not the only agents for the preparation of teachers, they would be the

state's chief agent; (6) the colleges and universities should not dominate the courses of study of the high schools to the extent of making
them solely college preparatory institutions; and (7) the curricula of
the normal schools should be broad enough to touch all phases of
special preparation demanded by the field.[7]

The Normal Department was really reiterating the fears of both
the normal schools and the emerging teachers colleges, as well as
much of the general public. The regional accrediting associations
were beginning to emerge, and they were largely controlled by college people. The high schools had not as yet been given the representation on the secondary commission of these regional associations
that they were later to achieve. The trend seemed to be toward
standardizing high schools to make them, not mass education institutions, but institutions preparing students for admission to colleges
and universities. The first step in this direction occurred when the
North Central Association of Colleges and Secondary Schools began
to enforce the standard that its member high schools must employ
college graduates as teachers. This hastened the conversion of the
normal schools to degree-granting state teachers colleges.

Effects of Transition on Teachers Colleges

Single Preparation for Elementary and Secondary Teachers

There was considerable sentiment among colleges and universities
that different standards should be set for the preparation of elementary and secondary school teachers; normal schools should be continued for the purpose of preparing the elementary teachers, high
school teachers should be prepared by accredited colleges and universities. (Not until about the mid-1950s was it generally accepted that
both elementary and high school teachers should be college graduates.) The normal school people believed that this proposal would set
the elementary and secondary schools apart as competing institutions
and divorce the high school, which many people saw as the "people's
college," from the vast majority of the people by making it an institution for the educational elite preparing exclusively for classical
colleges. Therefore, the proponents of the teachers college movement
fought the trend. They declared that it would be unwise to segregate
the preparation of high school teachers from that of elementary
school teachers, because it would cause a serious breach in the preparation of children as they moved from elementary to high schools.

Problems of Accreditation

One of the problems of the new teachers colleges was that the
only accreditation to which they could aspire was that set up for

general colleges and universities. These colleges existed for different purposes, yet they wanted to insist that teachers colleges meet their standards. This problem was alleviated by the creation of standards for teachers colleges in 1923 by the American Association of Teachers Colleges and later by the establishment in 1952 of the National Council for the Accreditation of Teacher Education (NCATE). There was a great temptation for the newly emerging teachers colleges to turn away from their basic functions and seek to become general or liberal arts colleges. Some did, but most did not; they began to establish their own criteria for accreditation.

The battle of the normal schools and teachers colleges to have some part in accreditation had begun as far back as 1899, when a report of the NEA Normal School Department distributed information on the practices of normal schools in regard to practice teaching, professional courses, and academic work. In 1902 the North Central Council of Normal School Presidents was formed, and in 1912 it became the National Council of Normal School Presidents, which later (1925) merged with the American Association of Teachers Colleges.

In the meantime, the new teachers colleges were improving the academic preparation of their faculties and developing four-year courses terminating in bachelors degrees. In addition, they were broadening their curricula to provide a wide range of electives and procedures for inaugurating new courses and curricula. All these developments were primarily aimed toward the preparation of high school teachers. In most states, degree programs were still a generation removed.

General Purpose Institutions: Final Step in Transition

All these efforts prepared the teachers colleges to take over the work of the normal schools and the preparation of high school teachers as well. At least they were forestalling efforts to abolish the normal school concept and shift teacher education to general purpose colleges and universities. This shift was to come in the 1950s and 1960s, but it came through the gradual transition of the teachers colleges to broad-based collegiate institutions; The basic philosophy of professional preparation for teaching was still a prime role of the colleges and universities that eventually replaced the normal schools and teachers colleges.

Two forces were at work in this later transition. The first was the furor over the Russian Sputniks in the late 1950s, which led to the bitter criticism that the teachers colleges were neglecting the sciences and concentrating on professional methodology courses. These criticisms convinced a large segment of the public that the state teachers colleges were inferior institutions.

The second force was the inundation of colleges by veterans of World War II and an increased college age population. State legislatures felt they had no choice except to change the teachers colleges to broader-based institutions offering not only teacher education but also general liberal arts and work in several other professional fields.

Notes

1. Newtown Edwards and German G. Richey, *The School in the American Social Order,* 2d ed. (Boston: Houghton Mifflin Co., 1963), p. 593.

2. National Education Association, "Report of the Committee on Statement of Policy Regarding the Preparation and Qualifications of Teachers of Elementary and High Schools," *Journal of Proceedings and Addresses of the Forty-Sixth Annual Meeting, Cleveland, Ohio, June 29-July 3, 1908* (Chicago: University of Chicago Press, 1908), p. 735.

3. Rees H. Hughes, "Changing Status of Teacher Education Institutions," *Journal of Teacher Education* (March 1951): 48-50.

4. *Manual on Certification Requirements for School Personnel in the United States,* published in the years listed by the National Education Association.

5. Adapted from *A Manual on Certification Requirements for School Personnel in the United States* (Washington, D.C.: National Education Association, 1951), p. 19.

6. Charles A. Harper, *A Century of Public Teacher Education* (Washington, D.C.: National Education Association, 1839), p. 130.

7. Ibid., pp. 137-38.

5

Teacher Education

as an

All-College Function

After a century and a half, teacher education has found its place as a respectable—if not always respected—discipline in higher education. A handful of lowly normal schools began the process of the professional preparation of teachers; full-fledged colleges and universities denigrated this effort and would have nothing to do with it. That has changed, and all types of colleges and universities are now engaged in teacher education.

Now that teacher education has passed from the normal schools and teachers colleges to the general colleges and universities, many are skeptical of the ability and willingness of these general institutions to produce effective teachers for the lower schools. One of the authors of this book has published his doubts in the form of twenty-three assumptions. Some excerpts follow:

Whatever is wrong with teacher education is wrong with higher education. With active student "help," colleges and universities have been exposed as unable to meet a double-barrelled challenge: relevance for individual students and action against societal problems. Most critics of teacher education naively fail to recognize that any criticism of teacher education can be strengthened and amplified to include the higher education that functions as its parent and protector.

If this contention seems to be a bit strong, it merely indicates that the clutching bear hug in which universities hold teacher education has dulled our senses. After a century of struggle to become respectable, teacher educators need critically to reexamine what we gave up in return for membership in the university club.

If we continue to act on unexamined assumptions, fantasy will continue to serve as program rationale. Our elaborate institutional coping mechanism (the university) helps us to make believe we are engaged in reasonable behavior directed at socially useful ends. Such delusions are not all evil; they sustain us in a complex world of powerful forces. . . .

Following are twenty-three assumptions—there are undoubtedly many more—we unthinkingly accept in the process of perpetuating the delusion that teachers can be educated for the real world in colleges and universities. Three kinds of positive change can result from discussing these assumptions openly: we might try to change a few of the university conditions that militate against teacher education; we might support rather than crush organizations outside the university that seek to prepare teaching personnel; we might revel in our irrelevance and seek to become change agents who educate teachers for the best of all nonexistent worlds—and how to get there.

1. *College-lower school cooperation is possible.* Slow-witted, lumbering elephants circle each other for a century only to discover they are both males and incapable even of friendship. Reports, books, and demonstration projects on how we can cooperate have not affected any reality. One simple example of this organizational gap is that lower schools seek to exploit these situations as vehicles for student teachers' growth. . . .

2. *Personnel in schools and colleges can work together.* As if working in mutually exclusive organizations and being reinforced by different reward systems were not enough, personality and value differences are quite common. Public school people regard college people as too theoretical and more concerned with analysis than solutions, not capable of working within legal structures, incapable of hard work during regularly scheduled business hours. College people perceive public school people as too conservative in accepting research or responding to great social problems. . . . Public school people evaluate themselves positively for improving present systems and achieving present goals more effectively. College people evaluate themselves positively for advocating basic structural changes in lower schools. In truth, both groups are experts in maintaining their own organizations and espousing radical reforms in the other.

3. *Academic disciplines are related to lower school curriculum.* More and more institutions have exchanged electives for requirements. Free choice, however, does not work magic on irrelevant fare. . . .

In order to put knowledge into the more integrated forms in which it is used in lower schools (and in life), universities have for decades tried to institutionalize interdisciplinary studies. These efforts break down for several reasons: team teaching does not meet the individualistic needs or the role concept of college faculty, more planning time is required than when teaching alone, graduate schools require advanced work in single disciplines as prerequisites, students and faculty have been conditioned to regard survey and interdisciplinary work as superficial.

The Office of Education and private foundations have spent tens of millions building heavy arts and science components into teacher education on the assumption that established disciplines can make themselves relevant (and upgrade) lower school curricula. But the simple truth is that sound elementary and secondary education is rooted in problems of living and in expanding personal consciousness while the higher education is carefully derived from clearly delimited fields of study. This gap is not a sinister plot but the inevitable result of the historical differences between common schools and universities.

4. *Professional knowledge can be acted on in lower schools.* Schools are organized for widespread public support and cannot afford the luxury of specific objectives. A riding academy, driving school, or farm for fat ladies can implement skills of teaching, a particular learning theory, and a standard program. Schools, on the other hand, try to be all things to all people to justify collecting everyone's taxes. . . .

In order for schools of education to implement professional knowledge, we would first have to abandon the myth that all can be admitted, all prepared in one smorgasbord, and all certified as good for all the boys and girls everywhere. . . . The likelihood that schools of education will specify parallel programs is as wishful as the expectation that lower schools will do so. In the absence of such specificity, we shall continue to pretend there is a universal professional theory undergirding our programs.

5. *Students who select themselves for teaching are open to change.* Whether an individual is just picking up a certificate or avoiding the draft is irrelevant since initial motivation does not in itself preclude anyone from learning to teach. The real problem is that large numbers of students self-select on the basis of their own previous schooling experiences, and as a result, have built-in, almost irreversible, rigidities. The assumption that teacher education students eagerly anticipate working in schools that are dramatic departures from those they attended cannot be supported by any data, while high positive correlations do exist between having a vocational orientation and a fit-in mentality.

6. *Late adolescents are in the most appropriate developmental stage for learning to teach.* Learners' growth and development are of critical concern to educators up through high school graduation. Following a ten-week summer, adolescents are transformed into mature men and women. Our acceptance of this instant metamorphosis is supported by our flimsy literature on college teaching. . . .

Professional teachers are capable of nurturing, eliciting, caring, supporting, empathizing, and deemphasizing their own needs in the process of enhancing others. Late adolescent Americans, if normal, are egocentric, self-indulgent, uncertain, and in need of massive doses of approval, self-confidence, and support. There is probably no worse stage of life in which to prepare for teaching than late adolescence. . . .

7. *College faculty are capable of relating theory to practice.* Most college faculty perform in a neverland that falls between sound theory and competent practice. Neither composers nor performers, we are Lawrence Welks in academe. The rare scholar with a unifying theory of learning or curriculum can be written off as "impractical" while the effective practitioner is inevitably "poorly grounded" (i.e., he lacks an advanced degree).

8. *College instruction can be a modeling process of the way students should teach in the lower schools.* Such shopworn abnegation should cease. Following are just a few of the reasons why parallelism in methodologies can be only the exception rather than the rule. . . .

A basic assumption of compulsory schooling is that teachers are responsible for finding better methods; the basic assumption of the faculty is that better students should have been admitted.

Schoolteachers assume motivation to be part of instruction; professors assume this to be the students' responsibility. . . .

School culture indoctrinates pupils to value teachers who are helpful; college conditions students to respect experts.

Schools are measured by pupil achievement; universities, by research activity and size.

And most critical of all, lower education is more concrete and couched in personal activity and experience; higher education is more abstract and supported quite well by reading, writing, formal experimentation, and discussion.

9. *The college environment supports a reward system that facilitates teacher education.* The real criteria of academe are . . . research, writing, consulting, teaching graduate seminars, teaching classes, administration, and working with students in field experiences. . . .

10. *Colleges are accountable for their graduates' performance.* Colleges and universities sell courses: no register, no tuition; no tuition, no faculty; no

faculty, no follow-up. In those rare instances when we do follow up . . . we get off the accountability hook by asking, How can we educate effective, creative, socially conscious teachers when the schools they work in are oppressive? . . .

11. *Colleges can change and improve themselves and schools through research, demonstration, creative proposals, and dissemination programs.* Laboratory schools have not been the only casualties of this assumption, government agencies and private foundations have placed universities in the role of "mover and shaker" only to end up in the same place at greater cost. After much time and money, there isn't a single example of school change which university faculty have researched and advocated that is now accepted practice. . . .

Our record for self-change is even more dismal. After decades of massive aid for innovation, which university has been significantly changed? What critics said of the total university in 1940 they could repeat in 1970, and ditto for teacher education. But this "and ditto for teacher education" is a much different assumption from that made by our most infamous critics, who assume the rest of academe as a yardstick for teacher education.

12. *College leadership—particularly in schools of education—is concerned and involved with problems of the lower schools.* After three years, my dean met the local school superintendent for the first time. In other cities they meet even less frequently—and what does it matter anyway? Deans are evaluated on five criteria: how they handle student disturbances; faculty work, scandal, and morale; the amount of outside research money they can generate; growth, as measured by irrelevant quantitative factors; the introduction of small, flashy innovation projects that take the heat off evaluating traditional programs. . . .

. . . any education dean who honestly took the position that his evaluation and budget should be based on the impact of his college on the lower schools and community would put himself and his school out of business. . . .

13. *The public sees and expects a cooperative relationship between colleges and lower schools.* Relationships are conceived in individual, not organizational, terms; that is, What will John and Mary need to get into Siwash State? not, What organizational connections can be made? That the university faculty would never dream of meeting with a local high school faculty in order to seek curriculum connections is, in part, a function of the fact that lower schools are local and higher education is statewide, regional, and national. But more fundamental is the assumption that the relationship is all one way—up. . . .

For teacher education, the tacit expectation of the public is that schools of education will prepare students to be successful teachers in present forms of schooling. They would be shocked if they knew the real level of noncooperation and the increasing number of faculty and school people who question the desirability of working together.

14. *Colleges influence teachers' future performance more than the situations in which graduates subsequently operate.* Teachers fit in, fight, or flee. They are not instruments of change that introduce great new ideas from college into the lower schools. Nothing we offer future teachers—whether skills, values, or theory—can withstand what they learn on the job as practitioners. If preservice preparation should prove more powerful than the situational press, the teacher would probably be fired. . . .

15. *Lower schools can change by educating individual teachers.* Teacher education is based on an individual entrepreneur model. If Susie Smith improves her ability to teach reading and then works anywhere she chooses, great social problems can be ameliorated. . . . We wasted a decade trying to equalize schooling by appealing to individuals. NDEA institutes, master's programs, sabbaticals,

etc., like all historical efforts to improve teacher education, are based on the monumental idiocy that each Susie Smith will, in the process of pursuing her own best interests, make a contribution that will cumulate into important social change.

16. *Colleges can relate to community groups and schools.* The recent growth of community schools, particularly black urban schools, has once again revealed the bureau-pathology of our university organization. We sell courses; even extension services cannot be made relevant to the needs perceived by the urban community. We lack the minority faculty members with the credibility, the know-how, the will, and the organization to help communities with their goals. . . .

17. *Colleges can work with professional organizations.* Which college makes student teacher and intern placements through its local teachers association? Where are association representatives involved in evaluating and revising teacher education programs? Which college offers inservice education and research under the auspices of local teachers' association? Which colleges are engaged in helping associations gain a share in the power to recommend for state certification?

18. *College programs represent and offer the best of what is now known about teacher education.* It is a rare treat to meet school of education faculty (or any others) who are conversant with the literature in teacher education. Faculties are composed of specialists in learning, reading, administration, etc. There are few who read and research the values and limitations of various new programs in teacher education. Fortunately, such ignorance in no way interferes with our willingness to discuss, vote, and exert exclusive control over programs. . . .

19. *College programs of teacher education can be evaluated, changed, and improved.* (Even our critics assume this.) Although accreditation teams usually make a few useful suggestions, their level of change is watered down by dealing with it on a literal rather than a spiritual basis. . . .

Self-evaluations are usually hopeless opinionnaires which demonstrate that our particular course received "very favorable" student reactions. In truth, changes in higher education are not planned; they are most frequently the result of chance or unpredicted events. . . .

20. *Colleges can upgrade inservice teaching personnel.* In a recent seminar with childhood education experts, we discussed Piaget, Bruner, and the implications of Skinner. That night, I was up until 3:00 A.M. with three of the best (by consensus) teachers of kindergarten in Milwaukee. They discussed chair throwing, starvation, love on the run, and the process of human caring between fits and starts of bedlam. The issue is not the simple-minded charge that we can't relate theory to practice but that disciplined academic knowledge is, by its very nature, not capable of transfer. . . .

21. *Colleges can evaluate each other.* They do, but on organizational rather than content criteria. A review of AACTE bulletins, as well as attendance at their meetings, will reveal that this association of school of education deans is concerned with the enhancement of an oligarchy. . . .

22. *Approved programs of certification should be confined to colleges and universities.* Sound teacher education is based on an interrelationship between fieldwork and conceptual activities. Although schools control the former and colleges the latter, the locus of program control is vested in the college. . . . no rhetoric can describe this situation as a partnership.

In the future, lower schools in need of fewer teachers will be less submissive to university exploitation than they have been in the past. Approved programs should not be limited to institutions of higher education; community groups, schools, and private enterprise should be permitted to compete with programs that have state approval. The assumption that college faculty have a corner on relevant expertise is not supportable by data. . . .

23. *Colleges can respond to great social problems by becoming directly involved in action programs.* Up to two years ago, militancy was a valid strategy for awakening a higher education that seemed responsible to only Rickoverish needs. . . . With this reaffirmed direction, the fact that schools of education are locked into universities is of ultimate significance. . . .

These twenty-three assumptions are merely illustrative of the basic issue. What is the potential of a teacher education ensconced in the university?[1]

Volumes could be written (and many have been) about the social, economic, and political ramifications of such an attitude. Whether America would ever have become the democratic nation it is had we not departed from the meritocratic concept of higher education is a highly interesting and debatable question. Suppose, for example, we had developed no normal school or any institution to prepare teachers for the common schools. Would our high schools have ever come into being? Would we then have adhered to the notion of higher education only for the wealthy or the extremely bright? Would the mass of our people have been condemned to common labor or lower-class designations as in some European countries? No one can answer these questions, but this we do know: by creating an institution that made it possible for every American to get some measure of education, we helped establish the first broadly based attempt at universal education.

Suppose our colleges and universities had simply refused to have anything to do with these lowly teacher training institutions or had refused them any kind of accreditation or transfer of credit. The door would have been closed. Before 1927 teachers colleges were barred from admission to the accreditation associations. It was only after the American Association of Teachers Colleges was formed in 1923 to define accrediting standards for teachers colleges that one of the regional associations relented and admitted such colleges to membership and accreditation. Thereafter, the others began accrediting these institutions one by one.

Of course, these single-purpose institutions had great support from the public. In the first place, most of them were located relatively near the homes of their students, and their tuitions were generally lower than those of most state universities or private colleges. These institutions had a ready-made clientele waiting to support them in state legislatures and give them the kind of support they needed to survive and flourish.

Now, the old shibboleths and prejudices have pretty much disappeared. The fact is that the single-purpose teacher education institutions (normal schools and state teachers colleges) have been rapidly disappearing; in 1970 only five public and eleven private teachers colleges survived. Teacher education is now a function of almost every type of college and university. In 1970 there were 1,246 colleges and universities providing teacher education programs out of a total of nearly 2,500 degree-granting colleges and universities. Part of the reason for this is that for two decades about one-third of all first degree graduates of all colleges and universities have prepared for teaching. Thus, the size of the teacher education clientele is a big attraction. Secondly, the single-purpose teacher education institutions have made a sincere effort to lift their standards of general education to a level equal to those of our best colleges and universities. Moreover, they have tried to accord liberal arts and other faculty members a voice in determining what should constitute the teacher education program of given institutions, whereas these decisions were once made solely by professors of education, state departments of education, and the teaching profession.

On most campuses today, there is an advisory council on teacher education that determines the components of the teacher education program. These councils include members from all departments having a role in the education of teachers. The approved programs approach, which is now used by most states, developed within this context. The essence of the approved programs approach is that, instead of following a state's prescribed course requirements for certification, each institution plans and offers its own program, subject to the approval of the state department of education. The institution recommends certification for the candidate successfully completing the approved program, and certification is granted rather automatically. The strength of this program is twofold: (1) the individual institution is not forced into a narrow prescription of courses laid down by certification requirements; and (2) it can plan its programs according to its own philosophy, clientele, faculty, and facilities. No two institutions are precisely alike. Therefore, great flexibility should be allowed in the planning of institutional programs.

There are some weaknesses in this approach, but there are many more strengths. The state department of education prescribes some minimum guidelines, such as student teaching, but details are left to the institution. This approach may lead to a diversity of teacher education programs, but that is not necessarily bad. In fact it may be good, since there is no general agreement on what constitutes a good teacher education program; there are too many variables. Programs should be flexible, and substitutions of courses should be made when justified by the background of a given student. Many education or general courses can be skipped after careful testing and analysis of students' reading backgrounds and experiences. Institutions may occasionally "cheat" on the approved programs, but state departments of education have developed a sampling technique in which the records of a small number of persons certified from given institutions are checked each year against the program approved for the institution. If a glaring number of deviations are discovered, the institution in question is asked to explain. In extreme cases, the privilege of the approved program approach may be taken from the institutions.

All these things have tended to eliminate the bitter differences that once existed between single-purpose teacher education institutions and general colleges and universities, and teacher education has become a function largely of the latter. But by far the greatest reason for this was expanding college enrollments, which forced legislatures to convert single-purpose institutions to multipurpose ones. Long before the postwar boom in student enrollments, teachers colleges in general had added other degrees than those for teaching.

What actually has happened is described by Commager:

Almost imperceptibly, the normal schools imposed their standards on many of the colleges. They have long abandoned the name "normal school" for "teachers colleges" and now are in the process of abandoning "teachers college" for "university." This change ... suggests how successfully the normal schools of an earlier day have carried their standards, interests, and attitudes into the colleges and universities. ... As for the teaching of subject matter—which traditionally belonged to the universities rather than to teacher training institutions—we need no longer inquire; for the controversy has been ended to all intents and purposes by the old familiar principle: if you can't lick them, join them. Teacher training colleges have joined, or have absorbed, or have transformed themselves into colleges and universities, and thereby have made their own teaching of subjects, on almost any level, respectable.[2]

Perhaps a word should be said here about the slowness of the universities to enter the teacher education field. There were sporadic efforts in the early years—largely in the West and by legislative action—to get universities involved. This was particularly true when public high schools began to become common. New York University established a chair for the philosophy of education in 1832, but it did not last long. A normal department was established at Brown University in 1850 but was discontinued when Rhode Island established a normal school in 1854. Normal schools developed early in the East and carried much of the load of preparing teachers for the common schools. In the West, however, normal schools developed slowly, and in the meantime pressures developed to establish normal departments in the state universities. Such departments were established at the University of Indiana in 1852, at the University of Iowa in 1855, at the University of Wisconsin in 1856, at the University of Missouri in 1868, at the University of Kansas in 1866, and at the universities of Utah, North Dakota, and Wyoming in 1881. Some of these were discontinued when normal schools were established in their states. Subsequently, teacher education in these universities was resumed, and chairs of education rapidly became departments of education. Thus, by 1970 there were 1,246 colleges and universities preparing teachers in the United States.

The belief persists that normal schools, and later teachers colleges, prepared all or almost all of the nation's teachers. This has not been true for a long time. In 1960, for example, the institutions preparing teachers were "85 teachers colleges (73 public and 12 private); 221 universities (93 public and 128 private); 891 general and liberal arts colleges (340 public and 551 private); and 122 technical schools, junior colleges, and unclassified schools."[3] Using the latest available data on the teacher education graduates of these institutions (1958), there were 114,411 graduates who had prepared for teaching. Of this number, 20 percent came from the teachers colleges (23.7 percent elementary and 17.6 percent high school teachers). About 44 percent came from the general or liberal arts colleges (43.3 percent of the new elementary school teachers and 45.1 percent of the new high school teachers). There was an almost equal division between the public and private general colleges. The 221 universities produced 35.6 percent of the new teachers (public universities, 25.3 percent and private universities, 10.3 percent). Public institutions of all types prepared about two-thirds and private institutions about one-third of the new teachers in that year.[4]

Of the 1,246 institutions preparing teachers in 1970, 36 were junior colleges (14 of these being two-year normals in Wisconsin that have now been abandoned), the others offered the first two years of work toward degree programs. A total of 631 offered the bachelors degree, 357 offered the masters degree, and 46 offered six-year programs leading to the specialist in education degree or a special certificate or diploma. A total of 171 offered either the Ph.D. or the Ed.D. degree.

With teacher education now largely a function of general colleges and universities, the great problem will be to synchronize the general and professional aspects of preparation. The integrity of the professional school or department must be protected and permitted to serve the needs of the teaching profession; it must not be restricted to meet standards and procedures prescribed by the general college.

Notes

1. Martin Haberman, "Twenty-Three Reasons Universities Can't Educate Teachers," *Journal of Teacher Education* (Summer 1971): 133-40.

2. Henry Steele Commager, "Challenges for Teacher Education," in *Frontiers in Education,* Nineteenth Yearbook of the American Association of Colleges for Teacher Education (Washington, D.C.: the Association, 1966), p. 55.

3. T. M. Stinnett, "Certification Requirements and Procedures Among the States, 1960," *The Journal of Teacher Education* (June 1962): 175.

4. National Education Association, Research Division. *Teacher Supply and Demand in the Public Schools, 1959.* Washington, D.C.: the Association, 1959, p. 14.

6

Selection of Students into Teacher Education Programs

The Need for Better Selection

Individuals differ in their susceptibility to college influences. Programs of teacher education exert a special kind of personal-professional influence, because they enhance and exaggerate the natural propensities and latent values already present in the students. Simply stated, whatever predispositions the students have are matured and supported by their programs. Students who are prejudiced will see their prejudices borne out in their pupils; they will use their experiences to intensify their bigotry. Students who perceive children as naturally vital and interested in learning will strengthen this perception. Whatever the value, attitude, or perception, the graduate will "be" more of it, and "have" more of it, than the beginner.

Selective perception is a self-fulfilling prophecy. The student starts with only hunches and inclinations but finishes with data; "I student taught down there and . . . ." Even if he starts with outright distortions—e.g. intelligence is racially linked—he will finish with a bibliography and experiences that support his misconceptions. Thus, while good students in teacher education are not exactly born, neither can they be produced from scratch. Many are naturally predisposed to learn what the faculty and future employers value, but others are inclined to perceive and reinforce what present representatives of the system do not value.

Admittedly, there are powerful forces that influence students to significant degrees. Almost every survey of attitudes and values indicates a difference between college and noncollege populations, as well as between entering and graduating students. It is our contention, however, that the direction and nature of these changes will be a function of the students' personality, values, and life style; certainly not inherent but shaped before admission.

The issue then is not simply an academic squabble regarding nature versus nurture; we must determine what kinds of people are influenced (reinforced and enhanced) in what ways by a particular program of teacher education. Then, assuming we know the purposes and influences we desire our programs to exert, what kinds of people should we select for them and how?

Processes of Selection

Two distinct processes of selection are critical in teacher education: (1) the selection of college students into preparation programs and (2) the selection of certified graduates into practice in public schools. During periods of teacher shortage the selection of students frequently becomes an outright recruitment program. During periods of oversupply, attention shifts to the processes and criteria by which public schools hire teachers.

Public School Selection

Public school selection is essentially a slot-filling operation; schools do not seek "good" people and then determine their functions. Specific positions, with delimited functions and, almost always, a particular state certificate requirement, are budgeted on an annual basis. Applicants are interviewed specifically to fill these clearly defined roles. This is an understandable process in a publicly budgeted, closely scrutinized, traditional public system.

The schools do not seek the most experienced practitioners, because they can rarely pay for more than eight years of previous experience. This is especially true in large urban areas where hundreds of thousands of dollars are "saved" each year by hiring beginners rather than experienced personnel. The cynical (realistic?) interpretation is that many cities could not afford their instructional staffs if they sought experienced teachers and paid for all the applicants' years of experience. Certainly, if "beginners can be as effective as experienced teachers," teaching would be a nonprofession, since by definition there is always more to learn in a profession and professionals grow continuously.

Interviews by employing districts usually involve clerical, educational-experiential, and human levels. Clerical items include the nature of the applicant's license; his place of residence, age, and sex; and all the things that can be quickly filled out on a form or answered by short, declarative statements. The professional-experiential level usually includes a review of work and college experiences. The interview process frequently permits the applicant to elaborate about a particular job or his student teaching. The "human" criteria are most important, although they are the kinds of things that personnel officers are reluctant to admit they use. These criteria include subjective reactions to appearance, speech, verbal expression, confidence, and appropriateness; that is, will this person fit into the role we have in mind? Race and ethnic background may produce preferential or discriminatory reactions depending on the setting and the times. The purpose of all this is always the same: personnel officers are successful if they select people who fit in (not fight), who do a better job achieving established goals (not introduce new purposes or drop established ones), and who get along with the present staff (not challenge or threaten them).

Although the tremendous number of applicants for each position enhances the public schools' ability to seek conformers, selection remains a vital concern. While increasing numbers of students are seeking to enter teacher education programs, quotas are being established in universities and regents and trustees are considering smaller programs in state colleges. Concern has shifted to the issue of equality of opportunity: Who should be permitted to prepare for teaching? Who shall decide? What processes and criteria should be used?

College Selection

College selection has been largely concerned with refining the procedures for predicting the successful *student* of education rather than the successful practitioner. Standardized instruments (e.g. Minnesota Teacher Attitude Inventory and National Teachers Examination) have been used more for descriptive research than as criteria of selection. Personal interviews are rare, because they require heavy investments of faculty time. Essentially, college admissions officers use clerical and standard college criteria, such as grades, courses completed, and proficiency exams. The simplest test for teacher educators who deny they are traditionally linked to success as perceived for college students rather than practitioners is to ask, "If a student has a 3.5 grade point average and has completed all the proper forms, what could prevent his entering your program? How often has such an exclusion occurred?" These questions immediately cut through the rhetoric to determine whether any human or personal considerations are actually implemented.

The state of the art of selection is presently poor, because follow-up is difficult if not impossible unless several conditions are recognized.

1. Assumptions of common purpose are increasingly less true. In

the past most teacher educators felt that the ultimate test of their programs was how well the graduates performed as teachers. Many of them, however, now advocate deschooling society; others are interested in community and alternative schools; and still others advocate preparing graduates who can radically change the present forms of schooling. With fewer jobs, most graduates are really being prepared to be more sensitive parents and taxpayers. Thus, it is no longer common sense to assume that all teacher educators perceive their job as assessable in terms of their graduates' work in the classroom.

2. Criterion variables are difficult to establish owing to the lack of common purpose. Because the evaluation of teaching practice is no longer the only assumed basis for judging programs, the achievement of specific skills (e.g., simulation exercises, micro-teaching, etc.), as well as knowledge, creativity, values, and personality tests, are being used for evaluation.

On-the-job evaluation is concerned with product, that is, "What can our graduates do as teachers to affect their pupils' learning?" Assessing graduates' behavior when they complete their training programs is a second level of product criteria. Here the behaviors students demonstrate are those assumed to lead to pupil growth, e.g., the ability to state behavioral objectives or use differentiated levels of reading material.

A third kind of evaluation criterion is advocated by teacher educators who are concerned with existential and humanistic concerns. They emphasize the processes of human interaction and consider their graduates are doing things that they perceive as meaningful in their own lives. Whether a student quits, starts a school, or teaches in an existing one, the issue is one of his individual congruence and whether he is living by what he values.

A fourth level of evaluation criteria has to do with social action and change. A growing group of teacher educators are less concerned with product in present schools or processes of human interaction than with changing the social setting that influences education. They point out graduates who have gone into community organization work or special projects or are activists for change within the present system as examples of the social utility of the teacher education program.

Religious, esthetic, and child-development criteria could also be cited, but the point is that faculty rarely agree on the yardsticks by which to assess programs.

3. Establishing causal connections is a research difficulty that is not readily overcome. There are too many factors that intervene between the time a student is admitted to a program of preparation

and the time he "produces," by whatever criterion. Given present research knowledge, the best we can do is correlate factors that seem plausibly related to subsequent practice. The obvious danger is that in the past intelligent researchers have thought of "plausible" reasons for connecting factors, such as relating whether it was the student's mother or father who wanted the student to become a teacher with the subsequent rating of school supervisors and principals. Connecting admission factors with later practice is so risky that it is seldom tried.

4. The expense of follow-up research is prohibitive to universities and schools operating on tight budgets. Follow-up is not supported by tuition.

5. Support and responsibility for graduates is closely related to expense. Universities feel responsible only for enrolled, paying students, and the schools feel no obligation to help track down graduates in order to improve college programs. In addition, school systems are reluctant to have outsiders assess "their" teachers, especially if follow-up involves personality testing and observation of the teacher's performance.

6. Enthusiasm is dampened by the profession's lack of control of entry requirements. Those of us who do research on selection pursue it as an interesting form of scholarship, not because we think it will change any practices. Students not admitted to one program seek another; students carefully screened in one university might be readily admitted in another, and the certification requirements of neighboring states differ. New knowledge in one area is not likely to affect the total entry into the profession.

7. The vested interest of many colleges in having as many teacher education students as possible in order to remain "multi-purpose" institutions hinders the collection and use of evidence on admissions. It is inevitable that the more we learn, the more selective we will become.

The foregoing raises selection problems that should be dealt with directly. "Too many" students seeking admission may mean several things. It may reflect a lack of overall opportunities for self-realization in other areas normally pursued by college youth. If sensitive, idealistic, educated young people want to interact with others and improve society, why should they be limited to teaching? The bumper stickers that ask, "After college—what?" reflect the general perception of college youth that there are few meaningful and relevant career alternatives.

A second reason for "too many" teachers is the assumption that a thirty-to-one ratio is the best criterion of teacher need. If our country spent 60 percent of the gross national product on education as some nations do (rather than the present 4 percent), this perception of needs would change. And if educators could successfully communicate the realities of individualization to the public, "normal" might be a three-to-one ratio.

In addition to the problem of too many applicants, there is always the belief that "the right people" are not applying. Advocates of this belief emphasize the need to recruit more minorities, men, activists, creatives, high I.Q.'s, or whatever, before setting quotas and limiting admissions.

Problems of Self-Selection

The advocates of self-selection cite substantial research evidence to support their contentions. They recommend wide experiences in teaching and related areas as the most effective means for helping students decide their own futures. This method, however, raises problems, including the need for more student time, greater university resources devoted to field work, and a more careful system for providing valid experiences on which students can make judgments. Ultimately, of course, there may still be an oversupply of self-selected individuals, because of a lack of meaningful opportunities outside of teaching. External judgments may be inescapable no matter how carefully we plan student field work and self-determination.

Problems of "Outsiders"

Another rarely considered issue is how selection and admissions policies affect transfer students and adult graduates who seek admission to certification programs. Admission criteria are usually established for undergraduates beginning as adolescents and working through a four-year program in the same institution. The same is true when quotas are set for "outside" students. Strange as it may seem, transfer and certification people are often regarded and treated like second-class citizens, even in public, tax-supported schools.

In addition to the problems discussed above, there is the ultimate question of purpose. If we really value change, then the predisposition to work as an innovator and change agent should be a critical component of the admission-selection criteria. The difficulties of establishing such predilections are obvious; should an interview, dress, rhetoric, or hostility toward systems people be used as evidence that a student is change oriented?

Principles for Developing Admission Programs
in Teacher Education

In an effort to set positive guidelines, it might be useful to state some principles of selection that take into account the issues and problems discussed above. The following seven concepts can provide direction for institutions facing the pressure to develop a rationale and procedures to guide admission policies for programs of teacher education.

1. All students have the right to general education. The right to pursue professional education may be extended only by the recommendation of professional experts employing selection criteria that have been carefully conceived, systematically applied, and regularly evaluated.

2. Clerical and bureaucratic requirements should be met before initiating any processes of admission and selection; these should be of a minimal nature, easily and quickly completed.

3. Self-selection is a necessary but insufficient condition for determining admission to teacher education programs; it occurs in stages over a one-year period.

a. The basis of initial self-selection is brief and varied observation of the work activities and professional life style of the teacher.

b. The basis of final selection is self-selection after an extended period of participation in all phases of the teachers' work.

c. Selection experiences should carry college credit and be designated as fieldwork, never as student teaching or internship.

4. Subjective judgments of professional experts (faculty and practitioners) regarding self-selected students are the ultimate basis for full admission to programs of teacher education.

a. Programs are schoolwide not the domain of individual faculty; genuine admission interviews are conducted by a committee of at least three, composed of faculty and practitioner-graduates who do not agree on their philosophy and practices in teacher education.

b. Subjective judgments are based on intensive interviews, oral examinations using simulated experiences, or direct observation of students' work and are never limited to cursory meetings or reactions to written documents.

c. Students' opportunities for self-selection based on their direct participation should precede any judgments by admission committees.

5. Traditional admission criteria such as college requirements and

objective examinations should be used after selection as a basis for planning subsequent work, not as a basis for determining admission.

a. All college requirements (e.g., grade point average, total course credits, specific course requirements, proficiency examinations in English and speech, and physical fitness), that are used in planning students' subsequent work should be explained by a careful rationale of their relationship to success in teaching.

b. All standardized tests (e.g., The National Teachers Examination or The Minnesota Teacher Attitude Inventory) should be explained by a careful rationale of their relationship to success in teaching.

6. Quotas for limiting admissions to the various programs should be established by a committee of faculty, practitioner-graduates, and others and should be approved annually by the total school of education faculty.

a. Specific quotas and their rationale should be current, public information.

b. Quotas for each program should include places for transfer students and certification-graduate students.

7. The selection process covers a period of up to one year, involves students in credit and noncredit activities, requires substantial clerical support, and involves a major institutional commitment of faculty time. Approximately the first half of the programs now offered as teacher education must be reconceptualized as the process of selection and admission.

The preceding principles deserve some elaboration. Principle 1 may not appear startling or worthy of mention to those unfamiliar with the history of teacher education. For more than a century, the lower socioeconomic strata have used teaching as an educational opportunity for their children. Teacher education did not even begin to equal a college education until after World War II; preparing to teach was the most widely offered opportunity available to large numbers of the urban working classes, the farm population, and women generally. The cumulative weight of these traditions makes us regard any effort to limit, selectively admit, or apply quotas as an abridgment of students' rights.

This traditional emphasis on college students' opportunities and rights rather than on the needs of the profession was until recently strengthened and rationalized by the great need for teachers and increased concern about minority members' rights to higher education. The seventies, however, have been characterized by job shortages and a wider participation of minorities in all areas of college and economic life, and it has become necessary to reiterate a basic concept of professionalism. Professional education is not an inalienable right of college students or applicants under which the university has the onus for explaining denials of admission. The "right" to higher general education is another matter entirely. The profession, acting through university programs of preparation, has the responsibility for using public criteria, applying them in an equitable manner, and carefully screening and selecting applicants for admission.

Principle 2 refers to the need for broad screening to expedite applications. Students who are not enrolled in the university, can only attend in the evenings (thereby precluding any laboratory experiences), or are unable to pass a physical examination can be helped to save their own time and the resources of the university. We must, however, ensure that this principle of initial screening deals only with basic minimum requirements for full-time university study, not with criteria of admission to programs of teacher education. This phase is merely for the purpose of establishing that the applicant has the technical right to apply for admission.

Principle 3 refers to the heart of the selection process. In most programs the students and faculty have a good idea who should be admitted just about when most are ready for graduation and certification. This guideline outlines a process that emphasizes self-selection.

a. The student must be provided with realistic substitutes for the memories and misperceptions that presently motivate students to apply. A real effort to help students gain an up-to-date view of the teacher's work and role will facilitate genuine self-selection.

b. The student should complete an intensive period of teaching experiences before full admission to teacher education. This will give them some basis for answering the question, "Do I want to be with children and other teachers in a building like this every day?"

c. Students who are not admitted to teacher education should receive credit toward general education and total college requirements. There is no reason to penalize students who spend time in direct experiences, determining if teaching is for them—especially since we now regard parenthood and the layman's consumption of educational services as dimensions of general education.

Obviously, much university time and effort will be devoted to structuring and supervising the early experiences of students, many of whom will never enter regular programs. It is our contention that such expenditures for selection of the best candidates are more valid than the present expenditures for the complete training of everyone.

Principle 4 refers to the need for open and equitable external judgments. Self-selection will not meet the full need, because some students are forced to lie to themselves about their real motivations and apply anyway. This principle establishes the right of the professional faculty to select, the wisdom of openly affirming that we use subjective judgment, and the safeguard of depending on more than one opinion. It stresses the intensive interview as the most critical and the final selection procedure.

Principle 5 relegates the traditional criteria we usually use first to the fifth phase of the selection process. The reason for this change of sequence is that students may perform well enough during the self-selection experiences and the interview to get some of the written criteria waived. By placing grades, tests, and proficiencies first, as we now do, we undervalue self-selection and faculty interviews. In the proposed sequence, traditional criteria become much more amenable to individualization and special treatment. Outstanding students can better demonstrate that they deserve special treatment in practice and interviews than they can in the present procedures, which define "outstanding" only in relation to grades.

Principle 6 deals with the future quotas to be established and the rationales for them. The issue of student involvement is cited to underscore the professional nature of these decisions. If we take the position that college students' rights are second to professional concerns, we must demonstrate that graduate-practitioners are heavily involved in the selection process. Annual reconsideration of these decisions will not only keep the policies current, but also emphasize the need for constant reevaluation of our publicly stated positions.

Finally, principle 7 is a restatement of the whole approach: we regard selection processes as at least equal in educative importance to the programs themselves; and the selection process is not a test, or an interview, or any simple one-shot decision, but an elaborate, time-consuming way to implement self-selection and the judgments of professionals and practitioners.

These "principles" are, of course, controversial. If our suggestions are not workable, field tests will establish more feasible guidelines. Our intention has been to generate a reconsideration of assumptions about selection, as well as a definitive set of rules by which to implement our views.

7

Content in
Teacher
Education Programs

Introduction

The content of teacher education has ancient roots. It is naive to try to trace a neat sequential development from skills, to morality, to basic fields of study. The notion of what a teacher is supposed to know is shaped by his culture, its stage of development, and the intelligence and sensitivity of its earlier teacher educators. Rather than selecting various discrete emphases in teacher education and trying to sequence them or credit them to particular individuals and cultures, the following synthesis attempts to demonstrate the eclectic nature of the content in teacher education.

If we were limited to one generalization about content, ours would be that everything teachers are supposed to know, in all societies throughout human history, is based on two essentially incompatible assumptions: (1) necessary knowledge, skills, and morals exist in the culture outside the learner and must be systematically taught to him; and (2) uninhibited and freely developed natural growth will elicit from individuals genuine, relevant learnings. The former assumption leads to the concepts of motivation and instruction; the latter to the concept that teachers need to work only on the settings, materials, and conditions that impinge on the individual.

These conflicting trends include overlapping and varied subgroups. Some of the particular influences on the content of American teacher education are found in bits and snatches of documents that deal essentially with the nature of children and the content to offer them.

Early American Influences

Charles Hoole, one of the earliest direct influences on American pedagogy simply recognized the need for varied instructional skills, in addition to the content being taught. "I shall therefore mention

71

sundry ways to make a childe know his letters readily, out of which the discreet teacher may choose what is most likely to suit with his learner."[1] He also recognized the effect of teacher attitude on pupil potential. The self-fulfilling prophecy and the relation of expectation to achievement are far from a new concern.

I have seen learners termed as meer blockheads, and rejected altogether as un-capable to learn anything; whereas some teachers that have assayed a more familiar way, have professed that they have not met any such as a dunce amid a great multitude of little scholars. Indeed it is Tullies' observation of old, and Erasmus' assertion of latter years, that it is as natural for a childe to learn, as it is for a beast to go, a bird to fly, or a fish to swim, and I verily believe it, for the nature of man is restlessly desirous to know things, and were discouragements taken out of the way, and meet helps afforded young learners, they would doubtless go on with a great deal more proficiency at their books than usually they do; and could the master have the discretion to make their lessons familiar to them, children would as much delight in being busied about them as in any other sport, if too long at them might not make them tedious."[2]

Early statements such as these support our contentions that peda-gogy is based on assumptions of instilling versus eliciting and that we have, with notable exceptions, tried to pursue both assumptions simultaneously and failed. Even Rousseau, who remains unparalleled in his arguments for natural development and nurturance of internal motivations, also assumes that "teacher knows best" about the con-tent of pupil learning.

Here is how I would go to work to get him to study of his own accord. At the hours when I wanted him to be busy I should take away every kind of amuse-ment and put the work for the hour before him. If he did not apply himself to it with good grace, I should not even seem to take any notice, and leave him alone without amusement until the weariness of having absolutely nothing to do brought him of himself to do what I required.[3]

We have a history of teaching our teachers how to control with devious means to delude ourselves that we are eliciting rather than instilling.

The moral content for teachers overlays both the input and elicit-ing approaches. On one hand, following teachers' directions is con-ceived of as God's work, on the other, morality derives from self-discovery in play activities. The following is an example of the "god's work" approach; note the authoritative style.

the instructor must be master in all places and at all hours. It is not enough that you govern and restrain them during school hours, but you must regard their conduct, at all other times when they are not under the care of their parents. By a proper course the master may as easily direct the amusement and play of his scholars as their studies, and it is hardly less important that he do so.... Such as may corrupt the morals or the taste,... should be discountenanced.... Every exercise that is immodest or unbecoming should be prohibited, and whatever would give offence to delicate minds, of either sex, cannot be approved.[4]

In contrast, the role of the teacher as a sensitive nonintruder is based on assumptions such as:

Play is the highest phase of child development—of human development and it is self-representations of the inner—representations of the inner from inner necessity and impulse. Play is the purest, most spiritual activity of man at this stage, and, at the same time, typical of human life as a whole—of the inner hidden natural life in man and all things. It gives, therefore, joy, freedom, contentment, inner and outer rest, peace with the world. It holds the sources of all that is good. A child that plays thoroughly, with self-active determination, perserveringly until physical fatigue forbids, will surely be a thorough, determined man, capable of self-sacrifice for the promotion of the welfare of himself and others.[5]

The input versus eliciting issue, therefore, refers not only to subject matter but also to morality; are good and virtue ordained, or do they emanate from unbridled nurture? Obviously, decisions about what teachers' need to know will derive directly from these assumptions.

The present emphasis on microteaching is actually a reincarnation of an age-old approach that emphasizes functions as the content of teacher education. Compare today's emphasis on teaching skills, such as establishing sets, structuring, questioning, assignment making, and closure, with Herbart's Formal Steps (below) and the difference is one of jargon rather than essence.[6]

1. Preparation. Essentially an application of the doctrines of interest and apperception, this gets the learner into a receptive frame of mind and connects previous knowledge with an introduction to what's coming.

2. Presentation. New material is introduced.

3. Association. Connections with old material are made.

4. Generalization. General principles are identified.

5. Application. Learner's knowledge is tested by practice and application of principles to problems and exercises.

Even today's concern with behavioral objectives has a well-rehearsed history. One example of a previous emphasis on exact instructional behavior for teachers is in Maxwell's *Hints to Teachers*.

1. This book should be placed in the hands of children as soon as they can read and write with some degree of facility; say a year and a half after entering school.

2. The book should be in the hands of each child. It is not a teacher's manual. It is a book for the child to use directly under the eye of the teacher.

3. There should be no preparation of the lessons by the pupils—no "home work." They should not see the book except when it is actually in use in the class-room; so that each new lesson may be fresh and interesting to them, so that their answers to questions may be spontaneous.

4. In using the Oral Exercises, allow the children as much as possible both to ask and answer the questions. Thus the book will be made to serve all the

purposes of a supplementary reader, while the work will be made more interesting to the children, and they will be given practice in the use of interrogative as well as declarative sentences.

5. All answers to questions should be given in complete sentences.

6. While following the general scheme of each lesson, do not confine yourself slavishly to the exercises thus given, but invent others of your own, specially adapted to the abilities and aptitudes of your pupils.

7. When exercises are to be copied, they should be copied from the book and not from the blackboard.

8. Until lessons are reached in which originality of expression on the part of the pupils is called for, all necessary corrections may be made by calling children's attention to mistakes while they write.

9. When originality of expression is expected, each paper should be corrected separately by the teacher. It is well, however, before doing this to give each child an opportunity to correct its own mistakes. For this purpose the compositions should be first written on slates, then corrected by the writers, then copied upon paper, then corrected by the teacher, and re-copied by the children.

10. In correcting do not confine your attention to mistakes in spelling, punctuation, and syntax, but mark every inelegance in language, every inaccuracy in thought, every defect in arrangement.

11. Do not accept or allow slovenly or inaccurate work of any kind—in spelling, in penmanship, or in punctuation; in thought or in language.

12. It is not enough merely to call attention to errors. Nor, on the other hand, is it ever well for teachers practically to re-write the composition, as too many do. If a child makes a mistake in writing, see that he understands its nature and corrects it himself. In language, as in everything else, the true plan is to learn to do by doing.[7]

Influence of Institutionalization

The systematic study of teaching received some early support with the advent of the Illinois State Normal University in 1857 and the Oswego Normal School in 1866, both of which were solely concerned with the training of teachers. The creation of chairs in universities, however, demonstrates that a legitimate body of scholarship has been identified and an expert is needed. Some historians credit the University of Michigan with establishing the first full-time chair in education in 1879.[8] Our research indicates that the University of Iowa established a chair of didactics and psychology in 1873, six years before Michigan's.[9] The first occupant of this chair was Professor S. N. Fellows, who promptly published a paper on what teachers should know. His paper, "Mental States or Acts Involved in Mental Activity," separated the functions of sensibilities, intellect, and will and was a precursor of later developments in psychology and psychiatry. Such independent theorizing without a systematic theory or research base continued for several decades. Interest and effort became the primary "stuff" teachers were taught, based entirely on the opinions of particular experts in the embryonic discipline of psychology. For example:

the two rules of educational method are: whenever direct interest in any constructive process fails to maintain the attention of the pupil, then the teacher should have recourse to those ulterior motives which are of an ethical nature, such as the desire of the pupil to do well in the estimation of his teacher, his sense of duty, and so on; and must never have recourse to the lower and unethical motives, such as fear of punishment or hope of reward, until all other means have failed. In the second place, he must endeavor gradually to make less and less use of these ulterior motives in order that indirect interest may pass into direct, for it is only insofar as, in any particular case, this result is reached that we can be certain that we shall attain our aim of establishing permanent and stable systems of ideas, which shall in after life function in the determination of conduct . . . when a succession of facts presented to the mind of the child have no internal bonds of connection—then the only way to retain and remember such a succession is to introduce some more or less artificial connection.[10]

This is a beautiful confusion of ethics and psychological understandings used to exploit pupil needs and control them. These threads are now more cleanly separated into Skinner versus Rogers; but the separation took a half-century to evolve.

Another universal theme has been the assumption that the content for teachers should be a thorough grounding in the basic disciplines of knowledge. While many, such as college instructors, have maintained that in-depth knowledge of a liberal art or science is all that is necessary, others have insisted that the plight of elementary and secondary education can be traced directly to teachers' ignorance and lack of scholarship in the traditional liberal arts.[11] Some have championed the need for specific knowledge to meet external threats.[12] More recently specific knowledge for teachers has been the panacea to combat internal threats.[13]

The outstanding attribute of those who emphasize traditional content as a cure-all is their durability in the face of evidence. Even those most directly concerned with educating the disadvantaged, i.e., the movers and shakers in the Office of Education who have supported NDEA institutes, have succumbed to the lure of academe.[14]

The decades since World War II have fostered a variety of rallying cries: "What teachers need to know are the key concepts in each discipline."[15] "What teachers need to know are processes of interacting with students."[16] "What teachers need to know deals with the development of affect and values."[17] These recent trends overlay the more traditional trilogy: the teacher needs to know his subject, the nature of youth, and the process of learning.

Teacher education programs have become so stylized, with each department of educational expertise getting its share of required courses and student teaching or internship serving as the integrating experience, that even nonteacher educators can easily come up with fairly good summaries of typical programs.

The founders of the first normal schools would be amazed to see how the content of teacher knowledge has burgeoned. Obviously, teaching pupils to parrot the Bible calls for considerably less pedagogy than teaching independence, problem solving, human relations, and varied academic skills. Much reorganization of what teachers need to know has come from inside the profession. In one highly sophisticated, but rarely used document, the five areas of teacher knowledge are outlined and justified as follows:

1. *Analytical Study of Teaching.* Topics include verbal and non-verbal forms of interaction; concepts of research or teaching; the classroom as a social emotional system; and the nature of leadership styles.

2. *Structure and Uses of Knowledge.* Here the student is expected to master the basic understandings related to the nature and use of all knowledge; its logical structures and how such structures affect the teaching art.

3. *Concepts of Human Development and Learning.* These aspects include knowledge of the structure of intellect, cognitive growth, learning styles, and basic concepts [e.g., motivation, readiness].

4. *Designs for Teaching-Learning.* Here the student goes beyond usual methods and is expected to learn how to form objectives, use strategies, develop learning units, and use instructional systems and programmed instruction.

5. *Demonstration and Evaluation of Teaching Competencies.* This study includes trial experiences in teaching, analysis of demonstrated competencies and even professional matters such as organization for instruction.[18]

The contribution of this document was not simply that it added new dimensions to what teachers need to learn but that it created a new point of view. Its emphasis on education as a scholarly enterprise dealing with the nature and structure of all knowledge makes it impossible to view teacher education in terms of discrete little programs for music teachers, home economics teachers, etc. The report also stressed the need to use materials and media beyond the traditional chalk and blackboard. While there are obvious weaknesses, e.g., lack of a personal growth component, the LaGrone document is an outstanding effort to reconceptualize what experts thought teachers needed to know, and it represents the thinking of most professional educators during the 1960s.

Previewing the development of content for teachers reveals several general patterns. Education faculty have consistently identified areas that should be added to training programs; few, if any, have advocated that anything be deleted. Outside "experts" have emphasized areas to be deleted, particularly those dealing with pedagogical concerns. Research and evaluation of practitioners inevitably shows both academic and professional gaps in their preparation. Finally, the education of teachers has been an outstanding example of the spiral curriculum with emphasis on the same ideas shifting in and out of fashion on a regular basis. For example, at first teachers received practical, on-the-job training; training then shifted to the normal schools and finally to the universities where student teaching became artificial rather than realistic. We now have many experts who advocate making training more practical by giving control over programs back to the public schools. For another example, in earlier times skills, behaviors, and specific teacher do's and don'ts were the rule. As knowledge in psychology, child development, and social science expanded, teachers were educated in principles and theory, not trained to perform unreflectively. Today's experts, however, quite frequently advocate a direct return to training teachers in the performance of specific behaviors and functions.

At present there seem to be at least twelve kinds of professional content for teachers. Since their advocates all claim to have the ultimate good of children, the community, the country, the teacher, and the profession at heart, it is difficult to treat these trends with much discrimination. Most of those concerned with the different contents are college faculty, who invariably are somewhat less than objective, since there is a very high correlation between what faculty teach in their particular courses and what they advocate as absolutely necessary for all teachers. It should also be noted that all these forms of content can be taught through diverse college teaching methods, i.e., lecture, direct experience, independent study, tutorials, and simulation. Most college programs offer several of these components, determined, of course, by the nature and needs of their faculty rather than by the compatibility of the components.

Components of Teacher Knowledge

Skills

One recent example of this component is microteaching. The original nine teaching skills, used in the secondary program at Stanford are (1) establishing set, (2) establishing appropriate frames of reference, (3) achieving closure, (4) using questions effectively, (5) recognizing and obtaining attending behavior, (6) controlling participation, (7) providing feedback, (8) employing rewards and punishments, and (9) setting a model. These nine were subsequently consolidated into seven skills: (1) reinforcement, (2) varying the stimulus, (3) presentation skill—set induction, (4) presentation skill—lecturing and use of audiovisual aids, (5) illustration and use of examples, (6) presentation skill—closure, and (7) student initiated questions.[19] The teacher-to-be learns these skills, and they comprise the basic behaviors that enable him to perform the function of instruction.

Another widely popular skills approach to teacher education involves the teaching and use of behavioral objectives. Teachers-to-be are taught to think in terms of, write, and conduct lessons using this approach. The essence of this content involves learning to specify pupil behaviors, terminal pupil behaviors, and criteria for determining the achievement of terminal behaviors.[20] "Good" teachers can state their objectives—what they expect of pupils, what precise activities will be practiced, and what level of pupils' final performance will be accepted—and "good" teaching is the execution of such preplanned specifications.

This content is less detailed than the seven microteaching functions but more widely applicable. Microteaching makes the teacher's behavior the central focus of training, while the behavioral objective approach makes the teacher's ability to specify the behavioral learnings of children and youth the central concern. Microteaching assumes "good" teacher purposes and effective pupil learning if the instructional skills are demonstrated. The behavioral objective approach assumes that the instructional methodology that induces the terminal behaviors is best. Both of these approaches emphasize the technical approach to the training of teachers, that is, teachers are people who can perform selected skills.

Ethics

Every teacher education program directly advocates and indirectly implies the way it wants its graduates to view children and youth. Early nineteenth-century training, for example, emphasized the work ethic. Children were assumed to be predisposed toward idleness, and they needed teachers to keep them actively engaged.

During the progressive era teachers-to-be were exhorted to value democratic participation, group living, and cooperative projects. Children were often viewed as an early but real manifestation of the communal ethic; competition and struggle were viewed as needless and debilitating. Much of the content offered teachers was aimed at this cooperative ethic and took the form of the activity program, the class unit, and problems of living.

More recently the age of individuality and "do-your-own-thing" has flavored many teacher education programs with a heavy taste for diversity, search for self, and cultivation of personal meaning. No value supercedes that of congruence or acting on the basis of how one "really" feels.

These three trends are not entirely historical. There are instances of programs in the same institution selecting, reinforcing, and turning out graduates who are passionate advocates of the work ethic, ethnic or community identity, or the self-actualized individual. The teaching of these value orientations, which eventually control the future teacher's performance, is accomplished by peer teaching, informal relationships, and direct experience rather than by formal lectures or faculty exhortation.

Disciplines

The main concentration of teacher education is not on professional studies but on the general education and specialization offered students as the basis for their professional studies. "General education" refers to all the introductory courses and experiences that develop the broadly educated man. Students are exposed to natural sciences, social sciences, esthetics, and humanities in an effort to give them broad, general concepts in all the major areas of human knowledge and help them choose a specialization. Specialization or "majoring" refers to the discipline or area of concentration that enables the student to pursue his interests and talents in depth. General education liberates, prepares the citizen, whets the appetite; specialization launches the student on the road to intensive scholarship. General education leads to intelligent citizenship and more pleasurable leisure; specialization to advanced studies. Both general education and specialization are necessary prerequisites and accessories to professional studies.

Formerly, these studies were carefully prescribed, as if to become an elementary teacher, a student automatically needed six particular courses in literature, three in mathematics, and so on. While such spurious accuracy is still practiced, many universities now permit open, freely selected general education. Specialization is also opening up but still tends to be more restrictive for secondary teachers than for elementary teachers. Since there is no evidence that what or how much students learn is related to their subsequent effectiveness as teachers, we tend to support college requirements on the basis of plausible and rational connections. For example, if a student can freely select his general education and then "turn on" in a specialization he has chosen, perhaps he will be more likely to help others develop a love of learning by offering them both the choices and the passions that may motivate them. In any event, since teachers are prepared in colleges, general education and specialization are in their programs regardless of whether these studies can be substantiated as subsequently useful for teachers.

Key Concepts

Some experts maintain there is a knowledge explosion. Since there is too much to learn, they argue, knowledge must be highlighted, not covered. Every discipline supposedly has a few major concepts or principles. Dance is essentially shape, effort, and time; mathematics is built around balance, infinity, and zero; history is a summation of critical events; art is the use of space, texture, and color; psychology is stimulus-response; economics is production, distribution, and consumption; and music is tempo, timber, and harmony. Scholars have so professionalized the disciplines that teachers are not faced with the dilemma of trying to learn everything. The American Association for the Advancement of Science has developed programs in biology, physics, and other areas organized around major concepts identified by experts in each area. Philosophers have carefully gone through all the fields of knowledge and attempted to do the same. The same efforts have been made in social sciences and humanities, although they have never realized the same level of expert consensus and translation into public school curricula as selected arts and physical sciences. A basic component of many teacher education programs is this analysis of the nature of knowledge and the professionalization or attempt to get at essences of knowledge.[21]

One basic reason for this "need" is that teachers must have guides for deciding which knowledge they might "cover" with pupils and which knowledge is so critical that time must be devoted to self-discovery. Obviously, not everything can be self-discovered. Therefore, what are the significant concepts worthy of this more inefficient but stronger form of learning?

Learners

A basic component of all teacher education programs is a course in early childhood, childhood, or adolescent development. The assumption is that the nature of the developing child or youth should be a basic variable in determining how teachers will interact with them. In physical education and in exceptional education—for the deaf, physically handicapped, retarded, etc.—even more emphasis is placed on the nature of the learner. Graduates of teacher education programs are expected to be able to describe, in general terms, the physical, emotional, and social development of the age groups they will teach.

The amazing thing about the universality of this component in teacher education is its widespread neglect in the schools. Situations that require small children to sit for long periods, deny adolescents high levels of emotionality, and refuse breakfast to hungry children are at least as frequent as programs that recognize the nature of development.

The "better" programs attempt to integrate studies of learners with fieldwork that illustrates development principles. Genuinely advanced programs integrate these studies with methods courses so that instructional strategies may be considered in terms of the learner's needs and predispositions.

Social Setting

At one time all teacher education programs required a course in the history or philosophy of education. It is now common to emphasize the social background of and social pressures on children. Spurred by funds from NDEA institutes for teachers of the "disadvantaged," the civil rights movement, and the national trend toward biculturalism, few programs fail to require some work in the social influences on children.

While development courses emphasize physiological and personality dimensions, this component stresses the values and culture of various groups with whom the teacher will work. In urban colleges the emphasis is frequently on black groups; in rural areas Indian youngsters may be studied. The educational sociologists and anthropologists have come into their own; courses in these areas are quite frequently required. Their net effect, however, is difficult to assess. The hope is that even if would-be-teachers learn little of direct application to their future charges, they will at least gain some perspective on their own backgrounds and values. A few programs require direct experiences in the school-community to enhance these studies.

Learning

Armed with principles of development and concepts of socioeconomic influences on children and youth, the future teacher is supposed to be ready for the real thing—the nature of learning. While no program lacks this essential, few programs give their students a rounded picture. Skinner, Piaget, Ausebel, Rogers, Hunt, Maslow, Bruner, Gagne, Torrence, Guilford, and others are common fare. Two trends are discernible: some students are "surveyed up" and are insufficiently schooled in any single system to behave consistently on a clear set of precepts; others are "trained" in one approach, such as Bereiter-Englemann's Behavior Modification, and never realize there are other alternatives. The great challenge to faculty who work in this area is to give students both the breadth of the field and depth in a single system. Many theorists, such as Piaget, do not lend themselves to immediate application, while others, such as Skinner, offer clear implications. The ethical question of which theoretic system to emphasize with students is never faced; no faculty has ever voted on what psychology to offer its students. The vacuum is frequently filled by a "be nice" approach that produces kindly graduates who demonstrate no systematically organized behaviors with children that are in any way different from the behaviors of kindly mothers who serve as volunteers.

A few programs develop a single approach. For example, the Bank Street College emphasized a psychoanalytic approach in educating teachers and pupils. Usually, however, the faculty of a particular educational psychology department fight it out among themselves with no clear-cut victor. Graduates suffer by learning principles that have been overgeneralized to secure agreement among warring schools of education psychology faculty or by taking courses that contradict each other. As a result, most concepts are not translated into practice.

Divisions are usually oversimplified into cognition versus affect: those educational psychologists who want to prepare graduates (i.e., "products") who can be effective (i.e., "teach kids stuff"), versus those who want to prepare teachers who will permit children and youth to develop in their "unique" ways. As if this schism were not destructive enough, the department of educational psychology also houses both researchers and the clinicians.

The basic assumption is well-intentioned. To know *how* pupils learn should be a basic guide for the teachers. We just never foresaw the multiplicity of learning theories and the monumental intolerance of their practitioners.

Pedagogy

Every teacher education program offers methods of teaching. These are usually broken down into teaching art, science, math, reading, driving, etc. The content of method originally required each subject matter to have its distinctive pedagogy. Horace Mann's Seventh Report to the Massachusetts Board of Education in 1837 includes a step-by-step guide for teaching reading (a quite "current" one, by the way). Penmanship, spelling, geography, ciphering, etc., were all carefully detailed with an accompanying how-to-do-it for teachers by nineteenth-century experts. During the 1930s and 1940s, however, the duplication became obvious. In response to charges of proliferation, educators introduced general methods.

Lately, in response to the persistent criticism that teacher education lacked "depth," general methods have once again been broken down into distinct courses. The recent emphasis on reading was the coup de grace. Elementary teachers benefit, or "suffer," more from this trend than secondary teachers, since they are now in programs that will become more specialized, or fractionated, depending on your values.

Process

The generally applicable methods of teaching have been well-documented and described in the research literature on instruction. These processes cut across all subjects but do not occur in the behavioral forms of microteaching. They include functions such as questioning, planning, assignment making, pupil evaluation, methods of individualization, procedures related to conducting open classrooms, affective education, and value clarification.

The thrust of this component has to prepare teachers who can supervise and change their own instructional behaviors. Prerequisite to this self-development is a systematic study of teaching. The basic difference between this element and the element of skills discussed above is that this component more frequently emphasizes the processes of teacher-pupil interaction in terms of the encounter or interpersonal dynamics.

The most popular systems are those of Flanders, Hughes, and B. O. Smith. Future teachers are expected to become more proficient at teaching higher orders of thinking, affect, and creativity in some systematic way. An incredible amount of research has been produced to support the simplistic assertion that students can learn and use these systems, but little evidence is available to support the contention that students will use these processes in subsequent practice. Practically no evidence exists to support the notion that if they do, their pupils will learn more. The justification of this component, which is one of the more recent additions to teacher education, is that teaching should be more carefully described and that teachers should be expert at categorizing their instructional behavior.

Technology

Every program includes some work in the use of materials, media, and technology. Some teach students how to thread a projector, others how to use videotape and television. Of all the weaknesses in teacher education, the theory and practice in the use of materials and media may be the most glaring. Faculty are ill-prepared or turned against use of media; colleges frequently lack equipment; students practice in schools that are ill-equipped or lack the motivation to develop media skills.

Teachers in the seventies are generally ill-prepared to use even phonographs and radio; the use of computors and videotape are beyond their frame of reference. Even the field trip has never been fully exploited beyond early childhood programs. In former years advocates of individualization were criticized for lecturing to large classes about that process, and we now have faculty who write about programming in conventional texts.

The recent breakthroughs in microfilm and Xerox equipment have influenced the college student to the point where there may be a carry-over into practice. The recent emphasis on consultants may also influence the behavior of future teachers regarding community resources.

Many universities have benefitted from government grants for the purchase of equipment, but we know of many institutions where teachers are prepared in programs that demonstrate only the use of chalk and blackboards, and even that somewhat uncreatively. Public school administrators frequently charge that when they do invest in tape recorders, science tables, or whatever, the equipment is locked up or underutilized, and the charge is largely accurate. Few teachers receive more than a once-over, if that, on the use materials and media. There are a few exceptions in fields that depend entirely on specific updated materials and equipment, such as swimming, typing, and driver education.

Self

Every teacher education program supposedly does something to enhance the development of self. Some programs do this directly through counseling and group sensitivity training; others claim this development is the result of the individualization offered in supervision, tutorials, or the advisement process. Some programs offer formal courses in personal growth; others hire faculty who claim this concern will permeate their contacts with students. No program ever states openly that they regard this dimension as unimportant or unrelated to their responsibility for educating teachers who will have a beneficial effect on pupils.

Few programs test formally for personality problems. All claim to have a mechanism for "guiding out" undesirables, although it is astounding how few students are ever "guided out." Either the large number of unhappy neurotics who teach developed their problems in service, or the universal claims of teacher educators about their diligence in nurturing students self-understanding and development are magnificently overstated.

As was carefully detailed in chapter 6, the issue of self-understanding is beyond the aegis of the college. The responsibility of teacher education programs lies more in the process of selection than in the hope of remaking personalities through college courses.

The use of self as the very content of teacher education is widely practiced in programs devoted to the psychoanalytic point of view. During the 1950s the issue was self-understanding; more recently the content has been expanded to self-study.[22] The best example of a total program of teacher education guided by these concepts was conducted at Yale.[23]

Change

The goal of equalizing educational opportunities is a thing of the past. With the advent of a new individualism, symbolized by pot, hair, and hippie life-styles, the entire educational enterprise has come under attack. Succeeding in dehumanized schools is no longer considered an "opportunity." In the past, it was a question of helping the "disadvantaged." Now that middle class youngsters are also disaffected, it is the system that must be changed. The antiestablishment writers are now the only ones that are widely published; it is almost impossible to find any popular book that supports the present system of schooling.

One result of this general discontent has been that a substantial group of teacher educators are now teaching students survival strategies for their first years of practice and change strategies for their tenure years. Other faculty are teaching "deschooling" methods and have led antischool strikes, meetings, and movements. A growing literature now supports students interested in deschooling society, community education, schools of the streets, and "outside" efforts.

The largest trend has been the actual teaching of methods of survival and innovation. In former years, educators engaged in frequent class discussions with teachers who argued, "My principal won't let me teach that way." Today, there is an open recognition of the need for strategies. Faculty who advocate new reading methods, individualization, or open classrooms now frequently teach the methods of subverting the system to gain this pedagogical elbow room. The change literature is aimed at parents as well as teachers.[24]

Organization of Components

The twelve kinds of content discussed above are pushed, squeezed, and somehow incorporated in 128 college credits and served up to masses of late adolescents. These courses are organized into semesters and years. In broad terms the programs are characterized by three components: (1) general education, or what every college graduate knows superficially; (2) specialization, or that area of study in which the student learns the language, methodology, and basic concepts of a particular discipline; and (3) professional education, which offers eleven of the preceding forms of content.

There are several ways to organize these three components. Figure 7-1 represents the internship, fifth year, or Master of Arts in teaching programs that are popular in many large universities. Professional education is "built on" a typical liberal arts education. The advantage of this approach is that would-be teachers are more natural, have a sound education, and are free to devote full-time to a professional year. The disadvantage of this program is that professional studies cannot be integrated with students' general and liberal studies.

Figure 7-2 represents a typical state college that emphasizes teacher education. Here there is some professional study from the very

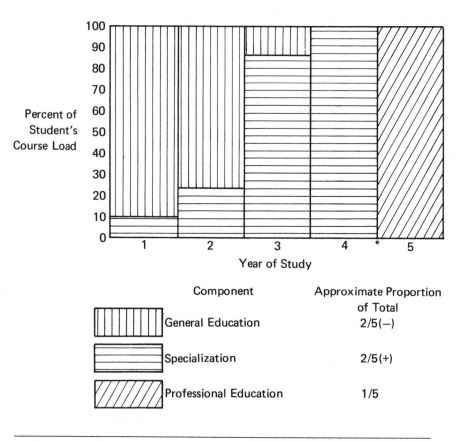

Figure 7-1. Relationship of general-special-professional education: pattern A

Component	Approximate Proportion of Total
General Education	2/5(−)
Specialization	2/5(+)
Professional Education	1/5

*Represents point of completion of Bachelors Degree.

Figure 7-2. Relationship of general-special-professional education: pattern B

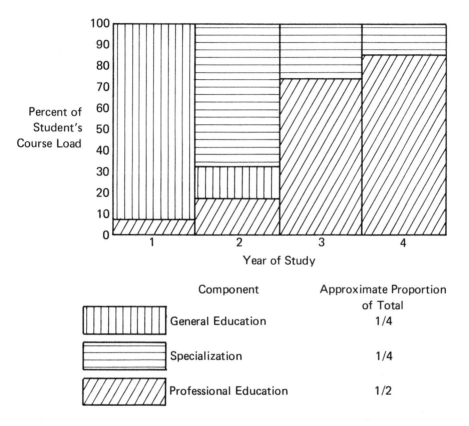

	Component	Approximate Proportion of Total
	General Education	1/4
	Specialization	1/4
	Professional Education	1/2

beginning. The advantage of this pattern is the great opportunity for integration of general, liberal, and professional education. There is also a four-year period during which students can achieve important growth in professional values. The disadvantage is the relatively smaller emphasis on general and liberal courses.

Figure 7-3 represents the undergraduate pattern common in larger multipurpose universities. Here, students do not enter professional studies until almost the third year. The advantages include little professional effort to large numbers of freshmen who fail or change their minds and a greater number of general and liberal courses than the state college model. The disadvantage is the great concentration of professional courses at the end of students' college careers. By the time students realize teaching may not be for them, they have

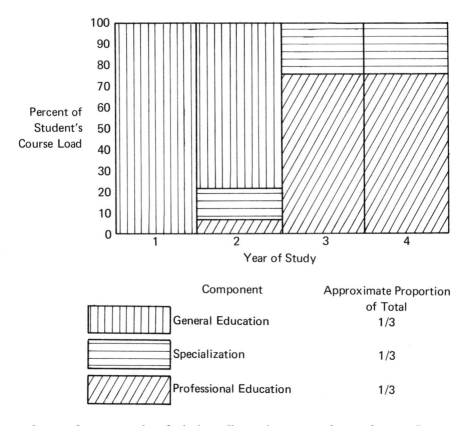

Figure 7-3. Relationship of general-special-professional education: pattern C

invested too much of their college time to quit or change. Large numbers are then certified and admitted to a profession they do not want.

Figure 7-4 represents a balanced five-year program. These are still rare. With present trends, i.e., too much to squeeze into four years and too few jobs, these programs may increase. Advantages are the integrated nature of general, liberal, and professional studies and the length of time for in-depth growth. The disadvantage will be that lower income students who cannot stay in college for five full years may be discouraged from becoming teachers.

The development of content in teacher education programs is an exciting pushing and shoving of pressure groups representing a vari-

Figure 7-4. Relationship of general-special-professional education: pattern D

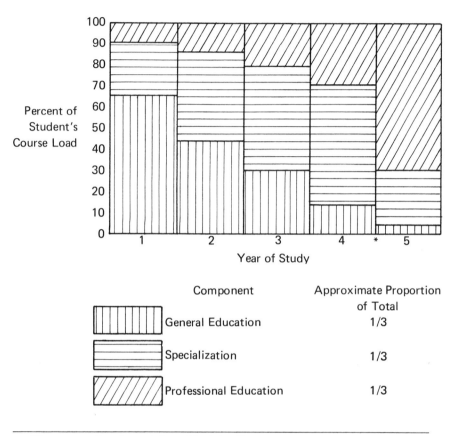

Percent of Student's Course Load

Year of Study

Component	Approximate Proportion of Total
General Education	1/3
Specialization	1/3
Professional Education	1/3

*Represents point of completion of Bachelors Degree.

ety of experts. Analyzing a similar condition in general education, Alfred North Whitehead once remarked, "The solution which I am urging is to eradicate the fatal disconnections of subjects which kills the vitality of our modern curriculum." This goal seems to be a good one for teacher education.

Notes

1. Charles Hoole, "How a childe may be taught with delight to know all his letters in a very little time," in *A New Discovery of the*

Old Art of Teaching School (1660; republished by Liverpool University Press, 1913), p. 5.

2. Ibid., p. 12.

3. William Boyd, ed., "Project for the Education of M. de Sainte Marie" (1740), in *The Minor Educational Writings of Jean Jacques Rousseau* (New York: Bureau of Publications, Teachers College, Columbia University, 1962), p. 54.

4. Samuel R. Hall, *Lectures on School Keeping,* 4th ed. (Albany: 1832), p. 43.

5. Friedrich Froebel, *The Education of Man,* trans. W. N. Hailmann (New York: Appleton & Co., 1907), p. 55.

6. Johan Frederich Herbart, *The Science of Education* (Boston: D. C. Heath & Co., 1893), pp. 143-47.

7. W. H. Maxwell, *Primary Lessons in Language and Composition* (New York: American Book Co., 1886), flyleaf.

8. Adolphe E. Meyer, *An Educational History of the American People* (New York: McGraw-Hill Book Co., 1957), p. 385.

9. Correspondence and original committee minutes secured from Reference Department, University Libraries, Iowa City.

10. Alexander Darroch, *The Place of Psychology in the Training of the Teacher* (New York: Longman's Green & Co., 1911), p. 133.

11. Arthur E. Bestor, *Educational Wastelands* (Urbana, Ill.: University of Illinois Press, 1953).

12. Hyman G. Rickover, *American Education—A National Failure* (New York: E. P. Putnam & Co., 1963).

13. James E. Allen, "The Right to Read Program" (launched during his tenure as Commissioner of Education, 1969).

14. Donald N. Bigelow, ed., *The Liberal Arts and Teacher Education: A Confrontation* (Lincoln, Neb.: University of Nebraska Press, 1971).

15. Jerome Bruner, *The Process of Education* (Cambridge, Mass.: Harvard University Press, 1962).

16. Anita Simon, ed., *Mirrors for Behavior—An Anthology of Classroom Observation Instruments* (Philadelphia, Pa.: Research for Better Schools, 1967).

17. Louis E. Raths, "Clarifying Values," in *Curriculum for Today's Boys and Girls,* ed. R. S. Fleming (Columbus, Ohio: Chas. Merrill, 1963).

18. Herbert LaGrone, ed., *Pre-Service Professional Component of a Program of Teacher Education* (Washington, D.C.: American Association of Colleges for Teacher Education, 1964), p. v.

19. James Cooper, Dwight Allen & Robert F. Schuck, *Microteaching,* ATE Research Bulletin no. 9 (Washington, D.C.: 1971), pp. 38-39.

20. Robert F. Mager, *Preparing Instructional Objectives* (Palo Alto, Calif.: Fearon Publishers, 1962).

21. Philip H. Plenix, *Realms of Meaning* (New York: McGraw-Hill, 1964).

22. Arthur T. Jersild, *When Teachers Face Themselves* (New York: Teachers College Press, 1954); Carl R. Rogers, "Some Issues Concerning the Control of Human Behavior," *Science* 124 (1956): 1057-66.

23. Seymour B. Sarason et. al., *The Preparation of Teachers* (New York: John Wiley & Sons, 1962).

24. Ellen Lurie, *How to Change the Schools* (New York: Random House, 1970).

8

Competency-Based
Teacher
Education

The most notable recent development in the preparation of teachers is the approach known as competency-based teacher education. In contrast to experience-based programs, which assume that when students complete certain courses and student teaching experiences they are ready to begin teaching, the competency-based approach requires students to demonstrate behaviors related to promoting learning in their pupils. Future teachers are held accountable, not for passing courses, but for attaining given levels of competence in performing essential tasks of teaching. The emphasis is on demonstrated output; that is, what can the future teacher actually do? Individual students can thus be held accountable for having particular competencies, and institutions can be held accountable for producing able teachers.

Definition

As is frequently the case with new educational developments, there is some ambiguity regarding the use of terms. The terms *competency-based teacher education* (CBTE) and *performance-based teacher education* (PBTE) are both used to refer to teacher education programs that seek to develop and evaluate specific teaching behaviors in their students. (*Students* refers to preservice or inservice teachers engaged in the process of teacher education.) These terms still retain enough of their meaning to differentiate their approach from experience-based programs. There is an overlap, however, between the use of the terms *competency-based* and *performance-based*. After an exhaustive review of current materials we found no basis for distinguishing between the ways in which both terms are used. Both CBTE and PBTE have been used to refer to preservice college programs as well as to inservice training. Both terms have been used by nonprofessional groups and state legislatures in dealing with issues such as certification and accountability. Both terms have been used in research studies, program descriptions, and expository writing. There are instances in which *competency* is used to refer to discrete, single skills and *performance* is used to refer to cumulations of competencies; in other instances their meanings are the exact reverse. Some scholars have used the term *competency* to refer to a particular ability or behavior the student may have learned in a professional course, in a general education course, or in a work or life experience, while the term *performance* is used to refer to the particular skills actually taught to students in teacher education programs. In sum, the present state of usage is that the terms are used in an overlapping and arbitrary manner.[1] To confound the issue, some state codes (e.g., Texas) use other terms like *proficiencies*. It becomes important, therefore—in research studies, program descriptions, and general writing—that the term used be operationally defined so that consumers of the professional literature are aware of just what is being advanced. Unless such care is exercised, PBTE and CBTE may become as vague and noncommunicative as so many other terms that frequently prevent rather than aid communication in education.

Basic Components of CBTE

There seems to be some general consensus that programs are competency-based if they meet the following criteria:

1. Competencies to be demonstrated by students must be derived from some explicit conception of the teachers' role, stated in ways that make it possible to assess student achievement of the competency, and made public before beginning the training.

2. Criteria for assessing competencies must be appropriate for measuring the particular knowledge or skill, explicit in stating the expected levels of student mastery under specified conditions, and made public in advance.

3. The actual assessment of students' competency must be based on his performance as the primary source of evidence; it must also include objective evidence of the student's planning, analysis, and evaluation of his teaching behavior.

4. Students' progress through programs of teacher education must be in terms of their demonstrated competency, not their completion of time requirements or "regular" course requirements.

5. The instruction offered students is for the purpose of facilitating their achievement of the programs' specified competencies.

These five components have been advanced as generic or essential elements for designating a program performance-based.[2] Various proponents add other components, which have become characteristic, if not essential. These include individualized instruction that provides for differing students' backgrounds and point of entry; some system of feedback that permits students to modify their performance; an emphasis on integration of components and systematic movement toward program goals; use of instructional modules; and student accountability for his performance. Other characteristics that are frequently, if not universally, advocated for CBTE programs include centering the program in the field; having public school groups work with faculty in organizing the program; using protocol materials to help students identify and use particular concepts of teaching in given situations; student participation in program design; and conducting follow-up research on graduates.

Some Basic Assumptions

Weaknesses in Experience-Based Teacher Education

Criticisms of teacher education are abundant and available from a variety of sources. Several of these criticisms are commonly grouped and used to establish the need for competency-based teacher education; they relate to inadequacies in the goals, processes, and evaluation of experience-based programs. These weaknesses are:

1. Limited conceptualization of the total program with no systematic or overarching view of the teacher's role
2. Vague program goals
3. Lack of research substantiating what is taught and advocated
4. The use of tradition rather than logic or research as the basis of program change
5. Little evaluation and follow-up of graduates
6. No accountability of the program to its students, their pupils, or the public
7. Inadequate faculty models in the university and in cooperating schools.[3]

Systems Approach

These criticisms do not automatically lead all who make them to conclude that CBTE is the solution. An additional assumption is needed to support the CBTE approach: that experience-based teacher education programs are weak because they are not systematic, and they cannot correct their weaknesses until they employ a systems approach.

A system is a collection of "interrelated and interacting components that work in an integrated fashion to attain predetermined purposes."[4] Assuming that experience-based teacher education is a series of unrelated courses and direct experiences, taught by faculty who do not communicate or are irrelevant to school practices, with no agreed on objectives for the program or the kind of teacher being prepared, obviously it cannot meet the systems approach criteria.

The purposes of a system, in this case CBTE, are realized through processes "in which interacting components of the system engage in order to produce a predetermined output. Purpose determines the process required and the process will imply the kinds of components that will make up the system."[5] The application of this systematic strategy to any human process is what is meant by a systems approach. The three components of a system—purpose, process, and output—become the guidelines for planning, offering, and evaluating CBTE. Advocates of CBTE are then capable of answering all the charges of weakness made against experience-based teacher education by using a systems approach. There is a clear conceptualization of program goals that specifically describes the teacher functions for which the students are being prepared. What is taught to students has an empiric basis. Research evidence rather than college traditions becomes the basis of program development. Follow-up of graduates' performance can provide real feedback for program revision. The program is accountable for teaching students to perform program objectives. Finally, since the behaviors to be learned by students have been identified and delimited, teachers who can model the behaviors are identified and utilized as teacher educators. Thus, having made and answered the broad criticisms of experience-based teacher education programs, the CBTE approach proceeds with the business of developing and teaching particular content.

Competency Behaviors

Wherever possible, the competency behaviors taught to teachers are attitudes, skills, understandings, and behaviors that research evidence suggests lead to intellectual, emotional, and physical growth in children. Recognizing the difficulty of making a large number of specific connections between teachers' behavior and pupil growth, the CBTE approach also requires clear statements of the teacher's role. Such specificity permits the development of program objectives, which provide a publicly stated, clear notion of the kind of teacher the particular program seeks to develop. Behaviors to be taught to students are actually the functions students must perform in order to fulfill the role of teacher that has been conceptualized as the program goal. Frequently, behaviors taught to students can be substantiated by the research literature as correlates of various forms of pupil growth; other competency behaviors are supported as having logical, theoretic connections to pupil growth. The basic assumption, therefore, is that the literature on teacher effectiveness, supported by logical connections between teacher performance and pupil growth, can provide a body of behavioral competencies to be taught to students.

An outgrowth of this fundamental assumption is the belief that clearly stating the specific knowledge and skills of a teacher to be developed will have several salutary effects. The argument is that faculty, students, the public, cooperating personnel, evaluators, and accreditors will be able to assess the quality of a particular program against what the program seeks to achieve. Further, a clear set of purposes will permit continuous self-evaluation and, therefore, greater independence by all who are involved as students. The value of clear, public objectives also assumes that open knowledge of goals will result in more substantial rationales for competency-based programs than is now true for many experience-based teacher education programs.

Buried in this assumption about the value of clear, public program goals, are several related beliefs that may seem unimportant to the uninitiated but are in fact critical: e.g., college faculty can agree on the specific role of the teacher to be prepared; public school teachers and others can participate and reach agreement with faculty in delimiting the competencies necessary for teachers; and this specification of role can be accomplished whether the program deals with the preparation of narrow specialists such as typing teachers or broad practitioners such as teachers in self-contained elementary classrooms.

A rarely discussed but highly significant assumption of the competency approach is that the pupil's role can be made as clear as the teacher's. Obviously, if pupils are to do what they choose to in their own ways, learning different contents to different degrees, there is no need for a competency model to prepare their teachers, except perhaps to teach the teachers the single behavior of not interfering with the natural inclinations of children and youth. The teachers at Summerhill, for example, must accept the school's philosophy and have some personal coping skills rather than any set of prescribed instructional skills.

The competency approach makes the tacit but critical assumptions that youngsters need teachers and that pupils will learn a common core of basic skills and knowledge to some minimal degree. In sum, the basic assumption is that pupils are learners who will change in ways specified by the curriculum objectives of the school. It is no accident that CBTE is a parallel development to the clarification and specification of the schools' curriculum objectives. The clearer the learners' roles are made, the easier it becomes to specify the CBTE for training teachers to work with those learners.

Another basic assumption of CBTE is that teachers will function more professionally if they perform logically derived operations than if they function idiosyncratically or in response to their personality predispositions. Arthur Jersild's approach, which was popular in the late 1950s, emphasized teachers' self-knowledge and self-awareness as the fundamental process for improving instruction.[6] It should be clear that CBTE stresses professional acts that can be performed by a *range* of teacher personalities regardless of their idiosyncrasies and predispositions.

The Instructional Module

The heart of the CBTE effort is the instructional module, which, in the final analysis, will determine how useful the competency-based approach will be. Instructional modules are the actual learning activities that teach students the competencies comprising the particular teacher education program. Ideally, an instructional module provides the student with (1) a rationale of the competency's importance and relationship to the rest of the program; (2) the objectives that specify the competency to be demonstrated; (3) prerequisites; (4) some pre-assessment and diagnosis of where the student is when he begins the module; (5) various learning activities that will help the student realize the module's objectives; (6) postassessment; and (7) remedial procedures and activities in case the student does not achieve the competency. In order to explain this approach, it is necessary to demonstrate how these ideal standards are actually implemented. Since one proficiency that seems to be a common component in all CBTE programs is listening skills, it might be useful to describe how this apparently universal skill is taught, bearing in mind the seven criteria against which an instructional module in a CBTE program should be evaluated.

Some of the most widely used CBTE programs are the Wilkits from Weber State College.[7] In June 1972 Wilkit's Listening Kit was revised to include:

Enclosure 1:
    a. A checklist that lists everything in the kit. This calls for the

student to fill in the date and to check "o.k." as he completes the various experiences and proficiencies in the kit.

b. An outline of the thirteen enclosures in the kit, the approximate time to complete the kit (in this case twenty hours), and the direct experiences to be scheduled in advance.

c. An introductory statement of why listening is important.

d. Four behavioral objectives that the student will have achieved at the completion of the kit.

e. Five experiences the student will engage in: (1) reading, (2) scheduling a discussion seminar with peers, (3) preparing charts and posters, (4) preparing four listening skill lesson plans, and (5) teaching one of the four plans.

f. Proficiency assessment. A statement of the actual proficiencies to be developed that will achieve the behavioral objectives of the kit. (In this case, the proficiencies are preparing two charts that demonstrate a knowledge of types of listening and listening skills; preparation of four lesson plans which demonstrate appreciative, creative, attentive, and critical listening skills; and teaching one lesson to a group of public school children evaluated by a cooperating teacher.

Enclosure 2: A self-test. Eleven items that assess, "Are you a good listener."

Enclosure 3: Thirteen pages of cartoons that depict concepts of listening.

Enclosure 4: Three pages of notable quotes and research findings related to listening.

Enclosure 5: Four page monograph on types of listening, definitions and examples.

Enclosure 6: a poem "Good Listening Manners" by Helena B. Watson.

Enclosure 7: A page listing of "The Do's of Listening Instruction" containing thirteen items.

Enclosure 8: A critique form. This page is used to evaluate student's actual teaching of a lesson and includes items such as the listening skill being taught, the behavioral objective of the lesson, the procedures and evaluation of the lesson, and the cooperating teacher's assessment.

Enclosure 9: Four lesson plan sheets. Spaces are provided for skill to be taught, behavioral objective, procedure, and evaluation.

Enclosure 10: A bibliography of eleven references. Students are required to read two items.

Enclosure 11: Propoganda—ideas for a unit. Lists seven common propoganda devices and seven pages of cartoons illustrating each.

Enclosure 12: Listening ideas. Contains twenty-four ideas of things to try with children.

Enclosure 13: An application for public school teaching experience.

This detailed example indicates the nature of instructional modules. Naturally, the actual written materials and student activities differ among various CBTE programs. All CBTE programs, however, specify the actual behaviors to be learned and demonstrated; indicate the criteria to be used in making this determination; and hold the student accountable for meeting the particular proficiency. The example on listening skills demonstrates that these competency behaviors need not all be related to the mundane skills of instruction. In most CBTE programs, skills include both content to be taught (e.g., phonics, new math, handwriting) and demonstrable skills for raising pupils' self-concepts, increasing motivation, and improving abilities for cooperative action among learners.

In order to make CBTE as effective as possible, proponents emphasize that competency objectives must always be public. Otherwise CBTE programs may make certain activities and experiences good "for their own sake" rather than ensuring that they remain means for achieving some clear, specific objective of teacher training. The preassessment activity is critical, because it permits individualization. Some students may test out of certain program requirements; others will, by virtue of the test, start the particular component at various stages of difficulty. Finally, it cannot be overemphasized that all components of a CBTE program should be as close to the real thing as possible. Whatever students study and practice should be similar, in all situational factors, to what they will be expected to do in their subsequent teaching.

Proponents of CBTE

Those supporting CBTE include members of diverse groups, from the public to teacher education researchers.

1. The public has increasingly supported efforts to ensure that education programs achieve their stated purposes and that educational personnel be held accountable for their services in these programs.

Various state laws specifying behavioral objectives in pupils' curriculum and requiring the evaluation of teachers' performance are examples of the public's growing interest in trying to make certain that they are getting something definite for their support of education. The great volume of critical literature recounting the failures of the schools in serving minority groups, the poor, the exceptional, the disaffected children of suburbia, and so forth, have fanned public concern for guarantees. Competency-based teacher education is more acceptable than experience-based teacher education to those who seek some specific reassurance about what teachers will actually be able to do for their children.

2. A large and increasing number of research-oriented faculty who teach in college programs also support CBTE. A few decades ago, only a small minority of teacher educators held doctorates. Individuals with advanced degrees now constitute a majority of the faculty in schools of education. This is not to imply that most teacher educators are in favor of CBTE, but the number of faculty who favor systems analysis and the data base required for CBTE has shown a notable increase.

3. Government support for regional laboratories and individual research aid program grants has required specificity of purpose, products, and evaluation. An experience-based teacher education program cannot possibly meet the usual funding criteria; CBTE programs are ideally suited to responding to government guidelines. The same is true for private foundations. Every funding agent needs precise, clear statements of what the grant will achieve. This influence from government and foundations has had a significant effect on schools of education, many of which must have these outside funds to survive.

4. A fourth group of proponents for CBTE are school administrators. Both on the organizational level (the American Association of School Administrators) and as individuals, school administrators frequently regard themselves as the consumers of teacher education programs. Because they hire the teachers, administrators feel they are held ultimately responsible for educational services in their districts and are therefore the most accountable. The CBTE movement gives many school administrators the assurance they need that when they hire particular teachers they will be getting particular skills. Many administrators feel that the graduate of an experienced-based program is "a shot in the dark," while the graduate of a CBTE program comes with a verified checklist of skills that he has actually mastered.

5. Some officials in the various state departments of public instruction have become disillusioned with trying to improve college courses on the wide variety of campuses in their respective states.

They see CBTE as a means of not having to deal directly with colleges in the usual way. If there is a competency or set of competencies that is established as a requirement, there is a greater likelihood of enforcing some minimum standards. These state officials believe that "3 credits in Elementary Reading" does not guarantee minimum proficiencies as well as a checklist of student competencies in phonetic analysis, construction of experience charts, etc.

6. More and more students who are members of minority groups are coming into teacher education. Many of these individuals feel they and their fellow group members have been hurt by poor teachers who didn't give them basic skills. Competency-based teacher education seems to these students to be a more hopeful means of guaranteeing that teachers who do not demonstrate minimum proficiencies will no longer be certified and inflicted on minority pupils.

7. Individuals who argue that college is not necessary for learning the skills of teaching often favor CBTE. We are all familiar with stories of teacher aides—particularly in early childhood—who are better than the regular teachers. The CBTE system permits "testing out." It questions experiences not only in professional education courses but also in general education. Since anyone who can demonstrate the proficiencies in the particular CBTE program is entitled to certification, this is perceived as a fantastic opportunity to many who have never had the opportunity to attend four-year college programs.

8. Finally, many deans of schools of education support the CBTE approach. While not all deans support CBTE, the number is sufficient for their organization (American Association of Colleges for Teacher Education) to take leadership in disseminating bibliographies and materials for helping interested schools move toward CBTE. There are several reasons for this support. Deans of schools of education must compete for university budget with other colleges in the university. The state legislators who appropriate these resources need greater reassurance that the schools of education are delivering some tangible results. As financial pressures force this kind of accountability, many deans see the CBTE approach as a helpful way to communicate their programs to lay legislators more positively. In addition, many deans have always harbored doubts about experience-based programs. The teacher education literature indicates that as many inside critics (i.e., deans and professional educators) as external critics have called for greater specificity of purpose, sequencing of teacher education curriculum, and clearer evaluation. Even during the greatest growth periods of their institutions, school of education administrators frequently advocated a more systematic approach.

For example, George Denemark, dean of the School of Education, University of Kentucky, and a past president of the AACTE, has long called for teacher educators to sequence direct experiences so that beginning students would learn prerequisites and lower level skills, while advanced student teachers would learn clearly identified, more difficult skills of teaching.

It is difficult to rank all of the above forces in terms of their respective pressures for CBTE. The public's concern for accountability, however, is clearly the most notable influence. As educational costs continue to increase, pressures are exerted on universities as well as on public schools. Fiscal pressures imply an accounting for services. The CBTE approach in teacher education is more suited than experience-based teacher education to explaining just what the student, his future pupils, and the public are getting in return for their support.

Criticism of CBTE

Recently, we accidently discovered a note in one of the books that has become a standard explanation of CBTE.[8] The note was from a colleague, Richard Western.

This is an interesting book in that it is long on advocacy and includes everything except examples of validated competencies. I would have guessed that empirically oriented systems types would *start* with the examples and would say, "Look, we have this and this and that competency and we know that each is necessary (sufficient?) for effective teachers of X, therefore, let's get a whole structure of such examples and use the structure to inform teacher training." I would have guessed . . . . Dick.

The most telling criticism of CBTE is that it is not derived from research on teaching. The competencies taught to students are justified vociferously with logic and theory but less frequently with research about what instruction causes pupils to learn. Experience-based teacher education cannot claim a research basis, but it is the CBTE approach that has made much of the deficiency and declared itself an improvement in this regard. The credibility of the physician who denigrates the faith healer and then talks about the need for patient faith is open to question.

Rosenshine and Furst conclude their definitive review of the research on teacher performance criteria with the statement:

Most studies on classroom instruction have been conducted by doctoral candidates, and there have been only a few large scale experimental or correlational studies on teacher behavior and student achievement. Because of this lack of research, we have little knowledge of the relationship between teacher behavior and student growth. Given the number of competent researchers in the American Educational Research Association, such a lack of knowledge is shameful.

Those responsible for teacher education have manifested their concern for the quality of education given our youth through the preparation of the model elementary teacher education programs. However, as of this writing, no one has shown that the behaviors identified in the models have any proven relevance to the real world. To be real, teacher behaviors need to be researched so that they are known to have some relationship to student outcome measures. Until this research is done, we can have little confidence that the models are providing any more hope that either teacher training or student education will be greatly improved in the foreseeable future.[9]

What is the rationale for a research-derived approach to teacher education without the supporting research?

A second group of critics attack CBTE as advocating training rather than education of teachers. Those in favor of general education in the university and those who define professional education as essentially the acquisition of principles of philosophy, human development, psychology of learning, and curriculum development reject the training emphasis in CBTE. In 1904, John Dewey summarized his objections to any teacher training that would give student teachers specific training at the expense of their intellectual development:

It ought to go without saying (unfortunately, it does not in all cases) that criticism should be directed to making the professional student thoughtful about his work in the light of principles, rather than to induce in him a recognition that certain special methods are good, and certain other special methods are bad. At all events no greater travesty of real intellectual criticism can be given than to set a student to teach a brief number of lessons, have him under inspection in practically all the time in every lesson, and then criticize him almost, if not quite, at the very end of each lesson, upon the particular way in which that particular lesson has been taught, pointing out elements of failure and success. Such methods of criticism may be adapted to giving a training teacher command of some of the knacks and tools of the trade, but are not calculated to develop a thoughtful and independent teacher.[10]

What Dewey perceived as too obvious to repeat—that professional preparation should develop independent, intellectual practitioners engaged in identifying basic principles rather than rehearsing specific methods—may no longer be quite so obvious. Critics of CBTE, however, still retain this vision of teacher education as emphasizing theory and the self-discovery of principles, rather than teacher training and performance of instructional skills.

A third major criticism of CBTE is leveled at its proponents' claim that it facilitates evaluation and follow-up of graduates. Critics argue that although the CBTE approach sounds as if it is accountable, what actually happens is that students are evaluated at the completion of their training (or in a few cases, a year later) only to ascertain if they have learned and retained the skills the program claimed to teach them. Students are not evaluated in ways that demonstrate that the skills they have learned and retained lead to growth in their pupils. Once again, while experience-based programs do not follow up any better, the CBTE approach was supposed to rectify this lack of connection between what graduates actually do and their pupils' learning. Critics argue that since the competencies taught in CBTE are not derived from teacher effectiveness behaviors to begin with, and since the evaluations of CBTE programs are simply a verification that graduates remember the skills included in their particular programs, this kind of follow-up does not demonstrate that pupil learning will be improved.

Essentially, those who criticize CBTE fall into two broad groups: (1) those who emphasize some form of personal development and (2) the advocates of a broad general-liberal education.

The basic assumption of the personal development approach is that teachers must know who they are and be able to deal with their own needs before helping others to do the same. The logic of their approach is that what teachers should want for themselves (i.e., self-understanding and self-actualization) is what they should want for children and youth. The process for realizing such a program is not training in skills advocated for all teachers but a personal form of education. This education may include in-depth experiences, such as psychoanalysis, and less intensive experiences, such as sensitivity training, various group activities, interactions with a broad spectrum of others, and even travel. This approach defines teaching as a process of human interaction that places no particular value on prior planning of specific objectives, either for teachers or their pupils. The emphasis is on the process and nature of relationships. Of all the forms of knowledge, personal knowledge is valued most. The most notable example of this form of teacher education was the Bank Street College of Education between World War I and 1960.

The second group of CBTE critics are all those who argue that teacher preparation must be built on a broad, basic general education. These individuals include more than the liberal arts and science faculties. There is a strong tradition in teacher education emphasizing the cognitive purposes of lower schools and the intellectual processes of a teacher education that would support such goals. This tradition is literary and oriented to the classics more than to modern disciplines such as systems analysis. The most prominent exponent of the traditional approach is Philip H. Phenix, who carefully explains how each discipline's way of knowing has a place in the curriculum.[11] An example of how this belief in broad liberal education is used to argue against CBTE is found in the critique by Harry S. Broudy.[12] Broudy argues in favor of theory for teachers; he supports studies of didactics (what the teacher teaches), heuristics (what pupils discover), and philetics (rapport) and claims that CBTE is disconnected and mechanistic without any total view of the universe, man, or the sweep of history.

It is important to emphasize that the critics, whether psychologically or classically oriented, frequently label themselves humanists. Since many CBTE advocates also claim this title, it becomes important to clarify "humanism" and not assume that simply supporting or resisting CBTE is a definition of the term.

Implications of CBTE

Content

As increasing numbers of teacher educators become more specific about what they want students and teachers to be able to do, it becomes more difficult to substantiate the attacks either of CBTE proponents on "traditional" teacher education or of its critics on CBTE. One reason for this muddling of differences is that some CBTE programs are teaching proficiencies that are not clearly behavioral (e.g., "Poetry for Today's Children" in the Wilkits material), while "traditional" teacher educators are teaching skills that would fit into many CBTE programs. A good recent example of this latter condition are the parallel teacher-pupil behaviors of informing, soliciting, responding, and reacting in a recent book on humanistic instruction. The protocol material and examples of Gestalt games could easily fit into several CBTE programs, yet it is presented as a means for realizing a philosophy of humanism.[13] There are numerous other examples such as value clarification techniques, sensitivity exercises, and strategies for teaching affective objectives, which are becoming common in teacher education programs but are difficult to classify as either competency- or experience-based. In future it will be more necessary than ever to cut through the claims and criticisms made by competency-based and experience-based educators and examine the actual contents being offered before attaching labels to programs.

College Control of Programs

Competency-based teacher education poses a threat to the present system of college control over teacher education programs, not by what it does directly, but by the kinds of processes it facilitates.

Pressure groups can influence departments of public instruction and state legislatures to introduce new behaviors that will become mandatory for the colleges to teach their students. In theory this is no different from the ways in which past pressure groups introduced courses dealing with the evils of alcohol, farmer and consumer cooperatives, or the history of a particular state. The difference is that in those times the assumption was that a new course was needed; now the emphasis is on the competency to be developed. A good example of this shift is a new statute in Wisconsin requiring that all teacher-preparing institutions provide their students with human relations skills by September 1973. The state department of public instruction is carefully checking the colleges to make certain they develop specific human relations proficiencies and do not simply require a new course in human relations.

There is a strong likelihood that some control over programs will be wrested from the colleges by this process of specifying competencies. Schools of education are geared to offering courses and providing machinery for the staffing, recording, and purchase of courses. Requiring competencies forces the leadership in schools of education to employ faculty who may be outside of the university establishment. Behavioral competencies may be gained under the aegis of public school classroom teachers in simulated experiences, or they may be self-taught. In addition, many local teachers associations are beginning to organize their own inservice education programs around the proficiencies teachers think they need, rather than those the faculty think they need.

This is called the renewal strategy. Renewal centers are places where such teacher-controlled programs would be offered. As more and more local teacher organizations put such inservice agreements into their contracts with local school boards, the schools of education's major control over approved programs will be somewhat diminished. The vehicle or process that supports this movement is CBTE. Obviously, if proficiencies rather than course experiences are best, and if teachers rather than faculty can identify those proficiencies, there will be some shift of control from the colleges to the organizations of classroom teachers.

Teacher Certification

As great as its impact on the content of teacher education, CBTE will have an even greater effect on the process of certification. Several states have gone on record with legislative acts or administrative code changes in their departments of certification that require all future beginning teachers to be certified on the basis of specified competencies rather than completion of college courses in approved programs.

The state that is furthest along the path of changing governance on the basis of CBTE is Washington. An interesting feature of their plan is that it deals with three constituencies: colleges, schools, and teacher associations. These troikas are expected to develop the competencies for particular programs on a regional or district basis so that competencies will not necessarily be uniform on a statewide basis. Just as state-approved programs now differ from college to college, they might in future differ on a district or regional basis. The difference, of course, is that the singular control now exercised by schools of education over recommending students for certification would be decreased to one-third control, and the basis for such certification would have to be competency.

The relationship between governance questions and CBTE is most clearly seen in the state of Washington's requirement for program approval and review.

The State Board will approve a program of professional preparation which:
1. Is based on an analysis and a description of the performance based expectations for the particular professional role for which the program is designed. Because roles change as new knowledge is created, analyses and descriptions of performance need to be revised periodically.[14]

Accountability

In June 1971 the California legislature enacted the Stull Bill, which made educational accountability a statutory reality. As a five-paragraph addition to the law on tenure, the key stipulations are:

1. Each school district must establish its own *objective* system of evaluation for the annual appraisal of probationary teachers and the biennial appraisal of all other teachers.
2. In devising its evaluation system, the district school board must seek the advice of the local teachers organization.
3. Each evaluation system must include—as a minimum—
   a. established standards and techniques for assessing student progress in each area of study.
   b. assessment of teacher competence as it relates to the established standards.
   c. assessment of duties performed by teachers as adjuncts to their regular assignments.
   d. established procedures for ascertaining that teachers are maintaining proper control and a suitable learning environment.

4. The evaluation must be conveyed to the teacher by a written evaluation plus a face-to-face meeting, and it must include any necessary recommendations for improvement.

Competency-based teacher education has established itself as a major force in teacher education. Since its primary support will remain the accountability movement, how influential it becomes will depend on how much pressure the accountability movement exerts on higher education and teacher education. Up to now, parents and citizens have held public schools, teachers, and administrators accountable. If their aim is broadened to include teacher education, CBTE will become a dominant force in teacher education. If the public concern remains fixed on the lower schools and their practitioners and does not broaden to include the institutions that prepare professional personnel, CBTE will become just one more of several approaches to be offered in programs of teacher education. Previous experiences indicate that no single approach has ever taken complete control over curricula at any level of education.

Notes

1. We would like to thank the colleagues and students who helped to research the use of this terminology: Al Solomon, Judy Kirkhorn, Alex Molnar, Will Roy, Pat Unterholzner, Larry Barnett, Jack Simpson, and Dorothy McGeoch.
2. Stanley Elam, *Performance Based Teacher Education: What is the State of the Art?* (Washington, D.C.: American Association of Colleges for Teacher Education, 1971), p. 7.
3. James M. Cooper and Wilfred A. Weber, "A Competency Based Systems Approach to Teacher Education," in *Competency Based Teacher Education,* vol. 2 (Berkeley, Calif.: McCutchan Publishing Corp., 1973), pp. 7-12.
4. Bela Banathy, *Institutional Systems* (Palo Alto, Calif.: Fearon Publishers, 1968), p. 4.
5. Ibid., p. 12.
6. Arthur Jersild, *When Teachers Face Themselves* (New York: Teachers College Press, Columbia University, 1956).
7. Caseal Burke, *The Individualized Competency-Based System of Teacher Education at Weber State College* (Washington, D.C.: American Association of Colleges for Teacher Education, 1971).
8. Benjamin Rosner, *The Power of Competency-Based Teacher Education: A Report* (Boston: Allyn and Bacon, 1972).
9. Barak Rosenshine and Norma Furst, "Research on Teacher Per-

formance Criteria," in *Research in Teacher Education,* ed. B. O. Smith (Englewood Cliffs, N.J.: Prentice-Hall, 1971), p. 72.

10. John Dewey, *The Relation of Theory to Practice in Education* (no. 17) (Cedar Falls, Iowa: Association for Student Teaching, 1962), p. 22.

11. Philip H. Phenix, *Realms of Meaning* (New York: McGraw-Hill, 1964).

12. Harry S. Broudy, *A Critique of PBTE* (Washington, D.C.: American Association of Colleges for Teacher Education, May 1972).

13. John A. Zahorik and Dale Brubaker, *Toward More Humanistic Instruction* (Dubuque, Iowa: W. C. Brown, 1972).

14. Theodore E. Andrews, *New Directions in Certification* (Washington, D.C.: Association for Teacher Educators, 1971), p. 35.

9

Research

in

Teacher Education

The uses and misuses of research in the process of evaluating teacher education programs is discussed in chapter 11. The purpose of this section is to analyze more specifically how teacher educators know what to teach future teachers. Where, for example, do the competencies in CBTE (competency-based teacher education) come from? What are the criteria on which teacher education programs can validly be held accountable? On what empirical evidence of effective instruction are teacher education programs based? Answering these questions will require a brief review of studies dealing with teacher effectiveness, the relationship of such effectiveness studies to teacher training programs and finally, the studies that seek to contribute new behaviors to be taught to future teachers in training programs.

Effectiveness Studies

"Effective" teacher behavior, in the technical sense, means that pupils learn x, y, or z in response to particular teacher acts. In other words, in the performance of specified instructional acts there is a predictive power related to pupil achievement. Theoretically, these effective behaviors would then become the competencies taught to future teachers. The several processes by which attempts have been made to identify effective behaviors have included teacher characteristic studies, laboratory studies, subject matter research, experimental classroom studies, and process-product research.

Teacher Characteristics

The earlier studies of instruction frequently sought to explain the success of teachers by assessing their personality attributes. These studies have been consistently denigrated in the summaries of research.[1] Nevertheless, the *manifestations* of such personality variables have been resurrected at least every decade as being more

111

completely verified in empirical studies than any of the others. David Ryans' designation of behaviors indicating warmth, enthusiasm, and businesslike attitude are still regarded as basic to an understanding of teacher effectiveness.[2] The search for teacher behaviors that can be separated from personalities is based on the need to support teacher training rather than any search for particular personalities who manifest the "right" characteristics. More recently, however, another premier summary of teacher effectiveness came up with several studies pointing to personality traits (e.g., "enthusiasm") rather than to learned behaviors capable of being practiced in training.[3]

Even though the majority of researchers do not like the idea, it seems quite evident that the study of behaviors that manifest particular teacher personalities is required for understanding teacher effectiveness. The best study in this area is that of Heil and Washburne.[4] These researchers used personality instruments for classifying teachers as "turbulent," "self-controlled," or "fearful" and their pupils as "conformers," "opposers," "waiverers," or "strivers." The results indicate that different kinds of teachers may be best (in terms of academic achievement and self-acceptance) for different kinds of pupils in particular subject matters. This study assumed that personality variables were paramount for both teachers and pupils; the obvious implication is that matching appropriate personalities to particular content studies may be more important than trying to train everyone to teach in all curriculum areas.

This fascinating approach to effectiveness breaks down in preservice teacher education, because we are, after all, normatively controlled. Which school of education, for example, would proudly defend their students who were classified "fearful" on the basis that "some children these students will teach will be conformers who respond best to fearful types"? Schools of education can neither change personalities nor simply function as conduits for all those who go through them, even if evidence does exist that anyone can probably be effective to some degree at teaching something to someone.

Another reason for playing down the characteristics approach is that data about inservice teachers and pupils is exceptionally hard to gather. The obvious need for guarding what is found out about teachers as personalities explains why so little information is available in this area.

Laboratory Studies

There are two reasons why this form of research is neglected: (1) most of what is known about learning is based on animal studies, and

(2) the laboratory studies on humans have limited generalizability to schools. The distinctive nature of school environments and the special nature of what is taught in schools have been clearly demonstrated. Even studies of human learning, therefore, are not clearly applicable to school learning. Laboratory studies are usually of individuals, learning over brief periods, about subjects that are frequently unlike school content, from people who follow more precise regimens than classroom teachers. If schools were more like these laboratories, teachers might be trained like those who conduct the laboratory studies and become equally effective. The basic problem, of course, is that real teachers have to teach the content given to them, while researchers select the content that will support their pet hunches about the uses of reinforcement, practice, or whatever it is they are studying.

Subject Matter Research

A third kind of study seeks to train teachers to use particular books or materials in a given content area. These efforts have been highly ineffective at getting teachers to use the same materials in the same way.[5] At first, these efforts were aimed at developing "teacher-proof" packages of curricular content that could be used in spite of alleged teacher ignorance in science, math, and other areas. It soon became obvious that teachers must be trained in the steps to be followed. This training was based less on effective teacher behaviors than on direct instruction of pupils and the precise steps teachers were to take in conducting lessons: the exact things to say, the questions to ask, and the assignments to make.

Two factors intrude on this approach:

1. The behaviors learned for using particular science materials will not transfer to other curriculum areas; they may not even transfer to other areas of the science curriculum.

2. Teachers frequently resent following instructions; even those who try, show greater variability than is permissible in controlled experimentation.

Many public schools value this approach to teacher education. They define inservice teacher education as training their classroom teachers how to use the specific books and materials that the particular system has adopted and purchased. Schools of education, on the other hand, would be hard pressed to take this approach with future teachers who will work in all kinds of school systems.

The important point here, is that studies of training teachers to use specific books and materials have not yielded many generalizable results to the body of effective behaviors to be included in teacher education programs. This is true no matter how limited the area.[6]

Experimental Classroom Studies

Experimental classroom studies seem to be the basic source of new data from which to derive effective behaviors, because experimental teachers are taught to engage in particular instructional behaviors and then compared with teachers who do not engage in these behaviors. While the pupils in the respective classrooms are evaluated in terms of their learning, it is the teachers who are the focus and, therefore, the appropriate unit of analysis and comparison. Before there can be valid generalizations, such experiments require a sufficient number of teachers; a system for seeing to it that the experimental teachers really stick to their "treatments"; a system for describing what the control teachers do, rather than sloughing them off as "following the regular routines"; and an assessment of pupils' performance at the end of the experimental period on a variety of tests. These straight-forward conditions seem simple enough to the uninitiated. It also seems likely that *The Encyclopedia of Educational Research, The Handbook of Research on Teaching,* the ERIC system, and other basic references would yield scores of such basic studies. However, owing to the problems of experimental design, getting permission to do such studies, and the intricacies of teacher training, they are the rarest source for deriving effective teacher behaviors. In 1971 an outstanding researcher and summarizer of studies was able to locate only ten studies that satisfied the basic canons of experimentation.[7]

Correlational Research

Since these studies attempt to relate teacher behaviors to student outcomes (or learnings) they are also referred to as process-product research. These studies have been the most numerous studies and most productive of effective behaviors. This makes the whole process of deriving competencies from research exceptionally tenuous since the researcher can correlate just about anything he wants in the way of teacher talk or gesture with pupil learning. Frequently, the researcher's guarded and carefully worded reservations about the pitfalls of teaching future teachers a specific behavior are ignored. After all, the researcher studied the behavior, his study was published, it *does* correlate with pupil gains, and, probably most important of all, it matches the particular prejudices of the teacher educators with the power to decide what future teachers should practice as competencies.

In this form of research the teachers' behaviors are the independent variables; the dependent variables are pupils' performance measures. If teachers are observed engaging in particular acts, these are considered low-inference variables, not because they are closer to having a cause-effect relationship with pupil learning, but because they are behaviorally observable teacher actions. High-inference variables sound further removed from a cause-effect relationship between teaching and learning, but the term simply refers to teacher characteristics that must be inferred by observers (e.g., warmth). While observers may consistently and reliably agree that they are observing "warmth" from a particular teacher, they will be less able to cite the exact behaviors that gave them this feeling while they observed a teacher "asking factual questions." At this point, there is no basis for believing that only one level of research is needed; both high- and low-inference studies can help define effective teacher behaviors.

Current Studies

There have been a wide variety of studies conducted in teacher education that are not directly related to either supporting or refuting CBTE or the experience-based approach to teacher education. In order to gain a fuller perspective of just what data base curriculum developers in teacher education have to refer to, it might be helpful to consider examples of these kinds of data.

There is no evidence that the general-liberal studies that comprise much of teacher education programs are necessary for performing as a teacher, although this component of the teacher education curricula has been generally accepted as desirable.[8] There is impressive testimony from students that they regard student teaching as the most practical part of their program; however, general or ill-defined student teaching experiences seem to have few beneficial and a great many detrimental effects. The positive studies seem to indicate that students will make gains in teaching performance (e.g., teaching reading) if their cooperating teachers have been selected on the basis of having such competencies.[9] Studies have also shown positive results on students in those cases where cooperating teachers were selected and given special preparation.[10] Recognizing these exceptions (i.e., specially trained and/or selected supervising teachers), the preponderence of evidence regarding experience-based teacher education is essentially negative.[11] This condition is in part the result of having to place large numbers of students with large numbers of supervising teachers who are selected for a wide variety of reasons other than their specific competencies and preparation. There are, however, additional reasons put forward as explanations for these negative influences.

It seems that as students move through their programs and get closer to becoming teachers, they become less humanistic and more custodial.[12] Studies using the Minnesota Teacher Attitude Inventory support this view that students become more authoritarian as they go through their programs and get closer to beginning as regular teachers.[13] Studies using other instruments have also supported this drift toward custodialism by describing students as more rigid and impersonal after student teaching than before.[14] The usual explanation for this condition is that students believe that most beginning teachers quit or fail on the basis of their ability to handle classroom discipline, and as they get closer to beginning their real teaching, they naturally begin to worry about possible failure. Whatever the causes may be, the condition has been sufficiently documented to make teacher educators more cognizant of this "natural" development in planning teacher education programs.

The most influential content in the teacher education program, at least in its impact on students' perceptions and values, seems to be the nature of the supervising teachers with whom they are placed, and the changes are largely in the direction of students' modelling themselves after their supervising teachers.[15] Unfortunately, the few studies that show some students moving in opposite directions from their supervising teachers indicate negative progress; for example, students who disagreed with their supervising teacher became less empathetic to pupils as a result of their experiences.[16]

All of the foregoing may seem to relate only to attitudinal factors, but when interaction analysis is used to assess what student teachers actually do, they seem to increase in more directive teaching (i.e., stating their own opinions and accepting students' ideas less frequently), and decrease in indirective responses (i.e., clarifying and praising students' ideas), during the course of their student teaching.[17] Studies that get at more personal data, such as students' logs, indicate that students start out being shocked and horrified at what their supervisors do but end up imitating them.[18] They justify their actions on the basis of pragmatic success (i.e., "it works"); unresponsive pupils are frequently classified as slow learners; pupils' individual needs are second to "getting the class through the lesson."[19]

Increased custodial emphasis, while the most documented and important finding regarding the influence of teacher education programs on students, is by no means the only generalization that can be made from the available evidence. Seven themes of research on teacher education have recently been summarized as follows:

1. A "systems" approach to teacher education improves its effectiveness. A good deal of research is clustered around three special cases of this general model: training teachers in interaction analysis, microteaching, and behavior modification.

2. When teachers are treated in the same way they are supposed to treat their pupils, they are more likely to adopt the desired style of teaching behavior.

3. Direct involvement in the role to be learned, or such close approximations as sensitivity training laboratories or classroom simulation laboratories, produced the desired teaching behavior more effectively than remote or abstract experiences such as lectures on instructional theory.

4. It is possible to induce a more self-initiated, self-directed pattern of learning, not only in teachers, but also through them in their pupils.

5. Traditional ways of educating teachers have some of the intended effects, but they also have some quite undesired effects.

6. There is no discernible research on training for college teaching in any field.

7. One long-needed methodological advance is beginning to appear in the research: the use of pupil-gain measures as the ultimate criteria of the effectiveness of any given process of teacher education. These include affective and behavioral gains as well as gains in subject mastery.[20]

While true of the studies that have been conducted about teacher education, these generalizations do not necessarily reflect actual practices. It may very well be that what is actually offered in many programs does not build on these generalizations.

Relationship of Effectiveness Studies to Teacher Education

One of the guidelines for deriving teacher education behaviors from the synthesis of research studies is that they must be viewed as supporting or refuting major contentions. No single study "proves" anything. They vary in quality and purpose and must be grouped and weighed. For example, if studies are categorized as dealing with normal children and with general methods that apply to all subject areas, the volume of available, appropriate research becomes highly abbreviated. Once the large number of subject matter studies and those dealing with special kinds of pupils are not considered, there are relatively few general studies remaining. It is starting to seem reasonable that there may be as many (or more) summaries and analyses of research on teacher effectiveness as there are actual studies seeking to derive generally effective teaching behaviors. One thing is certain. The real number of studies that support the installation of any specific teaching behavior as a competency for future teachers is smaller than prudence requires, if we accept the basic assumption that single educational studies do not prove or disprove but must be cumulated into weights supporting or refuting grand contentions. This problem of an insufficient number of general studies is complicated further by the reminder that essentially we are dealing with process-product research, which is correlational to begin with.

The teacher behaviors that seem to have the strongest relationship to pupil achievement are clarity, variability, enthusiasm, businesslike behavior, and student opportunity to learn (the latter may seem simple-minded but it is an often neglected notion). Teacher behaviors or conditions that are less clearly related to pupil learning include using students' ideas, criticism (negatively related), probing, using multiple levels of discourse, structuring comments, and perceived difficulty of the course. Except for the last item, it is quite clear that most of the recent studies have been ones in which researchers have chosen to study teacher talk using categories that they have chosen as the critical dimensions.

Behaviors that at this point seem to show *no* consistent relationship to learning include teacher absence, pupil absence, teacher knowledge of subject matter, teacher experience, nonverbal approval, praise, warmth, flexibility, teacher talk, and student talk.[21]

The problem of language in these various studies is now quite clear: What is the difference between "enthusiasm," which is a significant teacher correlate of pupil achievement, and "warmth," which is not? What is the difference between teacher "flexibility," which is not significant, and "variability," which is?" Consider the problem of taking such data and teaching minicourses such as the following:

CONTENTS AND TENTATIVE SEQUENCE OBJECTIVES[22]

I. Objective: To change teacher behaviors that will increase the pupil's readiness to respond to discussion questions.
Specific behaviors to be covered:
A. Ask question, pause 5 seconds, then call on pupil.
B. Deal with incorrect answers in an accepting, nonpunitive manner.
C. Call on both volunteers and non-volunteers in order to keep all pupils alert and distribute participation.
II. Objective: To change teacher behavior so as to decrease teacher participation and raise the level of pupil responses.
Specific behaviors to be covered:
A. Redirection—directing the same question to several pupils.

B. Framing questions that call for longer pupil responses.
1. Ask for sets or groups of information when framing information level questions.
2. Avoid yes-no replies.
C. Framing questions that require the pupil to use higher cognitive processes.
III. Objective: To increase the teacher's use of probing behaviors in order to guide the pupil to more complete and thoughtful responses.
Specific behaviors to be covered:
A. Prompting.
B. Seeking further clarification and pupil insight—this is a combination of two probing behaviors treated separately in the preliminary field test form of the course. Seeking further clarification and seeking to increase pupil awareness differ largely in terms of the quality of the pupil's initial reply.
C. Refocusing the pupil's response.
IV. Objective: To reduce teacher behaviors that interfere with the flow of the discussion.
Specific behaviors to be covered:
A. Teacher should not repeat her questions.
B. Teacher should not answer her own questions.
C. Teacher should not repeat pupil answers.

This is not to assert, of course, that there is anything "bad" about training future teachers to learn these materials. The goal, however, is for them to justify, with substantial amounts of varied research studies of normal youngsters in all general areas, that teaching these things is more valuable than teaching other things. It often seems that by changing one expert for another we can also change the behaviors that will be prescribed for students of teaching. The only real safeguard is to be aware of the need for more than one or a few studies that correlate particular teacher behaviors with pupil learning. This criticism is meant to support the behavioral approach and make it less vulnerable to charges of arbitrariness in the selection of behaviors, capriciousness in the selection of supportive research, and personality-proneness in the acceptance of the latest "expert" pronouncements on effectiveness.

All too often we substitute pupil behaviors of participation for pupil learning and then make plausible connections between teacher behaviors and pupil participation on the assumption that these participatory behaviors will influence pupil learning. There is probably nothing wrong with the logic of this approach, unless, of course, the people who use it criticize other teacher educators for not having a research basis for their programs. By this time, it should be obvious that "humanistic" teacher educators pursue their programs, while behaviorally oriented teacher educators pursue CBTE, but that neither group can demonstrate a greater degree of empirical foundation. Unfortunately for the behaviorists, however, it seems to be more incumbent on them to demonstrate research connections. After analyzing the sources of the behavioral competencies to offer future teachers, some of CBTE's leading proponents conclude by stating:

> Input must also come from empirical analysis of the act of teaching. Systematic analysis of the teaching act can lead to a determination of the skills, attitudes and knowledge necessary for effective teaching. Although this seems like a logical place to start, the difficulties of analyzing teaching must not be forgotten. Much documented research has failed to identify distinguishing characteristics of effective teachers. Process-product research has only been a bit more revealing to date. Up to now, research conclusions on teacher effectiveness have been so skimpy that educators may have been somewhat justified in basing their programs on tradition and mysticism. Of course, the lack of useful results thus far does not preclude the continuation of research efforts.
>
> The difficulties in specifying competencies often seem overpowering. However, many of the difficulties can be alleviated by careful preplanning and effective communication among those involved. The moves from program assumptions to teacher competencies to specific instructional objectives must be viewed as crucial. Merely adding "given" or "with 80 percent accuracy" to an identified competency does not convert it to a useful instructional objective. In too many cases, objectives are added to the program only because a particular competency can easily be translated into behavioral terms, or because instructional materials are readily available. Well conceived competencies are essential to competency based programs.[23]

What these expert supporters of CBTE seem to be heralding is an honest avowal that research in teacher effectiveness cannot serve as the only or even major basis for CBTE. Nevertheless, CBTE should be continued by following a process—in the above quote stated as "the moves"—which includes having a philosophic position and trying to synthesize what can be gleaned from empirical studies, various subject matters, and practitioners' experiences. A process of communication among several parties in various institutions is also proposed as part of the means for identifying the competencies to be offered.

At this point it might be useful to give two notable examples of skills to be offered teachers when there is a partial basis in research on effectiveness.

The first example relies heavily on "expert" analysis.

> Summary of Listening Skills for Teachers. From Phase 1 comes the most important set of skills: A teacher has the ability to perceive bits of information from pupil behavior, to classify these bits, to organize them into clusters with labels, and to formulate functional relationships using the labels. Phases 1, 2, and 4: A teacher reacts to expected events one after another and, at the same time, inductively processes information in such a way that the summary labels are kept tentative so they do not inhibit the receiving and processing of conflicting information.[24]

This model becomes even more esoteric. The point is that the process of identifying teacher effectiveness behaviors is just as frequently done by researchers' first deciding what kinds of teacher behaviors they will perceive and then taking in what practitioners do through a screen of preset categories. When researchers become sufficiently prominent, we may even skip the need to verify and just start extracting competencies from their conceptual models. Piaget and Bruner are notable examples of this most prestigious source of "competency" behaviors. Many other experts would like to achieve equal power to establish competencies by fiat.

Another example of what happens when there is a skimpy research basis indicates that we "compensate" for not being able to assess pupil learning by doing more research on our effectiveness in teaching future teachers to use and retain specific competency behaviors. Somehow, we hope this confirmation of the competencies will make up for our lack of proof that they are related to improved children's learning. Consider the data in table 9-1.

What this table indicates quite dramatically is, not only that teachers can be taught behaviors, but also that they will remember and strengthen them. For a complete foundation in studies dealing with teacher effectiveness with pupils we have substituted a partially empirical base and a partially expert-derived base, and for confirmation that the competencies we teach will actually affect pupil learning we are substituting evidence that teachers will retain and improve what they have been taught.

In concluding her analysis of the history of research's impact on teacher education practices, Clifford states:

Prevailing styles of teacher preparation have not adequately introduced prospective teachers to accumulated research, spelled out enough of its implications, nor developed attitudes favorable to inservice interest in applied research. The pervasive culture of teacher training is one of, in Mencken's term, "empty technic" of rapid method textbooks, of a disinterested educational psychology, of a survival training mentality among its participants.[26]

Although we must concur with this generalization, there have been model programs that did take into account what is known about teaching and the preservice education of students. This is not to contend that total programs—even model ones—have validated all their content as influencing learners. Nevertheless there have been efforts to support substantial components of programs with research and field testing.

One of the most important attempts to relate what is known about teaching to teacher education programming was the work of a blue-ribbon NDEA Institute involving some of the most knowledgeable researchers, planners, and teacher educators in the United

Table 9-1. Performance of treatment group (38 cases) on classroom videotapes made before the course, immediately after the course, and four months after the course[25]

Behavior	A Pre-Course Mean	B Post-Course Mean	C Delayed Course Mean	t-TESTS A vs B	t-TESTS B vs C
1. Redirection	24.71	38.18	36.94	4.53	.82
2. Prompting	3.97	7.15	4.47	3.05	2.37
3. Clarification	3.73	6.52	8.42	2.93	2.34
4. Repeating own question	14.34	4.73	2.31	6.62	3.78
5. Repeating pupil answers	30.05	4.50	5.34	10.30	.67
6. Answering own question	4.47	.71	.73	6.48	.07
7. Length of pupil response in words	5.70	11.55	12.46	5.08	.45
8. Number of one-word pupil responses	5.81	2.44	3.05	3.37	1.07
9. Length of teacher's pause	2.07	2.36	2.23	1.45	.50
10. Proportion of higher cognitive questions	26.16	52.27	48.58	5.72	.78
11. Proportion of teacher talk	53.18	29.44	30.20	7.17	.32

States.[27] From July 1966 through May 1968, this task force met monthly. They prepared working papers and invited position papers from consultants. Their basic charge was to develop a structure for clarifying the issues that confront teacher education. During this period, the major problem seemed to be preparing teachers for working with the disadvantaged. The major output of the institute, however, was one of the most notable works ever compiled on teacher education. The actual manuscript was written by B. O. Smith with editorial assistance from Saul B. Cohen and Arthur Pearl.[28] Individuals synthesized their own experiences, the research literature, and a set of values to make a statement that can serve as a guide for the preparation of all teachers. Among its most noteworthy characteristics are (1) the volume's cognizance of the existing research on teaching and (2) its development of a theoretic-behavioral approach, which immediately preceded the widespread interest and development of CBTE.

The institute took for a starting point the basic categories of situations faced by teachers. The following are the situations that students were to be prepared to face as teachers:

1. Classroom situations
   a. Instructional
   b. Classroom management and control
2. Extraclassroom situations
   a. Planning school programs and working with peers and administration
   b. Working with parents or other members of the community
   c. Working in professional organizations

In order to prepare for these situations, the planning involved teaching theoretic knowledge of pedagogy in the context of its use. Examples of protocol materials (on audio or video recordings) of actual classroom interactions were identified as the actual material to be analyzed in the teacher education program. The attempt is made to arouse the prospective teacher's interest in theory as he interprets these situations and at the same time to teach him skills, many of which have empirical validation.

The actual processes for developing this program involved ten steps:

1. Collect audio and video materials of the work of the teachers.
2. Review research on teaching and such other research as may be relevant, and formulate categories of the situations encountered by teachers.

3. Analyze, classify, and index the audio and visual materials into the situational categories that have been formulated.

4. Select concepts, generalizations, and facts relevant to the comprehension of the situations from appropriate sources.

5. Arrange the protocol or situational materials into courses of instruction.

6. Analyze protocol materials to make sure they are fundamentally understood for instructional purposes.

7. Try out protocol materials on a small scale with a few teachers in training.

8. Make revisions that the tryouts indicate.

9. Put the training program into operation for the total student body in training.

10. Make revisions in the program that wider experience and evaluation indicate from time to time.[29]

Obviously, this is not the usual process of curriculum development in teacher education. This procedure actually uses several sound research practices. First, material from the real world of teachers, rather than from experts, is the basic stuff of the program. Secondly, research knowledge about what teachers need to know is added to this pool of reality behaviors. Experts are used to analyze, select, and classify these materials, rather than to generate all the content to be learned. Finally, there are procedures for field-testing and revising the program to keep it alive and responsive to the needs of the practitioners.

This approach is based on the concept of feedback; that is, students can self-correct if they can systematically analyze their own instruction. Also, the particular systems recommended by B. O. Smith are among the most widely used and have had the greatest validation against the criterion of pupil learning.[30] Finally, there is an inherent logic to this approach, which begins and concludes with practitioners in the field rather than with college courses or the traditional organizers of teacher education curricula. This is not to contend that much of what is now offered would not find a place in such a program, but the locus of control over content shifts from the unvalidated expertise of college faculty to situations encountered by real practitioners.

Current Trends in Teacher Education Research

In spite of the fact that process-product studies are correlational, they do and will continue to comprise the major mode of educational research. Such studies assume that the most fruitful search is for a single set of behaviors that will be effective with all pupils. This single set of effective behaviors will then become the single set of competencies offered in teacher education. In a similar vein, most of the process-product studies also deal with analysis of affect or direct-ness of teacher control. There are literally hundreds of systems for categorizing teacher talk, and most of them emphasize affective rather than cognitive aspects of instruction.[31] Some researchers are suggesting a sequence of analysis where:

1. The relevance of the testing of pupils is judged against the na-ture of the instruction offered.
2. There is an analysis of the cognitive level of pupil-teacher inter-action.
3. There is an analysis of the affective level of pupil-teacher inter-action.

It is almost hopeless to persist in the present situation of teaching one thing and testing another, meanwhile evaluating the whole proc-ess of instruction with primarily affective instrumentation.

While characteristic or personality studies are constantly deni-grated, it is quite likely that there will be a return to them in some new form. The interaction of teacher, pupil, and content is suffi-ciently different for different kinds of teachers, pupils, and contents to motivate at least some researchers to return to seeking *differential* sets of effective behaviors for instructing different students in differ-ent subject matters.

It is essential (which means it will probably remain undone) that experimental studies also attempt to follow up CBTE graduates in practice, not simply to confirm that they remember what they were taught, but to find out whether their behaviors actually do differ from those of teachers who were never taught the competencies in college programs. If, for example, formally trained actors do not do different things from self-taught actors, there is little sense in perpetu-ating formal training. In teacher education, we do not make such comparisons; we merely assume that if the formally trained learn, remember, and demonstrate the competencies, formal training is justi-fied.

At this time and in spite of the research (largely comprised of one-shot dissertations), there is still little connection between teacher behavior and pupil learning. The necessary research can never be fully done before CBTE takes over teacher education. It seems reasonable, however, to recommend that at least part of the time, energy, and resources devoted to CBTE should be spent seeking em-pirical substantiation of the competencies put into programs. It is

interesting to note that the CBTE movement has generated less research on effectiveness than has the humanistic, or open education,
movement. Because it is more systematic, more behavioral in style,
and more frequently offered by research types, it has escaped the
criticisms of being a new form of mysticism with as little real empirical support as "the child development" point of view, the traditional
curriculum of methods classes and student teaching, or the internship
emphasizing trial and error learning.

The most important research problem facing teacher education,
however, is not directly related to CBTE or the lack of research on
effective teaching; it involves the more fundamental and pervasive
issue of whether instruction itself is of much import. The first warning came with the Coleman Report,[32] which used a monumental pile
of data to support the contention that teaching accounts for less
than 15 percent of the variance in pupil learning. Factors in students'
socioeconomic backgrounds and the nature of their peers seemed to
matter much more than the quality of school facilities, curriculum,
or competence of teachers. As if this were not enough, the study
unleashed a whole raft of research on school integration that con-
firmed that student and peer groupings are the single most potent
factor that schools can manipulate to affect pupil learning.[33]

Christopher Jencks delivered the coup de grace when he published
his summary of research and his own study, which clearly indicated a
lack of relationship between the entire process of schooling and
pupils' subsequent income and status.[34] These data went far beyond
the evidence of the Coleman Report, which merely questioned the
power of instruction (when compared to background and grouping
factors), and seriously jeopardized the assumption that schooling itself is a useful process for subsequent living.

It is nothing short of amazing to note the blinders on those educators who are supposedly devotees of empirical validation. The
heavy evidence that the grouping of pupils has much greater impact
on pupil achievement than instruction is met with resounding
apathy. Even the shattering contention that schooling may be unimportant is ignored. Once CBTE is set as the objective, "other" forms
of research that question traditional analyses of instruction, such as
teacher talk or teacher questions, cannot be tolerated.

In sum, the present is no different from the past; more research is
needed on effective instruction. Now, however, we need additional
evidence that *connects* effective behaviors with competencies taught
to teachers. Competency-based programs can make a solid contribution to teacher education by remaining a change effort rather than
becoming a bandwagon. This will require diverting some resources
from change efforts to basic studies of teaching.

Teacher characteristic studies should also be resurrected and done more carefully. Efforts to differentiate effects on learners in different content areas remain a basic need.

Finally, research in related areas of sociology and psychology cannot be ignored. The evidence that out-of-school factors and peer influences control learning more than teachers do cannot be disregarded. It should be included in CBTE. At this point, in fact, the most well-founded "competencies" on which to train future teachers should deal with different ways to group, subgroup, and regroup learners. Such competencies can be specified on the basis of the learner's age, achievement, and motivation and the content to be learned. There is nothing more certain in the very complex search for meaningful teacher competencies than the need to teach future teachers to differentiate assignments for varying groups of pupils.

Notes

1. N. I. Gage, "Teaching Methods," in *Encyclopedia of Educational Research*, ed. R. L. Ebel (London: Macmillan, 1969), pp. 1446-58.

2. D. G. Ryans, *Characteristics of Teachers* (Washington, D.C.: American Council on Education, 1960).

3. B. Rosenshine, "Research on Teacher Performance Criteria," in *Research in Teacher Education*, ed. B. O. Smith (Englewood Cliffs, N.J.: Prentice-Hall, 1971), p. 46.

4. L. M. Heil and C. Washburne, "Characteristics of Teachers Related to Children's Progress" (Report to American Educational Research Association, Chicago, February 1961).

5. J. J. Gallegher, "Three Studies of the Classroom," in *Classroom Observation*, AERA Monograph no. 6 (Chicago: Rand McNally, 1970).

6. J. Fey, "Classroom Teaching of Mathematics," *Review of Educational Research* 39 (1969): 535-51.

7. Rosenshine, in *Research in Teacher Education*, p. 42.

8. G. W. Denemark and J. B. MacDonald, "Preservice and Inservice Education of Teachers," *Journal of Educational Research* 37 (1967): 233.

9. W. G. Bradtmueller, "An Investigation of the Development of Problem Solving Skills Related to Teaching Reading during Student Teaching" (doctoral diss., Indiana University, 1964, Ann Arbor: Microfilm No. 64-1671).

10. A. F. Perrodin, "In Support of Supervising Teacher Education Programs," Journal of Teacher Education 12, no. 2 (1961): 36-38.

11. *Evidence* is here defined as excluding testimonial evidence and refers to the systematic data gained from studies employing the commonly accepted research designs.

12. W. K. Hoy, "Organizational Socialization: The Student Teacher and Pupil Control Ideology," *Journal of Educational Research* 61 (1967): 153-55.

13. R. E. Muuss, "Differential Effects of Studying vs. Teaching on Teachers' Attitudes," *Journal of Educational Research* 63 (1969): 185-89.

14. E. B. Jacobs, "Personal and instructional variables as related to changes in educational attitudes of prospective elementary school teachers" (doctoral diss., Northern Illinois University, 1967, Ann Arbor: Microfilm No. 67-12 898).

15. A. H. Yee, "Do Cooperating Teachers Influence the Attitudes of Student Teachers," *Journal of Educational Psychology* 60 (1969): 327-32.

16. R. G. Underhill, "The relation of student teacher empathy change to supervising teacher empathy and student teacher success" (doctoral diss., Michigan State University, 1969, Ann Arbor: Microfilm No. 69-5980).

17. C. C. Matthews, "The classroom verbal behavior of selected secondary schools science student teachers and their cooperating teachers" (doctoral diss., Cornell University, 1967, Ann Arbor: Microfilm No. 67-1394).

18. L. Iannaccone, "Student Teaching: A Transitional Stage in the Making of a Teacher," *Theory Into Practice* 2 (1963): 73-80.

19. Ibid., p. 79.

20. Robert F. Peck and James A. Tucker, "Research on Teacher Education," in *Second Handbook of Research on Teaching,* ed. R. M. W. Travers (Chicago: Rand McNally, 1973), p. 943.

21. Rosenshine, in *Research in Teacher Education,* p. 55.

22. Sample material obtained from the Far West Regional Laboratory, Berkeley, Calif., 1968.

23. J. M. Cooper, H. L. Jones, and W. A. Weber, "Specifying Teacher Competencies," *Journal of Teacher Education* 24, no.1 (Spring 1973): 23.

24. N. Flanders, "Basic Teaching Skills Derived From A Model of Speaking and Listening," *Journal of Teacher Education* 24, no. 1 (Spring 1973): 37.

25. W. R. Borg, "The Minicourse as a Vehicle for Changing Teacher Behavior: The Research Evidence" (Paper presented to the American Educational Research Association, Los Angeles, February 1969).

26. Geraldine J. Clifford. "A History of the Impact of Research on Teaching," in *Second Handbook of Research on Teaching,* p. 36.

27. Hobart Burns, Saul B. Cohen, Wm. E. Engbretson, Richard L. Foster, Vernon Haubrich, Wm. C. Kvaraceus, Arthur Pearl, F. George

Shipman, B. Othaniel Smith, James B. Tanner, Matthew J. Trippe, Mario D. Fantini, Anthony C. Milazzo, Harry N. Rivlin, Donald N. Bigelow, David D. Darland, Rev. Joseph P. Owens, E. John Pole, Richard E. Lawrence, and James Kelly, Jr. Special consultants included Harry S. Broudy, Rupert Evans, James Hall, Jr., Paul Ward, and Joseph Young.

28. B. O. Smith, in collaboration with Saul B. Cohen and Arthur Pearl, *Teachers for the Real World* (Washington, D.C.: American Association of Colleges for Teacher Education, 1968).

29. Smith, *Teachers for the Real World*, pp. 64-65.

30. B. O. Smith et al., *A Study of the Strategies of Teaching*, U.S. Office of Education Cooperative Research Project No. 1640 (Urbana, Ill.: 1967); N. A. Flanders, *Teacher Influence, Pupil Attitudes and Achievement*, U.S. Office of Education Cooperative Research Project No. 397 (Minneapolis, Minn.: 1960); A. Bellack et al., *The Language of the Classroom* (New York: Teachers College Press, 1967).

31. A. Simon and E. G. Boyer, eds., *Mirrors for Behavior: An Anthology of Classroom Observation Instruments* (Philadelphia, Pa: Research for Better Schools, 1967-1968).

32. J. S. Coleman et al., *Equality of Educational Opportunity* (Washington, D.C.: Office of Education, 1966).

33. See, e.g., I. Katz, "Review of Evidence Relating to Effects of Desegregation on the Intellectual Performance of Negroes," *American Psychologist* 19 (1964): 381-99; N. St. John and M. S. Smith, "School Racial Composition Achievement and Aspiration," mimeographed (Cambridge, Mass.: Graduate School of Education, Harvard University, 1969).

34. C. Jencks, *Inequality: A Reassessment of the Effect of Family and Schooling in America* (New York: Basic Books, 1972).

10

Faculty

and

Administration

Introduction

In order to understand present conditions and future prospects of teacher education in America, we must devote some attention to what the faculty and administrators of schools of education know and do. The distinction between those who prepared teachers and those who served on college faculties used to be much clearer than it is now. The former were stereotyped as doers without substance, and the latter as theoreticians without utility. As professional education was advanced into higher education and integrated with the general and liberal studies of undergraduate education, these distinctions became less accurate.

(Originally, the faculty that prepared teachers did so by teaching arts, letters, sciences, and humanities. They did not view students as future teachers] The unspoken assumption was that if one were forced to use his education in some vocational manner, keeping school was one possibility, which, it was hoped, would only be a temporary detour on the road toward more advanced studies.

The assumption that pedagogy is nonexistent or self-discovered through direct experience, still claims numerous adherents. "Two ends of the log with Mark Hopkins at one end and me at the other" is the illusion not only of some anachronistic academicians, but also of a surprisingly large number of professional educators. Less defensive and more open educators easily grasp the complexity of the schooling process and recognize that in addition to knowing his subject, the would-be teacher needs further knowledge about: /

1. The aspects of the subject matter worth teaching; the organization of the material into theory, concepts, information, and skills;

131

and the relation of these forms of knowledge to students' levels and interests

2. The processes of learning

3. The impact of human growth and development on students' motivations, expectations, and predispositions

4. The nature of interpersonal dynamics among peers and between groups of students and adults, and how such social forces impinge on learning

5. The processes of instruction with their attendant complexities of questioning, assignment making, grading, verbal and nonverbal communication, and how various teacher acts shape learning activities and outcomes

6. Materials and media that facilitate and control the teaching-learning situation in particular ways

7. The study of curriculum, that is, the clarification of purposes, school organization, and systematic evaluation that gives perspective and a total view to what otherwise might be a twelve-year series of unrelated "lessons"

8. The administrative processes of decision making, school-community relations, and organizational change that structure the setting and permit or prevent the other seven processes from occurring

These and other "complexities" have long convinced all except the most narrow that mere knowledge of subject matter is insufficient for good teaching. Actually, the problem now facing teacher education is quite the reverse: How, and on what basis, can we delimit and exclude all human concerns from becoming a legitimate field of inquiry for professional educators? Is the mere connection of any human activity with learning sufficient justification for its inclusion in professional education?

Early Influences

The first American schoolkeepers were not considered to need sound grounding in what we now refer to as traditional subject matters. The Massachusetts Law of 1642 required every town of fifty householders to provide instruction in reading and writing, because it was "one chief project of the old deluder Satan to keep men from a knowledge of the scriptures."[1] Therefore, the teacher needed a knowledge of reading, writing, and moral characteristics. Horace Mann's twelve reports to the Massachusetts Board of Education between 1837 and 1849 indicated in no uncertain terms both the content and practices for improving the work of teachers. In addition to calling for new schools and libraries and urging public support, Mann

spelled out the teaching of reading and the humanization of discipline in great detail. The sections of his reports directed at teachers
reveal both the clarity of today's behavioral objectivists and the humanism of child-centered educators. While no "faculty" in education
existed in this period, the real teacher educators were the renaissance
educators who philosophized, taught, and politicized. They succeeded by cloaking sound ideas in personal charisma. A long list of
notable early American educators, including Henry Barnard, Calvin
Stowe, and James G. Carter, were all directly concerned with upgrading teachers. Inevitably, this improvement centered on teaching basic
skills and developing moral character.

The second important new content for teacher educators developed from expansions in the fields of psychology and philosophy.
While each had many predecessors and universal roots, E. L. Thorndike and John Dewey were largely responsible for the bodies of
knowledge that became the expertise of teacher educators in the first
half of the twentieth century.

Dewey

Unlike the nineteenth-century giants, Dewey contended that the
child is trained morally by meeting the demands of living properly
with his mates. The teacher's job is not to fix the moral habits, as
formerly advocated, but to devise situations from which the child
will draw his moral concepts. Since the school is a social institution,
these situations should be the basic concerns of real life. In addition,
the school was expected to (1) derive from the child's home and play
activities that are the source of his life experiences and (2) reflect
and anticipate a better world, not merely present conditions.

The two pillars of Dewey's philosophy are his contentions that the
school was the institution for social reform and that its approach to
such reform was the treatment of content in a scientific manner. No
content was sacred, no truth immutable; education became the continuous "reconstruction of accumulated experience."[2] Adolphe
Meyer sums up Dewey's contentions in four basic premises:

(1) education is actual living and not merely getting ready for eventual living; (2)
education is the process of growing, and so long as growth is at hand, education
is at hand; (3) education is the constant organization and reorganization of
experience; (4) education is a social process and to promote and further this
process the school must be a democratic community.[3]

There are three obvious implications:

1. This view was radically different from the views held by the
skills-oriented Puritans.

2. Teacher educators needed knowledge of children, their experiences, society, and the scientific method.

3. In place of moralistic commitments, teacher educators needed varied kinds of commitments: to democracy, to growth, to change.

As a result of Dewey's influence, teacher educators needed to learn and specialize in educational history and philosophy; child growth and development; the selection, application, and integration of knowledge; the connection of concepts and students' interests (methods of instruction); the structuring of laboratory and clinical experiences; and the systematic evaluation of programs. Eventually, most of these forms of expertise were taken over by specialists in curriculum and instruction; the historians and philosophers remained aloof and developed departments of "foundations."

Thorndike

The second blast of the double-barrelled attack on nineteenth-century pedagogy was leveled by E. L. Thorndike. Although not the first important psychologist, he conducted the first investigations in the field of educational measurement,[4] made a comprehensive and quantitative study of learning and the transfer of learning, and studied and documented the nature of individual differences and mental capacities. His ideas and experiments on the nature of skill development and growth are still worthy of implementation and extension into further research. His experiments wiped out the myth that learning is the prerogative of youth and beyond adult capabilities. He proposed and documented the support for the stimulus-response formulation. Although the field of educational psychology has splintered into structuralists, functionalists, behaviorists, gestaltists, and psychiatric and existential specialists, there has been constant interest and, recently, a resurgence in Thorndike's stimulus-response approach. In addition, there are now educational researchers and statisticians whose specialties are commonly housed in departments of educational psychology, largely owing to Thorndike's delimitation of the field of study.

The common weaknesses of the nineteenth- and early twentieth-century psychologists were not using systematic observation and experimentation as the source and substantion of their theories, using too many categories, and framing explanations moralistically. They defined human instincts with words like *wit, curiosity, revulsion, flight, pugnacity, self-abasement, self-assertion,* and *parental instinct. Fear, love, and rage* were also common terms. Thorndike put man's instincts into three classes: (1) those related to food and self-preservation, (2) those having to do with responding to others, and (3) those related to cerebral and body activity. This clarity of categorization led not only to developments in theory, such as Maslow's Hierarchy of Needs, but also to experimentation and research in such fields as behavior modification, practice-skills sessions, and learning and forgetting cycles.

Relationship and Continuing Influence of Thorndike and Dewey

Thorndike and Dewey were united in the sense that Dewey emphasized clinical experiences in real settings for teachers, while Thorndike stressed the point that transfer of learning depended on the common elements in learning and life situations. Their combined influence established the student teaching structure as the essence of teacher education. Teacher educators were to become expert at conferencing, demonstrating, and all ways of helping future teachers identify the basic elements of their practice situations with the principles they would espouse in later practice. Future teachers were also to practice the skills of teaching they would later employ.

Thorndike's penchant for measurement, i.e., "whatever exists, exists in amount and hence is measurable," is not at all remote from Dewey's belief in "mastery as the basis of creativity." In any event, the similarities and differences of these giants become more than academic exercise. They and their disciples pushed forward both the subdisciplines of education and the nature of the contents to be included in education. This delineation of the field of education was concretized in doctoral programs, first at Teachers College, Columbia University, and then across the country. Many of the distinctions that divide teacher education derive from the different viewpoints of Thorndike and Dewey; much of the consensus in teacher education is a legacy of their overlapping interests.

Thorndike and Dewey solidifed two main philosophies that have always contributed to the study of education: the concepts of education as a system of individual learning and as social growth. Educational psychology and its substudies concentrate on the individual learner, while educational philosophers, historians, and curriculum planners emphasize the school-community. While educators can use either model to analyze problems, the content and practice of teacher educators is quite clearly divided by the assumption a scholar makes to begin his analysis. Is the goal of education to develop individuals who enhance the common good or to change society to enhance individuals? Lest the reader too quickly believe this a completely artificial distinction, we must point out how readily the following practitioners can be classified. Guidance counselors, remedial reading teachers, and teachers of the retarded are trained by teacher educators who obviously hold a psychological viewpoint: individuals must somehow be made better as to improve themselves and society. Other teacher educators are concerned with community organization, community and alternative schools, racism, sexism, and bureaucracy. Their goal is to change what they perceive as debilitating societal forces in order to free the individual of social obstacles to learning. The psychologically oriented inevitably perceive learning as individually based; it is not strange for them to use a concept such as motivation. The socially oriented more typically perceive social impediments, dislocations, and inequalities as obstacles to learning. They believe that all can learn when these outer obstacles are removed. The open education movement, for example, eschews the concept of motivation.

The Thorndike and Dewey legacies, therefore, are still quite apparent in schools of education, both in their psychological and sociological ways of conceptualizing the processes of education, and in their suggested practices. The trainers of teachers tend to approach education as a system of treatments, technologies, and methods to be worked on individual learners or as a system of change strategies, social practices, or bureaucratic behaviors to manipulate the setting in which schooling occurs. While the belief that real analysis must incorporate both frames of reference is laudable and theoretically sound, we have organized schools of education into disciplines and then into departments in order to function in the university setting. The content and bases of these divisions are the legacy of those who translated the psychological and philosophical-social theories into educational terms. To practice integrating both forms of knowledge in teacher education programs would require integrating the psychological and philosophical-social foundations of education. This is difficult, not only because of the departmental structure of universities, but also because the people who become specialists in technical, research, and psychological matters are different from those who are interested in historical, social, and philosophical matters. In sum, the university structure, the differences in experts' predispositions, and the basic concepts all seem to make it difficult to perceive children as both learners and products of society.

The first phase of development among teacher educators was the triumph of professional-political educators over moralizing school-keepers. The second phase might be viewed as the development of disciplines in education that parallel the social science divisions throughout the university. The third and present phase is the specialization and, perhaps, overspecialization of these disciplines in the graduate schools that prepared our present teacher educators.

Faculty Characteristics

The preceding sketch of content development is important background for understanding the present forms of expertise that legitimize faculty and administrators in schools of education. As a group, faculty can be characterized as diverse, specialized, and isolated. Each of these attributes bears a direct relationship to how faculty are trained and what they are taught.

Diversity

Specialization is a necessary condition for advanced study and research. On the other hand, the specialist risks being unable to deal with total problems and real programs because of overly narrow concepts and methods of analysis. The initial scientists, philosophers, and others who began the systematic study of education and legitimized their studies as disciplines worthy of university support inevitably had broader and more general viewpoints than the faculty who are now trained in these fields. Perhaps Parkinson's Law—work expands to occupy the number of people hired to do it—has an educational counterpart. It may well be that educational studies expand to meet the interests of those who pursue them. If this is true, it would explain why, as increasing numbers of different individuals become professional educators, content expands into ever-increasing branches of specialization.

The obvious implication of this analysis is that real problems in society and schools and among learners are not always the reasons that new forms of specialized study develop. In an effort to be more systematic about this contention, we interviewed faculty in two departments (educational psychology and social philosophical foundations) in a well-known school of education. The following are the self-reported areas of their interests and expertise.

Social Philosophical Foundations Faculty

1. Philosophy of nationalism; cultural pluralism; humanistic approaches to schooling
2. Manpower uses in Brazil; international education, particularly in Latin America; urban education problems of local Latin community
3. History of American education, particularly its religious development
4. Philosophy of sociology as a basis for teaching social studies
5. Philosophy of education with a special emphasis on the philosophy of counseling; urban environment as it affects schools' goals

6. Sociology of education with particular interests in delinquency, rehabilitation; social environmentalism

7. Political science and the relation of community organization to problems of urban education; Labor movement

8. Philosophy of instruction

9. Sociology: values in society and schools

10. Renaissance man; modern technology and its effects

Educational Psychology Faculty

1. Behavior modification; draft counseling; drug abuse

2. Vocational choice making; theory and techniques of counseling

3. Computer systems and their use in socioeducational problem solving; measurement and evaluation

4. Clinical psychology; projective testing

5. Infancy and relevant preschool programs; aides training

6. Child development; inservice leadership training for day-care centers

7. Applications of technology to instruction

8. Learning theory; open education

9. Therapeutic uses of behavior modification; learning problems

10 & 11. Research design; program evaluation

12. Adolescent learning; research design and statistics

13. Information retrieval; computer-based guidance

14, 15 & 16. Learning principles and their applications in schools

These self-selected areas of interest are now the basis of the courses, research, and community service performed by these faculty. Assuming our perception of this trend has some general validity, the faculty in teacher education is certainly more diverse in what they care about and actually do than the colleagues or immediate disciples of Thorndike and Dewey. The diversity of interests, which will continue to increase, is, therefore, the first characteristic of present faculty.

Specialization

In order to pursue the analysis of the department members cited above, it is necessary to examine their actual graduate courses and experiences. Generally, they have had little teaching experience; the newer Ph.D.'s have rarely had any direct experience teaching in public schools. In addition, they have achieved an exceptional level of narrowness in their dissertations. The development of precision, clarity, and systematic research design has brought with it a great specificity, which seems to be increasing in the major universities that prepare education faculty. The dissertation topics chosen seem to lose interest, since (1) no faculty member could be found who had ever pursued his dissertation with follow-up or even related research, and (2) no faculty member was using the knowledge gained in his dissertation in some active way in the field. A faculty member's dissertation is generally used only as a bibliographic or lecture source in some course he teaches, and, most frequently, it is never mentioned or referred to after it has gained him admission to regular faculty status.

The combined result of narrow scholarly dissertations and little actual teaching experience is a highly specialized group of people. (While teaching experience does not guarantee a relevant faculty, it does provide a common, unifying background and thus counteracts the natural drive to specialization that inevitably results from successful graduate study.) Therefore, the second major characteristic of education faculty is great and intensifying specialization.

Isolation

The natural result of increased diversity and specialization is that services are performed by individuals who function alone rather than in teams or groups. If one values this, it is called independence; if not, it is called isolation.

Faculty achievements are based on previous success as individuals. Everything they are recognized and rewarded for is a result of independent effort. Graduate faculty, for example, make no pretense of hiding their disapproval of doctoral dissertations done in groups. "Who actually did which part? How can we be sure each team-member is totally competent in the full range of research design?" Difficulties in team teaching and interdisciplinary efforts, therefore, are not all due to the way colleges are organized; much of the explanation lies in the emphasis on individual achievement in the training programs that prepared the present faculty.

Institutional Characteristics

In addition to the general characteristics of the faculty as individuals, there are characteristics of the university setting that impinge on and control the nature of faculty services. These conditions of the setting are related to the integration and relevance of programs to school problems, the system of faculty rewards and recognition, and the administration of schools of education.

Program Disintegration

In natural combination with the diversity, specialization, and isolation of faculty, the university tradition of constructing programs composed of separate courses offered by discrete departments makes the lack of integration complete. This tradition is so entrenched that to suggest even a small change in the concepts of departments or courses is a challenge of threatening proportions. Faculty easily fall into the university traditions and solidify their diversity, specialization, and isolation by supporting the departmental system, because it justifies and legitimizes their interests and expertise. Without departments that legitimize their own criteria, the faculty might be required to demonstrate the relevance of their courses to practitioners in real schools, and no doctoral program has such applicability as a real goal of its training. Simply stated, the school of education's program objectives, e.g., "to prepare elementary teachers who can do x, y, z" or "to prepare guidance counselors," are never in line with what individual faculty choose to do. The university setting, with its protection of individual departments and courses, inevitably makes faculty desires more important than program needs. Even if all faculty could be forced to "cooperate" in a given program, their competencies would not add up to a program any more than a lot of random cells add up to an organism. In practice, we claim that the special interests of faculty add up to the programs listed in catalogues; in truth, the programs are disparate pieces consisting of whatever individual faculty choose to teach. Any college program is actually a conglomeration of talks by individual faculty on their favorite topics. In professional schools this dilemma cannot be ignored, since relevance to real socioeducational problems is an obvious public concern.

Faculty Reward System

In addition to program disintegration, the higher education setting is also characterized by a reward system that enhances the faculty's diversity, specialization, and isolation. There is no need to outline here the emphasis on rewarding all the wrong things in professional schools that seek academic respectability over applications to field and school situations. The conception of the reward system is particularly corrupt in schools that claim field relevance by working with student teachers but neglect practicing professionals. Once again, the natural proclivities of individually trained, highly specialized faculty are better accommodated by the university reward system, which values publication and research, than by a system that values field involvement. Even the present reemphasis on high-quality teaching as a basis for faculty reward is often bogus. Frequently, the evaluation is based on the teaching of preservice teachers or of individuals *preparing* to be administrators, counselors, etc. This is simply an evaluation of college teaching, which is common throughout the university. A more realistic evaluation would come from the reactions of students engaged in the *practice* of teaching or administrating. This would more clearly assess faculty relevance and usefulness to real problems, which is, after all, the supposed goal of professional education.

Administration

Disparate programs and irrelevant rewards are characteristics supported by a final condition of university settings: the professional administrator. The administrators in schools of education are usually better than those in other colleges. They tend to respect the study and application of administration, while much of academe still deludes itself that scholarship in English or history or chemistry is the primary and major requirement for running a multimillion dollar operation involving tens of thousands for broad social service purposes. Without being overly negative then, there remain several common characteristics of administrators in schools of education. They tend to (a) be more permanent and career oriented as administrators, (b) regard administrative posts as promotions or above faculty, (c) be conversant with the organization and politics of educational issues, and (d) be the few generalists remaining in schools of education staffed with increasingly specialized faculty. The actual dimensions by which we might evaluate them can be seen on the continuum for evaluating leadership, which concludes this chapter. As administrators become professional managers rather than scholars, there are positive and negative effects. On the positive side, they become more proficient in managing funds, plant, and personnel; more capable in dealing with student organizations and school and professional groups; and more efficient in managing limited amounts of change within the organization. On the negative side, professional managers lose touch with the quality of ideas, do not always recognize the best people to hire or reward, and do not always select the best new ideas and approaches to support.

The need for scholar-administrators is clear; the problem is their scarcity. If it is possible to find the thousand such leaders who are needed, it is most desirable for them to be sound managers who can implement change as well as maintain present operations. They must also be scholarly enough to consume ideas and recognize ability, if not to generate new contributions or movements. At present, most administrators are more successful at maintenance than at innovation. Their ability as scholars is more difficult to characterize, because some of the younger deans and chairmen have made notable contributions.

Summary; Looking Forward

In this section we have tried to build on the previous outline of the development of content in professional education. After the giants legitimized the study of education, numerous substudies evolved. As a result, present faculty are diverse, specialized, and isolated in function. The university setting also exerts three major forces, which easily combine with these characteristics: programs are fractionated pieces of faculty preference rather than responsive to field needs; rewards are in the university tradition rather than realistic recognition for professional service; and administrators are professional managers, not necessarily facilitators of the most relevant programs.

Other generalizations become apparent as we examine faculty and administrators. There seems to be no common value system, set of purposes, body of knowledge, or even concerns among those who serve in schools of education. Finally, teacher education is no longer the main purpose in many institutions, particularly the most prestigious ones.

The administrators of schools of education are products of the content heritage described above. In addition to having whatever personality attributes drive some to become administrators, deans, chairmen, and administrative officers share a common preparation with faculty. The one distinction from other colleges is that administrators in arts and science colleges are often downgraded as mere handlers of nonscholarly and clerical matters, while deans and chairmen in schools of education are considered to be "promoted." Even this distinction is blurring and will be less accurate in the future.

We can make some easy, short-term predictions and some difficult, long-term projections about the future of faculty and administrators in schools of education. In the immediate future there will be more candidates with doctorates for fewer positions. There will be some token promotion of females to administrative positions. Faculty will be less willing to shift positions, and less value will be placed on "broad experience in various institutions." The long-range implications for faculty and administrators will deal with purpose, the nature of content, departmental organization, and the reward system.

Reexamination of Purposes

Purposes will be severely reexamined. We are already overcoming our traditional assumption that the school of educations' major purpose is to prepare beginning teachers, with little regard for their inservice training. Many institutions have already so broadened their purposes that they spend much time preparing nonteacher personnel. Moreover, the drive to regard some professional education as general education for all citizens will enhance the disposition of many faculty to regard what they do as basic and universal rather than technical. Finally, those faculty who are antiestablishment and alternative school minded will gain recognition and legitimize much of their education for new forms of schools. All these forces should combine to make the next decade one of vital and persistent struggle to reexamine purposes. General conditions such as changing job markets, state support, and open enrolment policies will certainly encourage this struggle. Two trends that should be expanded but are likely to diminish in intensity are student involvement and the recruitment of minority faculty. Present faculty and administrators are going through a new cycle of rejustifying themselves and their prerogatives in response to public pressure. The resulting defensiveness will not permit increased sharing of power with students or a search for colleagues who might be "less than qualified."

Broadening of Content

The nature of content will be broadened; that is, the trends toward diversity and specialization will be intensified. In addition, many new types of content will be added to schools of education. Experts in the various social sciences, communications, urban affairs, architecture, environment, religion, and presently undefined studies will appear in schools of education. The graduate student who plans to be a faculty member may be wise to change from an area such as elementary education to a field that will be expanding or beginning. The range of content has certainly come a long way from Thorndike and Dewey; its quality and applicability, of course, are still debatable.

Organization

Organizationally there will be two kinds of pressure: interdisciplinary studies and the breakdown of narrow departmental lines. These trends have always been present and active. The pressure for relevance to real educational problems will cause a new surge toward faculty cooperation. In many institutions the issue will be decided on the basis of whether departmental lines can be bent or must be destroyed. Most faculty have too much to lose to destroy departmental conveniences and rewards. Therefore, interdisciplinary work will probably be achieved by organizational innovations that add to or circumvent departmental structures.

Standards

Standards for the accreditation of teacher education have been developed and refined to a sophisticated level. In the last decade the National Council for the Accreditation of Teacher Education (NCATE) has evaluated approximately 500 institutions using 46 standards and 156 substandards as criteria for evaluating the curricula, faculty, students, and evaluation of all programs that involve state certification. All this complex organizational machinery is intended to guide the profession into controlling and upgrading itself.

It is truly amazing that nowhere is there so much as a footnote devoted to administration and leadership. The very thoroughness of the NCATE standards makes the absence of any mention of the functions performed by deans, directors, and department chairmen a dramatic omission. There are two possible explanations of this "oversight":

1. Administrators in schools of education are not considered to have any real impact on the quality of programs offered.
2. This is a conscious, deliberate omission to protect administrators from being evaluated and held accountable.

Since I have never met a school of education administrator who believed he had no influence on programs in his school or department, I find the second alternative more plausible.

Article 7, section B, of the NCATE constitution states:

Responsibility for carrying on a systematic program of evaluation of standards and development of new and revised standards shall be allocated to the AACTE.[5] The AACTE shall ensure the participation of institutions, organizations, and fields of study concerned with teacher education, and the Council. The AACTE shall receive and consider recommendations about existing or revised standards from institutions which prepare teachers and from individuals and organizations concerned with teacher education.[6]

The examples of criteria below are a constructive effort to suggest to the AACTE specific dimensions of leadership that they might include in their next revision of the standards. Naturally, they will seek to secure a broad-based reaction to the final standards they actually adopt. (The number 6 has been selected for this example, because present standards go only to 5.)

6.1 *Administrative Competence and Use*

Standard: An institution engaged in teacher education has full-time faculty serving in administrative positions with doctoral level preparation, and demonstrated scholarly competence and experience in appropriate administrative specializations. Such specializations ensure competent supervision of undergraduate and graduate programs; research and experimental programs; laboratory, fieldwork, and extension services; fiscal management; long-range planning; selection and promotion of faculty.

6.1.1 What evidence indicates that the administrators performing the special functions are appropriately prepared and competent to do so?

6.1.2 If administrators are "acting" or not qualified by preparation and experience, how long and why has this been permitted?

6.1.3 What is done to evaluate the effectiveness of administration at departmental and schoolwide levels?

The last standard may be realized through various kinds of data gathering. I would like to recommend that each department chairman, dean, and other administrative officer be assessed on the following set of continua. Chairmen might be assessed by deans and members of their departments; deans by their superiors, department chairmen, and a random selection of faculty.

Figure 8-1. Continua for evaluating administrative officers in schools of education

Directions: Place an X at the point on each continuum that most closely approximates your point of view.

Decision Making

Unaware of past experiments, programs, and traditions of the institution	Highly cognizant of institution's history and its implications for present and future directions
No theoretic, experimental, or experiential basis for decisions	Great knowledge and evidence to support positions
No coherent plan or objectives for decisions	Carefully conceived, publicly stated set of priorities

Arbitrary and idiosyncratic regarding programs supported	Involves faculty, students, and others in setting program priorities
Communication Shares little to explain decisions, values, and purposes	Open and public in sharing rationales for actions
Is poor, unrepresentative spokesman of school to remainder of institution and public	Is accurate, positive representative of school
Operates with clique of confidantes	Makes good use of regular channels for communication
Closed and vindictive with those who disagree	Open and receptive to all points of view
Inaccessible	Available
Faculty Selects new faculty poorly	Chooses excellent faculty
Makes unfair merit recommendations	Is equitable
Promotes wrong people	Makes wise promotion recommendations
Professional Values Places little value on teaching	Values excellence in teaching
Has little interest in community service	Values close working relations in community projects

| Unconcerned with scholarly developments and research | Vitally interested in new ideas and findings |

| *Change* Essentially maintenance type who will keep present system functioning | Genuine change-agent who will influence basic programs and their impact |

Scoring: Administer test annually. X's that move to the right are +; those that shift to the left are –. Continua should be analyzed item by item, in each category.

Analysis: Total scores (e.g., 9–, 4+, 2 no change) can also be cumulated and analyzed in terms of median change. A simple sign test will determine significance.

Growth Potential

No analysis of the faculty and administrators in schools of education can be complete without a generalization about our growth potential:

· Faculty are frequently liberal, do-good, social-service, and humanly oriented on issues outside the university; they know why and how just about anything should be changed.
· Within the universities they are archconservatists, defending ancient truths and traditional faculty rights.

This may seem to be an overgeneralization, but it is substantially true. I hope that it will become less true in the future. Living up to Goethe's carp that "Everyone wants to be somebody, nobody wants to grow," is of no advantage to faculty, who should be the students of their subjects.

Notes

1. Nathaniel B. Shurtleff, ed., *Records of the Governor and Company of the Massachusetts Bay in New England* (Boston: 1853), vol. II. pp. 203.

2. John Dewey, *Reconstruction in Philosophy* (New York: Henry Holt & Co., 1920), p. 122.

3. Adolphe E. Meyer, *An Educational History of the American People* (New York: McGraw Hill, 1957), p. 255.

4. E. L. Thorndike, *Educational Psychology* (New York: Teachers College, Columbia University, 1920).

5. The American Association of Colleges for Teacher Education (AACTE) is the association of schools that prepare teachers. It is composed of several institutional representatives from each university or college. Essentially, it represents the deans of schools of education.

6. NCATE, *Standards for Accreditation of Teacher Education* (Washington, D.C.: 1971), intro.

11

Evaluation

of

Teacher Education

Introduction

Evaluation is a peculiar process. The knowledge, desire, and power to implement the results of the process are frequently found in disparate groups. Students who have experienced a teacher education program and then tried to teach are in the best position to assess the applicability of a program, but many students feel no responsibility or have no opportunity to do so. Faculty supposedly know the most about the processes and conditions under which programs are offered, but many faculty are more interested in maintaining their present functions than in supporting evaluative processes that may expose them to different, new, or more functions. Administrators and regents have the financial and policy-making power to implement the results of evaluation, but they are frequently so remote, uninformed, or misinformed that their ability to utilize program evaluations intelligently must be seriously questioned. While these various constituencies do not have monopolies, they do represent different amounts of insight; resistance; and control, not only of what will be evaluated, how, and by whom, but also of what will be done with the results.

Essentially, the myriad of evaluation approaches can be grouped into presage, process, and product criteria. By presage we mean all the common characteristics usually used to predict in advance that an educational effort will be effective. Family background is a presage criteria for evaluating pupil learning; years of teaching experience is a presage criterion commonly used to evaluate teacher effectiveness: consider the ubiquitous query, Why place beginners in the inner city and experienced teachers in middle-class schools? A common criterion in teacher education programs is, How many faculty have doctorates?

Process criteria are used to evaluate what actually happens during the program, on the assumption that particular activities lead to desired goals. Some examples of process criteria are: Do pupils decide their own activities? Do teachers ask questions that require conceptualization on various levels? Do teacher education programs offer courses on how to teach reading?

Product criteria are usually referred to as "hard-nosed" and many consider them the only valid ones for assessing any educational program. Product criteria include pupil achievement scores, teacher behaviors related to pupil scores, and teacher training activities that lead to specific instructional behaviors.

The following sections contain analyses of these three kinds of criteria as they apply to the evaluation of teacher education programs. We refer to presage criteria as "institutional," while "process" is used synonymously with "program" criteria. Product is reserved for use in its traditional sense.

Institutional Criteria

Institutional, or presage, criteria, which are perhaps the most common ways of evaluating teacher education, do not deal directly with the education programs; they deal with characteristics that supposedly predict in advance without the need to see what students do in training or as graduated practitioners.

Professional Criteria

Professional criteria have been developed and codified by the National Council for the Accreditation of Teacher Education (NCATE). These standards are used to accredit total programs every ten years. While some of the standards deal with process and others with product (i.e. follow-up of graduates), the total approach is one of applying these standards to schools of education and then expecting that the graduates will be at least minimally prepared. This total presage approach to evaluation is so critical to our profession that it will be discussed in a separate section and each standard will be analyzed in detail.

Another form of professional criteria deals with the reputation of the particular school of education in various professional organizations, cliques of prestigious educators, and grant-giving private foundations. Over the years various schools have developed good reputations in early childhood education, reading, special education, educational psychology, curriculum, administration, and research. Such reputations can usually be traced to some outstanding researchers and theoreticians. Unfortunately, the institution's reputation sometimes continues long after the resident giants have left, retired, or simply stopped their thinking and research to become national lecturers and full-time "experts."

Grants have also made selected institutions famous as centers for particular specialties. These reputations may or may not be justified.

In some cases an innovative program can put an institution in the limelight. The first Ford Internship in the late 1940s did this for the School of Education of the University of Arkansas. Such prestige bases for judging "goodness" are short lived.

In other cases a dynamic dean places a school of education in the news. The University of Massachusetts School of Education in the late 1960s is one example. The validity of this criterion depends on its relationship to other presage criteria, such as good faculty, new programs, and funds, and, ultimately, to process and product criteria.

Generally speaking, the institutional criteria commonly used within the profession may or may not be related to quality. They represent a set of internal values typical of a professional community rather than values connected to social-educational service of children and youth. The assumption that connections exist between the values of professionals and the education of children and youth is a victory of expectation over experience. We reward each other for new ideas, knowing full well they cannot or will not be implemented. The best example of this is the burgeoning new literature on the change process itself. The very strategies that are supposed to help us implement new ideas have become a form of inapplicable scholarship. We now study and write about change just as we study and write about the I.Q., the teaching of reading and the disadvantaged, and so on, knowing that the end product will be the study or book rather than new forms of service in the field.

Legal Criteria

A second set of institutional criteria for evaluating programs is state legislation on licensure and the process of certification. In recent years the approved program approach has led the majority of states to accredit total programs. This enables most major institutions to file their programs with the state department of teacher certification and then merely forward the names of students as they complete the programs. Such a process makes it unnecessary to check transcripts or count credits. This is the states' way of recognizing that some of their institutions can be "trusted," while others that do not offer approved programs—usually small private colleges— must have their graduates checked against the specific minimum requirements for each course.

Such legal predictions of quality are becoming increasingly important, since more and more states have reciprocity agreements; that is, a student who is certified in his state can be certified in over thirty others on application. These advance predictions of quality are based on the state departments' version of minimum standards for certification in the "usual" areas. In specific terms this means that the institution offers an accredited bachelors degree, professional courses with key words in their titles (e.g., learning, child development, methods), sufficient liberal arts courses for secondary teachers, and a minimum number of hours in supervised student teaching. These criteria deal with the form rather than the substance of programs. State departments do not have sufficient staff to make sure that the programs are offered as advertised or to justify their use of these standards in the first instance.

Public Criteria

The public applies its own criteria to evaluate teacher education. Included among these are program costs, admission practices, and local needs for various kinds of teachers.

Lower schools have felt the taxpayers' wrath for decades. This concern is now reaching the schools of education. Shrinking needs and a drive to economize make the public increasingly critical of schools of education, particularly those with booming building programs and enrollments. Related to this but acting in the opposite direction is the desire of parents to get their children into schools of education. In spite of the declining job market, increasing numbers of students are trying to enter teaching, because they believe it to be one of the few areas in which they can "make a meaningful contribution." In other words, as a taxpayer or consumer of teachers, I might evaluate the local school of education in terms of its budget or the local need for teachers; as a parent, I will evaluate the same school on the basis of whether it will admit my child.

University Criteria

Finally and most bizarre, there are the criteria imposed by the university setting of the school of education. Now we are in the never-never land of the image makers. The total university image may be shaped by the economic level of its students; its religious affiliation, football teams, treatment of activists, tuition, location, graduate school of law, and traditions; the notoriety of its faculty; and whether the evaluator is an alumnus. This list is only a sample; the point is that the reasons, excuses, rationalizations, hunches, stereotypes, feelings, and experiences people have had, or think they have had, in an institution will color their evaluations of the school of education within that institution. While most presage criteria are nonsense, these "common sense" reasons actually determine where people send their children and which institutions get state and personal support.

Institutional Criteria as Predictors

Predicting quality in advance by using the foregoing criteria is, at best, a risky, ill-advised procedure. Nevertheless, we must recognize that fund-givers and professional educators are not much different from lay citizens in using many of these characteristics as evaluative criteria. We "know better," yet, in the process of informally sharing ideas, we frequently fall into the trap of assuming these irrelevancies are actually predictors. Next time you meet a professor tell him you would like to send your son to prepare for teaching in the very best school. The institutions he suggests are likely to be the places of image. At this point ask, "Have you any firsthand knowledge of their teacher education program?" To some degree, we are all victims of the popular criteria for evaluating universities, and the school of education is an inevitable recipient of the kudos and brickbats extended to the larger university setting on the basis of inappropriate criteria.

Process Criteria

The easiest, least expensive, and, therefore, most common assessments of teacher education programs are based on process criteria. Any of the activities of the institution is assumed to support "good" teacher education—if it is done "well." Precisely what these criteria are and the standards for determining how well they are achieved depend on the constituency conducting the evaluation. Students, faculty, and administrators establish their own criteria, use their own ways of measuring, and set their own levels of minimum or desirable standards.

Since process criteria do not deal with the ultimate effects of programs, they must be supported on the basis of reasonableness. Theoretical explanations of human behavior, related research, or the systematic analyses of experienced writers can be used as a program's rationale, but they do not provide the same firmness as product criteria: i.e., What can the graduates do? We must replace unevaluated traditions, chance, or expedient reaction to outside pressure with criteria that are both rational and plausibly related to some theory, research, and experience. "We've always done it that way," or "We had a grant that left us six videotapes, and we should make use of them," or "The program reflects adding or dropping a course in response to outside demands," are real examples of the processes that have shaped programs in teacher education.

Attempts to support college programs on the basis of human behavior theories, research related to adult change, or the experience and analyses of outstanding experts are not based on any hard data either. But the basic assumption of these kinds of rationale is that thinking is better than not thinking, related forms of evidence are better than no evidence, and experienced experts are sometimes insightful. Unfortunately, the process criteria commonly used by administrators, faculty, and students have no rationale other than custom, chance, or expediency. Perhaps by opening them up to public scrutiny we may be motivated to abandon some and find firmer support for others.

Administrative Criteria

Administrators in schools of education are not essentially different from other college administrators. They may handle more outside funds; respond to more agencies outside the university, e.g., state departments, public schools, and professional associations; or confer more degrees than other college administrators, but these are differences in degree rather than kind. The criteria on which they are judged successful are certainly not unique. Listening to them describe their schools, reading what they write, and observing what they work on reveals that administrators of teacher education programs are generally rewarded and criticized on the same set of process criteria as are used by other college administrators. The following criteria and the values they express, could easily be the outline for an Education Dean's State of the School Annual Address.

Size

Size is important. Large is good. Small is bad. Expanding programs are "doing well." Shrinking ones are "in trouble." This view unites all who sell anything, whether munitions, beer, or college credits.

The criterion of size is not altogether irrational, since larger classes and programs pay for smaller ones. The confusion arises from unthinkingly equating size with quality. In the past, "the largest teacher-preparing institution in the state," "the biggest graduating class in the college," or "the school that has tripled its size in four years" were offered in all seriousness as indications of quality and importance. Actually, it is as reasonable to assume that size leads to depersonalization and bureaucratic oppression.

Class sizes are often used within schools to compare departments. Such comparisons often overlook the variety of real reasons for students taking particular courses, namely, state certification requirements, university degree requirements, the salary policies of public schools, the course's reputed lack of difficulty, etc. The truism "Undergraduates register to meet requirements, graduates choose convenient times and places" is also worth considering.

The shrinking need for new teachers in many areas is shaking administrators' faith in size as a criterion of quality. Traditionally, the need for teachers was used to justify rapid, careless expansion. Such "growth" was offered as a form of public service and, therefore, a positive process. This logic has now come home to haunt its perpetrators. If size and expansion are good, can schools of education that drop some programs and decrease others be "good"?

Newness

Newness, in the form of totally new programs, is a second kind of criterion commonly advanced as evidence of quality. Furthermore, the changes are easily ranked: a program for aides is not as good as one for teachers, a new program for undergraduates is not as much "progress" as a doctoral program, and a revision of existing programs is not as good as something the school never offered before. As foolish as this criterion may seem, its application is even crazier. It is more prestigious and a sign of greater progress for a school in the southwest to introduce a totally new program in international education than to revise the existing program for teachers of Indians and Chicanos.

While newness is considered a positive value for total programs, it is viewed negatively on the course level. Any new offering begins from the defensive position of answering a charge of proliferation and duplication. The same dean who takes pride in reeling off the titles of six new programs would never dream of mentioning the number of new courses the expansion requires. Strange as it seems, the idea apparently is to generate new programs, which is "good," without increasing the number of components, which is "bad."

Facilities; Personnel

Facilities and equipment are cited by administrators as indicators of improvement. A new building, a new suite of offices, more classrooms, even a new parking lot are offered as prima facie evidence of progress. Equipment of all sorts—whether office, research, or instructional—is an indication of "moving ahead." Personnel to manage facilities or equipment is another indication of advancement. Getting a Xerox copier is surpassed only by getting a copier *and* the funds to hire a girl to do the copying.

These "advancements" are seldom questioned. Our experience,

however, indicates that students who move directly to computers and never go through the process of hand scoring data with a mechanical calculator miss some learnings along the way: the feel of the data. Another of our old-fashioned beliefs is that students who never search the library because everything is handed out by instructors with access to copiers also miss some necessary learnings. In any event, equipment and facilities are not thought of in terms of their use and potential influence on students; they are generally presented and accepted as improvements per se.

Obviously, a projector where none existed before is a potential good. The same can be said for videotape equipment, a bookcase, or a library. The question is whether expansion at the expense of other items can always be accepted as improvement.

Faculty appointments and promotions are often cited as "gains"; retirements and resignations as "losses." It is common practice to start every academic year with an introduction of new staff and congratulations of those who have been pushed ahead in the professional hierarchy. No one rises to question whether we need another person in mental retardation, or whether his new Ph.D. from Illinois means anything. Similarly, no one questions the "fact" that professors will do a better job than associate professors, even if we are referring to the very same individuals. Obviously, more is better, and senior faculty are better than junior faculty. To question the system is to cast aspersions not only on ourselves, but also on the criteria by which we reward ourselves and the system that enhances and supports us.

In the past new administrative additions were cited as progress. (The appointment of our new *second* associate dean" brought a standing ovation from the faculty just five short years ago.) Today, chopping administrators is evidence of efficiency. (An assistant to the dean in charge of relations with public schools and the director of research were recently cut from the same faculty without any objections.) In the future summer sessions cuts and increased retrenchments will be made across-the-board, and the board will include all the areas of expansion we heartily applauded in the not-so-distant past as "evidence" of progress. Simply stated, we confused unsystematic expansion with positive growth.

Grants and Special Projects

Government grants and special projects are the administrators strongest criteria of improvement. They bring status and money, new ideas and money, and changes and money; they solve critical problems and bring money. It is interesting that a hierarchy has developed by which these grants are commonly ranked. An Office of Education grant trumps an OEO one; a research grant is better than a training grant; a graduate program beats an undergraduate or noncredit one; private money is better than public; long-term beats annual funding; support for additional regular faculty is better than temporary positions. Most of all, and this is never avowed publicly, the project with the largest amount of unencumbered overhead money, which permits the administrator "flexibility," is obviously tip-top.

Administrators are fond of newsletters and publicity releases that announce plans, the receipt of funds, and the initiation of activities. They rarely make any announcements at the end of things. To the uninformed (nondeans) it might seem more valid to announce how the half million from TTT, Headstart Leadership Training, or whatever, changed the school of education in important ways, instead of announcing the project's initiation and nothing thereafter. The usual practice, however, is to take credit in advance but hire enough javelin catchers (called project directors—black if possible) to take the blame for the inevitable "no significant change."

The worst part of this criterion is that the administrators never point out how all the regular programs will suffer. In the staffing of grants it is inevitable to raid existing programs for staff. About the only consistent result of outside funds is a brain and effort drain from regular offerings. No school of education is capable of withstanding funded wealth. As soon as grants are accepted, a number of creative, hardworking people move into the special projects, and the traditional are left to become more traditional. While this process does not always occur, it is sufficiently likely to make intelligent administrators very careful about which funds to accept, for what projects, and how to staff them.

New Policies

New or revised policies are commonly cited by administrators as evidence of improvement. Doing away with the grade point average as a criterion of admission, eliminating some required courses, or abandoning grades are frequently proferred and accepted as evidence that the administration is removing restrictions on student learning and tuning in to the students' rights movement. Administrators and faculty have become notorious for confusing laissez-faire with expanding actual opportunities to learn. The point is not that policies are too liberal or in violation of some ethic but that they ignore the need for some evidence that "swinging" new policies will achieve institutional goals. Even worse, this new policy syndrome frequently flies in the face of existing data (e.g., permitting open enrollment for students preparing to teach social studies may be in tune with the rights of college youth but in opposition to the need of the university to use its resources most efficiently).

We sometimes get so caught up in our own little worlds that we point to processes for determining processes as "evidence" of improvement. A new balloting—including students, of course—to select a committee to decide X is evidence of more involvement, more representation, more equity, and, therefore, inherently good. Conversely, calling a year-long halt to all committees—as some institutions have done—is accepted as evidence that the institution will engage in a total and intensive reconsideration of itself. The whole concern with decision-making processes seems to have become an institutional neurosis; just as some individuals become transfixed with self-study and disconnected from reality, institutions can become little islands of committees and organizational structures, playing at processes that are evaluated by processes that we no longer even try to connect with life.

Student Criteria

Students in teacher education programs are supposedly different from college students generally. This contention may have been truer when institutions were more clearly specialized. With the advent of larger and more generalized institutions of higher education it has become more difficult to identify differences in the specific attitudes, values, and abilities of teacher education students and students in general. What once may have been differences in kind are now more likely to be differences in degree, and differences in degree are becoming nonsignificant differences. Charles Silberman indicates that a substantial number of arts and science graduates who specifically did *not* prepare for teaching entered teaching some time after graduation and may actually exceed those in the profession who were prepared formally. Perhaps a major and hitherto overlooked distinction, is that education students simply develop their interest in teaching earlier than other students and are not different kinds of personalities. In any event, there seem to be four groups of students in preservice teacher education programs that are similar to student groups throughout the university. Before discussing the process goals on which students evaluate teacher education programs, it would be useful to describe these student groups.

Influence of Student Groups

Activist, problem-oriented, socially conscious students are becoming quite common in teacher education programs. They are vitally concerned with community schools, free schools, and all forms of alternatives to the present "system." These students are not necessarily interested in working in such schools on a long-term basis; rather, they want to learn about and lend support to all forms of education that they believe are preferable to the present form of "oppressive bureaucracy."

In their college lives, particularly in the teacher education program, these students are the driving force behind free electives and the breaking down of all selection criteria, formal standards, prerequisites, requirements, and traditional systems of evaluation. Formal rules are anathema. The freedom to learn is predicated on the destruction of the concept that students are institutional houseboys.

Their major concern is the process of going through the program: the here and now rather than the past or the future. Their efforts and attention are focused on participation—if possible, control—in all decisions affecting their present existence in the college and the teacher education program.

Academically oriented students are somewhat similar to the activists in that they use here and now criteria. They differ in that the process of involvement and questions of political power over programs interest them less than the content of the program. Academics also identify with a broader intellectual, conceptual, and historical world then the problem-focused activists.

Students in the academic group regard the teacher education program as a sequence of experiences dealing with bodies of knowledge. They evaluate in terms of logical connections between arts and science, the branches of pedagogy, and the goals of schools in American society. Students in this area are intellectually oriented; they use the criterion of personal interest more readily than that of social relevance.

Vocationally oriented students are not concerned with changing the existing system; they simply want to meet all its requirements and get a teaching job. They see college as a set of hurdles, not to be evaluated or changed, but simply to be overcome.

Students in this group evaluate their experience in utilitarian terms. It does not matter whether a college course in the teaching of reading will help solve community problems or offer another basis for understanding language and thinking; the issue for these students is more likely to be whether the course is really needed for certification and whether they can earn a high enough grade to impress future employers who might check the transcript.

Another group is composed of students whose basic interests and lives lie outside the university. They may be married students who work full-time, drug-addicted students who must focus on outside activities to survive, minority group students deeply involved in community activities, or adult women with job and home responsibilities. Many of these students seek neither relevance to social problems, academics, nor a specific job; because they have strong out-of-college ties that are of infinitely more importance to them, they become children of convenience. The time at which a class meets becomes more important than the content; a student strike becomes an opportunity to avoid a final examination; and the content choices demanded by academic students means only that they get out of some requirement. Even the shortage of certain kinds of teaching jobs, which is so crucial to the vocationally oriented students, is of less interest to these students, who might be more interested in the fact that majoring in social studies makes it easier to find open sections at registration periods. College is something to graduate from—a generalized good. In future years many of these students may be better than other students at solving social problems, in graduate school, or at work. Throughout their college and teacher education careers, however, they are more concerned about other things.

Specific Criteria

Having identified these student groups, it is now possible to look at the kinds of processes that teacher education students commonly use to evaluate their programs. Essentially, they develop criteria around the answers to three questions: What do I have to do to get in? What do I have to do to pass and get certified? What happens now? These are neither capricious or pedestrian questions. Their simplicity masks a deep concern and a wealth of assumptions. The real criteria of students can be better understood by examining these questions in depth.

Genuine product criteria (i.e., How well did my preservice program prepare me to function as an effective practitioner?) are seldom translated into meaningful action, since graduates are long gone and in many cases far away from the institution that prepared them when any insights regarding the value of their programs finally hit them. Those working close to home who can be evaluated in terms of how the institution might have done better are also helpless; they are as ignorant as most faculty about effective change strategies, assuming they have a clear notion of what to change. Superficial product criteria (i.e., Were my undergraduate grades high enough to get me into graduate school?) are also inadequate, since few education students make grades so low that they are barred from subsequent studies. Essentially then, students use process criteria. Recognizing the earlier distinctions between student groups, it is still possible to make some overall generalizations about the process criteria commonly used by students in all the schools and colleges throughout the university.

The role of student, with its concomitant rigid set of functions, do's and don'ts, status relationships, and values, is an inevitable given. Our belief that such a formal role should not exist does not change the fact that it does exist. While there are variations in degree of lowness, from institutional "nigger" in the anonymous general studies programs of large universities to soon-to-be gentleman in a particular house at Yale, the student is encased in a caste relationship, subservient to faculty and administration. As a result, students tend to use process criteria that will help them survive this temporary state of debasement.

Assuming this subservient role for students, what do they value? What criteria do subordinates in an inescapably inferior status seek in order to survive? Student survival depends on the ability to use the student role to get in easily and out successfully. To experience minimum "hassle," students require at least five conditions, and, strange as it seems, these conditions are transformed into the criteria by which students judge their institution. Thus, the following five process criteria are a natural outgrowth of being the disadvantaged class in a hierarchical system.

1. Clear directions. Activists notwithstanding, college youth have been conditioned by twelve years of schooling to expect rewards for dependent behavior built largely on accurate compliance with directions. To skeptics we can only suggest that they try writing a catalogue with suggestions rather than directives; making parking recommendations in place of regulations; and offering some informal advice in place of the recipes for admission, grading, fee schedules, and library use. The trend toward increasing student involvement in making these decisions, codes, and policies does not mitigate the cumulative effect on students' perceptions: that one, and perhaps the most important, criterion of goodness is the clarity of the orders they must follow.

2. Specific requirements. This is related to the foregoing but pertains to the clarity of curriculum requirements. Are specific courses required? Are there particular prerequisites? Which ones? How many? Are there distributive requirements? Can the number of credits per course be added to make full loads? Are there specific requirements for admission to the school of education? For graduation? To graduate school? How many credits make a minor or major

area of concentration? Which courses can be substituted for which? Which courses can be waived, credited by examination, or taken by correspondence? How many credits may be taken per session or per summer? What are the absolute minimums and maximums?

These are just a few of the common questions that indicate the students' need for clear directives. The quality of the answers they get to such questions leads students to trust or doubt that their institution "knows what it wants."

3. Carefully circumscribed time. Students' time must be carefully controlled, not only because they work and engage in a wide variety of activities but also because their role demands it. The Carnegie unit is still the currency of higher education. The number of hours of class time, lab time, outside study time determines the number of credits, and the number of credits is the single indicator of passage through the system. Students "give" or "spend" their time in return for this carefully apportioned credit. This makes it natural to seek and to emphasize the minimum time requirements per course.

Students are not evil, stupid, or uninterested in learning; they are conditioned to respond to the system in a dependent style. Initiating a course-free program, for example, leads to the following responses: type A discovers that no one is taking attendance and disappears; type B sets up his own schedule and follows hours as if he were still taking courses; and type C is very uneasy with his new freedom and is always hanging around, more dependent on the faculty than ever.

4. Clear and specific paper work. Beginning with an application for admission, and continuing through chest X rays, transcripts, registration forms, references, and placement papers, students know that paper progress through the clerical-records world must parallel their actual progress through the school. We all have "funny" stories of how computors rather than people decide whether a student has completed a course. A student may teach for a full semester only to learn that the machines never punched his card for a student-teaching course. The situation can be straightened out, of course, but the price of not doing the paper work may be anything from delayed graduation to not getting a job interview because of incomplete placement papers. The blood, sweat, and tears involved in fighting the clerical hassle widen the gap in academe; the faculty is oblivious, and the students feel brutalized. This paper work criterion also deals with whether the "forms" are publicized in advance; whether they are clear and reasonable to complete; and whether the institution has a good record for retaining rather than misplacing them.

Graduate students are doubly conscious of this criterion. Many of their programs are individually planned. Since faculty change roles, resign, etc., it becomes critical for graduate students to have programs formally approved and filed.

5. Clear and constant roles. As low status occupants trying to move through a system, students have a vested interest in keeping others in their respective roles. Having mastered the art of schoolsmanship—i.e., how to negotiate through the system, quite apart from any learning—they have an obvious need to keep the game the same. This is consciously true in the case of students we have categorized as academic, vocational, and convenience oriented. It is equally true—but less consciously so—with the students we have called activists.

Summary

In essence we have argued that a rigid role set is operative in higher education; that this leads to an established set of student expectations; and that these lead to a pragmatic set of process criteria by which college students generally evaluate their experience, to wit, Do they know what they want? Can I give it to them?

Faculty Criteria

Faculty criteria cannot be discussed without reminding ourselves that professional educators are university faculty first and teacher educators second—in some cases a poorer second than in others. The faculty role supports a value system with implicit dangers for teacher education: e.g., doctoral study is more valuable to teacher educators than experience with children; publishing is a more meritorious contribution than service in schools; and undergraduate teaching (i.e., service to late adolescents, most of whom will not get a job or remain in teaching) is a greater contribution than working with nonmatriculated "specials" (who might be inservice career teachers working with real pupils). Such distortions are only possible when the values of academe are given precedence over professional values. We term these organizational dislocations *bureaupathologies* of teacher education, attributable primarily to the fact that the ethic of higher education is more potent than any professional influence on faculty. Recognizing this fundamental condition, what are the criteria commonly used by faculty?

The reward system for teacher education faculty is not simply publish or perish; it is much more intricate and interesting. Figure 11-1 indicates the two fundamental dimensions: how many students are contacted (i.e., taught, advised, observed), and what level are these students? (A) faculty are those who might teach introductory and basic courses in social-philosophical foundations and in educational psychology to large classes but for only nine-to-twelve hours

Figure 11-1. Two dimensions for determining faculty status in teacher education programs

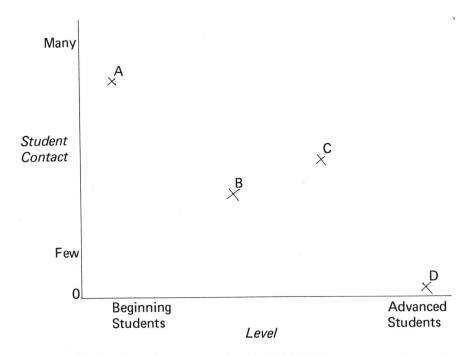

per week. Faculty who are out in the field (B) have more advanced students but a smaller number that they actually supervise. (C) faculty usually teach inservice and graduate students. Finally, the (D) faculty are those who work with a few doctoral students.

These two dimensions lead to rather than constitute the operating prestige gradients. Three kinds of behavior result from being (A), (B), (C), or (D): (1) faculty are on or off campus; (2) faculty gain control (a form of institutional "squatter's rights") over certain courses and specialties, or they remain outsiders; (3) faculty write and do some organizational work on the national level, or they remain localized. The level an individual teaches on and the nature of student contact are important, not for themselves, but because they control the three subsequent behaviors, which in turn control the criteria commonly used by faculty in teacher education programs.

What are the implications of these three dimensions? Stupid as it may seem to the "commonsense, noncollege type reader," the first contention is that a realistic criterion of faculty (in this case teacher educators) is whether they are off campus and respond to other people's schedules or work in a university office and control most of their own time. In addition to these territorial and temporal imperatives, faculty have a second kind of power need; to lay claim to and control selected courses. This is similar to the first factor except that the territory is not an office or time but a piece of the catalogue.

The third implication is the well-known publish or perish rule. In actual practice "publication" may include a variety of organizational publications, conference papers, speeches, and consulting reports. If it's someone we really want to promote, a book of edited readings will be treated like a final draft of *Les Miserables*. Actually, this third dimension is the faculty member's lifeline; should he want to change jobs, he needs to be known. Publications, conferencing, organizational work, etc., are not done to advance the field as much as to keep the faculty member's escape hatch ready and open.

In sum, faculty members evaluate the teacher education programs in terms of their career goals, not those of the administrators or the students. They seek less rather than more student contact with advanced rather than beginning students. Building on this limited role, they seek to control their schedule and place of work and any courses or programs that they can, and they cultivate a form of national recognition that is most convenient. It takes little imagination to note that these faculty criteria are not directly related to teacher education. However, the fact that any relationship between what we seek to do and the program goals is unplanned, coincidental, and spurious does not prevent us from taking credit when some good people do get some adequate preparation.

Product Criteria

Can we imagine a group of irate parents surrounding their local school of education to protest their children's lack of achievement, poor self-concept, or drug addiction? Can we conceive of a school of education having to defend one of its graduates for using corporal punishment? Would we dream of an urban community protesting to the school of education that beginners prepared there quit or failed in their first year of service?

These questions seem ludicrous only because the concept of actually holding schools of education accountable is so far removed from reality. There are many reasons for this condition, the most notable of which is the "competitive-individual-practitioner model" on which the profession is built. As long as graduates work where they please and systems hire competing individual applicants, it is difficult to follow up graduates. There are numerous other excuses, all leading to the inevitable conclusion that schools of education remain disconnected from the students who support them and not responsible for the professional quality of their graduates who become practitioners. The ideal standard for evaluating teacher education is a product criterion that connects the services of educational personnel with their programs of preparation. Realistically, it is not feasible to connect performance with program, and we lapse into four types of second-rate product criteria that are related to the nature of the individual graduate and what he does after graduation.

Student Types

Although the four kinds of students discussed above (activist, academic, vocational, and convenience-oriented) use process criteria for evaluating their programs, it is possible to base some program assessment on what happens to these individuals after graduation.

Activist students might be evaluated in terms of their later involvement in programs aimed at ameliorating a wide variety of social problems. Whether they are within some present system (e.g., social welfare, VISTA) or outside the established institutions (e.g., a community school project), their purposes and styles of engaging in teacher education seem to be appropriate criteria if they continue to practice their interests.

Vocationally oriented students might be judged by their willingness to enter and remain in established schools. Once these included all, or at least most, teacher education students. Now they are only one segment of them.

Academically oriented students might be evaluated in terms of their entrance and success in graduate schools. Many will remain lifelong students, others will become faculty, and some will remain on the periphery but in touch with academe.

While convenience-oriented students might do anything, they might be judged on whether they continue to seek the most readily available alternatives, e.g., teaching if they can work in a school near home or entering a particular business because "an opportunity presented itself."

All these outcomes of our teacher education have one thing in common. They are unplanned and individually determined. They cannot be considered product criteria, because schools of education never incorporate accountability for individual success or lack of it as part of their offerings. The teacher education program can receive neither the blame nor the credit if the activist goes on to stop the war in Vietnam, the academic does the definitive study on "how to teach reading to poor children," or the convenience-oriented student goes on to happiness as an insurance salesman. Even the vocational student may or may not get a teaching job and may or may not succeed in teaching for reasons beyond his power. There can be no product evaluation of teacher education programs as long as success is based on individual solutions to the question, "After college, what?" It is nothing short of amazing how frequently otherwise intelligent, rational educators assume that education students are all vocational; that all faculty are preparing their students to improve present forms of schooling; that employing systems are fundamentally equivalent situations; and that the performance of comparable pupils in equivalent systems can be connected to the instruction of these teachers and their preservice teacher education programs.[1] It is like walking a piece of thread from Boston to Washington, D.C. and not expecting anyone or anything to snap it.

Generalized Product Criteria

The difficulty of connecting an individual practitioner's behavior with his program of preparation does not preclude other forms of product evaluation. These forms most commonly take the form of generalizations extrapolated from the research and doctoral dissertation literature. Such analyses can be divided into three types: (1) pupil learning, (2) the teacher as change agent, and (3) teacher behavior.

Pupil Learning

Pupil learning is most commonly explained by heredity, background, parental, and out-of-school factors. The relatively small amount of potential school influence is further subdivided among such factors as facilities and equipment, grouping procedures, and the quality of instruction. When the quality of instruction is finally studied, only a very minor part of the variance in school achievement remains unexplained. (It is important to remind ourselves that "school achievement" here refers to scores on standardized achievement tests, not to how much or what students actually learn in schools.) At this point, pupil learning is often correlated with background factors (e.g., what kind of college the teacher attended) or, in a few cases, something as narrow as the teacher's scores on a verbal skills test.

It should be noted that many characteristics of teachers were not measured in this study; therefore, the results are not all conclusive regarding the characteristics of teachers that are most important. Among those measured in the survey, however, those that bear the highest relationship to pupil achievement are first, the teacher's score on the verbal skills test, and then his educational background—both his own level of education and that of his parents, On both of these measures, the level of teachers of minority students, especially Negroes, is lower.[2]

What we have, then, are attempts to correlate teacher-related factors with some form of pupil learning. The problem, of course, is our inability to draw a causal link because of contaminating factors. One example, if any are needed, might be the following. A fourth grade teacher spends much time and know-how encouraging a girl who has developed a block against mathematics. After being encouraged, rewarded, and helped for a ten-month period, the girl begins to be willing to try again. Summer comes. In fifth grade, with another teacher, who offers group instruction on one level only, the girl moves three years ahead in math achievement scores. Which is the effective teacher? We also have problems of regression, in which the very lowest nonachievers invariably show artificial increases; "bright" youngsters who learn more rapidly than average students; and organizational procedures, such as grouping patterns, which frequently affect learning more than the actual instruction.

Pupil learning can be related to instruction and to teacher education if (a) pupil learning can be broken down into specific behavioral objectives to be achieved in short time periods such as one hour; (b) instruction can be defined as the teacher's specific behavior in that hour; and (c) teacher education can be defined as training the teacher for a short period before his demonstrated instruction. We now have a training period and an instruction period immediately following. Under such "laboratory conditions" it is valid to relate teacher training, instructional behavior, and pupil learning.[3]

As this laboratory method gains popularity, it raises some real questions (e.g., How similar are laboratory and real teaching situations? Can we assume transfer?) and some value issues (e.g., Should we help make teacher education technical training?). The former can be answered by further study, the latter are not researchable.

The present method of connecting teacher education programs with pupil learning remains focused on correlations between factors that can be associated on the basis of face validity: e.g., teachers who know more content have the potential to teach more; teachers who know more about their pupils have the potential to personalize instruction. These "common sense" factors are usually related to gain scores, but whether these and similar factors cause pupil growth remains to be determined.

Teacher as Change Agent

With the growing availability of beginning teachers, many schools are consciously seeking "fit in" types rather than "fighters." Hippies;

activists; and deviants from middle-class modes of dress, grooming, speech, etc., are finding placement more difficult than beginners who seem more "adjustable" to schools as they are. This contention is based on the assumption that most school leaders believe they can improve schools if given the resources and better personnel and do not actively solicit radical reforms such as educational vouchers and decentralization. It is also based on numerous interviews with personnel officers who went through their interview procedures item by item. This is not to say that schools do not seek creative, imaginative people in any form. Most personnel officers seem to desire such types, provided they are committed to the system in some basic ways (e.g., they believe that schools are essentially good for children) and will not be too offensive to a hard core of teachers and/or parents.

Increasing numbers of school of education faculty and students, however, are questioning the basic assumptions of public education in America. One admittedly small piece of evidence to support this view is that the MTAI scores of education students are becoming more like those of college students generally (i.e., less permissive). In addition, more students claim to be willing to support radical reform. Not that Holt, Kozol, Goodman, Coles and Harold Taylor, and the like are actually changing anything, but they are being read by teacher education students.

Just as we can make valid and invalid generalized connections between pupil achievement and teacher education, we can connect teacher education and the willingness of schools to change and reform. Are beginners more likely to support organizational, curriculum, and personnel reforms than experienced teachers? Are they more willing to support community control and decentralization efforts? Such generalizations will be confounded by the increasing selectivity of school hiring officers, but if today's youth are genuinely different—rather than merely passing through a "phase"—there will be significant differences no matter who is hired. It is important to remember, however, that if school change becomes a criterion measure for programs of teacher education in the future, the evaluation will be confounded by all the other factors that facilitate and prevent change: funds, minorities, wars, urbanization, mass media, etc.

Teacher Behavior

The third category includes truncated "product" criteria, since teacher education leads only to instructional behaviors, not to student learning. In this category are the host of instructional schemes currently in vogue in our preparation programs. These behaviors can and will be connected with the accountability movement in the future. It began with Marie Hughes, John Withal, and Ned Flanders, and we now have a sixteen-volume encyclopedia cataloguing these systems.[4] As accountability practices grow, it will become easier to correlate teacher evaluation with preservice preparation by using the same system to describe instruction. This trend may support teacher "education," if learning the system also involves learning its psychological and sociological foundations. On the other hand, it might emphasize behavioral "training" in which students learn a given set of responses and practice replicating them in subsequent teaching. Naturally, this issue divides the profession; it will be interesting to watch this trend develop in future. The behavioral competency trend ("training") is currently on the upswing.

Notes

1. Richard L. Turner, "Conceptual Foundations of Research in Teacher Education" in *Research in Teacher Education,* ed. B. O. Smith (Englewood Cliffs, N.J.: Prentice-Hall, 1971), chap. 2.

2. James S. Coleman et al., *Equality of Educational Opportunity* (Washington, D.C.: Dept. of Health, Education and Welfare, Document OE-38001, 1966), p. 22.

3. Barak Rosenshine and Norma Furst, "Research in Teacher Performance Criteria" in *Research in Teacher Education,* chap. 3.

4. Anita Simon and E. G. Boyer, *Mirrors for Behavior: An Anthology of Observational Instruments Continued* (Philadelphia: Research for Better Schools, 1970).

12

Accreditation

of

Teacher Education

Like other recognized professions in American life, teacher education has established a national agency for accrediting acceptable programs. As one might expect from other historic struggles in education, this effort was vigorously opposed by college and universities already accredited by general accrediting bodies. One argument was that no national accrediting body was needed, since six regional or general accrediting agencies cover the nation. Other professions, however, have found this claim invalid, because the variations in quality from one institution or state to another make it impossible to enforce reasonably uniform requirements for admission and preparation and practice. The big argument about accrediting teacher education arises, of course, from its close affiliation with the general or liberal arts program. Can professional education, which is integrally related to general studies, and specialization be evaluated separately?

Definition

Accrediting is an almost exclusively American term and experience. In most other countries, standards are fixed and enforced by the state. Our first colleges and public schools developed independently and close to the people, who wanted the government to stay out of the business of education, except at the local level. A workable definition of accrediting as we know it in the United States is "approval of an education institution, usually by an association of educators who have voluntarily banded together to enforce reasonable standards." One major purpose is to protect the people and students against inferior institutions, some of which would offer the cheapest possible programs with inferior teachers and facilities. In other words, accreditation seeks to protect the integrity of the program of education offered.

Need for Accreditation

Diploma mills have existed at one time or another throughout our history, in almost all states, and some still exist in a few states, largely because those states were and continue to be reluctant to supervise colleges and universities too closely. One of the reasons for their reluctance is that all our early colleges were established by churches to train ministers, and because of their troubles in Europe the churches fought state interference. Another reason can be found in the precedent set by the *Dartmouth College* case. Many of the early private colleges were given state subsidies, which often led to a state takeover of the colleges. One of these was Dartmouth College. However, since Dartmouth and the New Hampshire legislature were controlled by warring political factions, when the state took over, the legislature so changed the college's charter that its original purpose was annulled and it was renamed the University of New Hampshire. The college brought suit to retain its original rights and privileges, and the case reached the United States Supreme Court, which held that a college charter was a contract and could not, therefore, be impaired.

For these reasons states have generally been very careful in their initial accreditation of programs offered in some private colleges and universities. This caution varies widely from state to state, and we still have a few states in which diploma mills can operate to sell doctors degrees with virtually no requirements other than a fee to be paid for the degree.

Origin

The process of accreditation began in Western Europe with the church granting certain privileges to the guild of masters at the University of Paris or the guild of students at the University of Bologna. These masters became powerful enough to obtain papal sanction for granting licenses to teach, thus controlling admission to their ranks. They both prepared the students and licensed them to teach. In time both the church and the princes chartered these two institutions and accorded them certain privileges. After the Reformation and the growth of nationalism the universities (particularly in protestant countries) were controlled by the state, but this control varied widely among countries. In England, for example, the faculties were in almost complete control, and presumably, this tradition was transplanted to the new world. The doctrine of laissez-faire as applied to education in the United States is illustrated by two things: (1)

Education was not mentioned in the constitution of the new union, and (2) Over 200 colleges and universities were chartered by the states between 1860 and 1890 with little or no restriction on their standards and functions.

States do exercise legal controls over accreditation for teacher education, because the bulk of teachers are prepared for the tax-supported public schools. Selden identifies the Board of Regents of the University of the State of New York as probably the first accreditation effort. In 1787, the legislature required this board to visit every college in the state once a year and report to the legislature.[1] Selden also mentions the University of Michigan, the Association of American Colleges, the American Association of University Women, and the University Senate of the Methodist Episcopal Church as possible claimants for being first in the field.[2]

This was a century before voluntary accrediting associations, as such, developed in the United States. These associations came about because of the proliferation of colleges, graduate schools, and high schools. The first step in this direction was a procedure adopted at the University of Michigan in 1870. That university was then the only one of twenty-three universities that did not also contain a preparatory department. It borrowed a plan from Germany in which the university sent selected members of the faculty to inspect high schools throughout the state and to recommend which high schools seemed to warrant acceptance of their graduates by the university. At that time the admission requirements to colleges and universities were diverse and often without validity. The basic purpose of this kind of accreditation is to provide a means of admission to colleges from high schools, transfer of credits from one college to another, and admission to graduate and professional schools.

From the 1870s through the 1890s the situation became so confused from school to school and from state to state that members of the Massachusetts Classical and High School Teachers Association sought a conference in 1884 with Dr. Charles W. Eliot, president of Harvard, to try to work out some degree of uniformity in the admission requirements of colleges and universities. The teachers were finding it impossible to interpret admission requirements in different sections of the country. The conference with Dr. Eliot led to the formation of the New England Association of Colleges and Secondary Schools in 1885: the first of six regional associations later to be formed. This was not a regional accrediting association in the present meaning of the phrase until 1952. Its purpose in the beginning was to bring some degree of uniformity to the content and terminology of examinations given by colleges and universities for the admission of high school graduates. The chief influence in the New England Association was the high schools and academies, but the chief influence in the later associations was that of the colleges.

The success of the New England venture led the Michigan Schoolmasters Club to propose a similar regional association in the Midwest. This resulted in the formation of the Northcentral Association of Colleges and Secondary Schools in 1895. The Southern Association of Colleges and Secondary Schools was formed in the same year.

The Middle States Association was established between 1889 and 1892. It serves the middle Atlantic states and Puerto Rico and the Canal Zone. The North West Association of Secondary and Higher Schools was formed in 1918, and the Western College Association (including Hawaii and Guam) was formed in 1948.

In addition to these regional accrediting associations, the College Entrance and Examination Board was established in 1900 to supplement the work of the regionals. Some colleges still put great reliance on test scores of this organization for admission purposes.

Accrediting for the Professions

The professions (of which there are now about thirty in the United States) refused to rely on regional accrediting of a high school as the sole criterion for admission of high school graduates to professional schools. Thus, the professions began about 1904 to develop national accrediting agencies. The American Medical Association was the first.

American Medical Association

Although there were a number of good medical schools in the country, the accrediting practices of medicine never amounted to much until the famous Flexner Report in 1910, a study done under the aegis of the Carnegie Foundation for the Advancement of Teaching.[3] Although the American Medical Association had been organized in 1847, the demand for doctors was so great that too little attention had been given to improving medical education. Most of the 162 medical schools existing when Flexner made his survey were privately owned and operated as profitable enterprises. Schools were poorly housed, their incomes were from student fees, and entrance requirements were meager or nonexistent. Flexner's report shocked the American Medical Association into action. Although it had adopted accrediting standards in 1904, very little had been done to enforce them. By two or three years after the Flexner Report appeared, the 162 medical schools had been reduced by at least half.

Proliferation of Agencies: NCA

The continued proliferation of national professional accrediting agencies has caused great concern to higher education institutions since the 1930s. According to opponents, there were too many accrediting agencies invading the rights of the individual institutions and destroying institutional freedom, encouraging uniformity and limiting experimentation, raising costs excessively, and demanding too much duplication. The situation had become so bad that in 1938 collegiate associations banded together to form a Joint Committee on Accrediting to pass judgment on any new body seeking to establish a new accrediting agency. This committee was not too successful and was succeeded in 1949 by the National Commission on Accrediting, a joint body sponsored by seven large and important national college associations. The commission consists of forty-two members, six from each of the constituent associations. The commission is not an accrediting agency as such; it accredits authorized accrediting bodies. Its policy is to recognize only one accrediting agency for a geographical area (such as a regional association) and only one agency for a given professional field.

The following professions now maintain national accrediting agencies approved by the National Commission on Accrediting or the U.S. Office of Education: business administration, business, chemistry, dentistry or dental hygiene, engineering, forestry, journalism, landscape architecture, law, librarianship, medical record librarianships, medical technology, music, nursing, occupational therapy, optometry, osteopathy, pharmacy, physical therapy, podiatry, psychology, public health, social work, speech pathology and audiology, teacher education, theology, and veterinary medicine.

Efforts to Establish Accrediting for Teacher Education

The normal schools and early teachers colleges found themselves ostracized by the regional accrediting associations, because they were not classified as standard colleges. As early as 1855 the normal schools had formed their own association. Rather than accrediting, it studied how standards might be raised. In 1870 the Department of Normal Schools became one of the original departments of the National Education Association. In 1917 this organization became the American Association of Teachers Colleges, which merged with two other associations interested in teacher education to form the American Association of Colleges for Teacher Education (AACTE) in 1948.

The first real effort to establish a national accrediting body for teachers colleges was made in 1923 when the American Association of Teachers Colleges, after appealing many times to the regional associations to accredit their members, developed their own national standards, which it began applying in 1927. Then the North Central Association of Colleges and Secondary Schools relented and began accrediting teachers colleges. Over the years most of the other regionals also began admitting teachers colleges to membership. By 1948, when AACTE was formed, only 284 of the more than 1,000 teacher education institutions then in existence had applied for accreditation in the national association, being content with regional accreditation. Thus, between 1948 and 1952, those interested in national accreditation of teacher education struggled to establish the National Council for the Accreditation of Teacher Education. As Selden says,

in the entire history of accreditation, probably the most intense, bitter, and widespread struggle developed once the question of accrediting programs of study in teacher education was introduced. Conditions during the earliest days of the labor negotiations could hardly have aroused more passion and unreasonableness than was expressed by the extremists over this issue. As in the case of the labor movement, the development of teacher education had a long historical background. Imported from Europe, the idea of schools devoted only to the preparation of teachers took root in this country when the first private normal school was established in 1823, soon followed, in the 1830s by the first public normal schools. With an expanding population and a corresponding increase in school enrollments, in time supported by compulsory school attendance laws, the demand for teachers, on which the liberal arts colleges turned their backs, encouraged the growth of normal schools. Socially ostracized by the liberal arts colleges, these schools formed their own organization ... when NCATE was organized in 1952, the smoldering broke into a conflagration. The liberal arts people ... made plain their opposition—first to the extension of professional accrediting into an area which they insisted could be adequately served by the regional associations, second to the acceptance of the argument that teaching is a profession like medicine, law, or nursing, and third to the relationship of the certification of teachers with the accrediting of liberal arts colleges by a national professional teacher education accrediting agency.[4]

Formation of NCATE

The leading organizations in the formation of NCATE were the Council of Chief State School Officers, the American Association of Colleges for Teacher Education, the National Commission on Teacher Education and Professional Standards, and the National Association of State Directors of Teacher Education and Certification.[5] It began with a constituency consisting of a joint council—somewhat like that of the American Medical Association—of an equal number of practitioners, representatives of teacher education schools, and representatives of the state education legal authorities, plus three members of the National School Boards Association (the consumers of teacher education).

Structural Problems

Although there were several arguments concerning NCATE, its opponents from the first attacked the makeup of the council. As a result of this hassle over structure and certain dissatisfactions about procedures, there have been three different structural organizations:

Representation	1954	1956	1966
Practitioners (teachers)	6	6	6
Members of Teacher Education Faculties	6	7	10
State Legal Educators' Authorities	6	2	2
Local Legal Educators' Authorities	3	1	1
Academic Disciplines	0	3	3
Total	21	19	22

It should be noted that the more than 2 million practitioners still have six representatives on the council while the number of college and university representatives has risen from six to thirteen, and the state and local legal education authorities have been reduced from nine to three. NCATE began as a cooperative affair with equal representation from the major sections concerned. It has now become an organization which is, or can be, dominated by the colleges. This is a significant departure from the general structure of most of the national professional accrediting associations.

The National Commission on Accrediting has insisted that a majority of the membership of NCATE should represent colleges and universities, which is not true of some of the national professional accrediting agencies it has approved. On the other hand, there are those who believe that accrediting of teacher education should be lodged in the hands of the practitioners. This is a struggle which will continue. At the moment, no one can foresee the outcome.

Institutions Accredited

The number of institutions accredited by NCATE has increased from 254 in 1952 to 470 in 1970 (this had increased to 498 in 1971). Institutions accredited by NCATE currently prepare about 80 percent of the newly graduated teachers each year. Over the years, the nature of the colleges approved for teacher education has changed materially, as can be seen in table 12-1.

It can be noted that the number of teachers colleges has declined

Table 12-1. Types of Institutions Preparing Teachers
in Selected Years[6]

	1957	1964	1970
Teachers Colleges			
Public	113	35	5
Private	13	12	11
Universities			
Public	79	116	180
Private	127	145	172
General Colleges			
Public	145	197	206
Private	511	580	636
Technical Schools	39	29	
Junior Colleges	189	50	36
Other	10	9	
Total	1,226	1,173	1,246

from 1964 to 1970, the number of universities has increased, and the number of general colleges has also increased. Most noticeable of all is the virtual disappearance of teachers and junior colleges. The former has already been explained by the shift of the teachers colleges to general state colleges; the latter is attributable to the general raising of state certification requirements to the degree level.

Possibility of Government Intervention

One possibility in the future of accreditation is that we shall see more state and federal intervention in the process. Actually, the states have the legal authority for accrediting and certification, but states have generally sought to join with voluntary agencies in exercising this function. It is conceivable, however, that if the fight over NCATE cannot be resolved by cooperation and agreement, the states could vest almost complete power in their departments of education. Indeed, NCATE may ultimately become a consultant and advisor to the state departments of education.[7] Forty-one states currently report that they have developed their own standards for accrediting teacher education, drawing heavily of course on NCATE and regional accrediting associations.

The U.S. Office of Education may also be propelled into this field, in an advisory or direct capacity. Under current federal law, the U.S. Commissioner of Education is required to publish a list of nationally recognized agencies and associations found to be reliable in appraising the quality of education offered by institutions. This provision protects against the possibility of federal funds going to unqualified institutions. As a result of this legislation, the U.S. Commission of Education has created a staff whose functions are (1) continuous service of USOE practices and procedures in the areas of accrediting and eligibility for funding; (2) administration of the process whereby accrediting associations secure initial and renewed recognition by the commission; and (3) consultation services to institutions, associations, other federal agencies, and Congress regarding eligibility for funding. The commissioner has established a committee of nongovernmental educators to assist him in determining institutional eligibility.

Whether the continued infusion of federal funds into education will become heavy enough for further interference in accrediting is a moot question. Certainly, the possibility is there. In the past the U.S. Office of Education has relied almost completely on existing accrediting bodies, but this could change.

Notes

1. William L. Selden, *Accreditation: The Struggle over Standards in Higher Education* (New York: Harper & Bros., 1960), p. 30.

2. Ibid., pp. 29-36.

3. Abraham Flexner, *Medical Education in the United States and Canada* (New York: Carnegie Foundation for the Advancement of Teaching, 1910).

4. Selden, *Accreditation,* pp. 63-64.

5. For a fuller account of the founding of this organization, see T. M. Stinnett, *Education in the States: Nationwide Developments Since 1900* (Washington, D.C.: Council of Chief State School Offices, 1969), pp. 407-24. Also see John R. Mayor and Willis G. Schwartz, *Accreditation in Teacher Education: Its Influence on Higher Education* (Washington, D.C.: National Commission on Accrediting, 1965).

6. W. Earl Armstrong and T. M. Stinnett, *A Manual on Certification Requirements for School Personnel in the United States* (Washington, D.C.: National Education Association, National Commission on Teacher Education and Professional Standards, 1957, 1964, 1970).

7. See T. M. Stinnett, "The Accreditation of Teacher Education Institutions and Agencies," *Phi Delta Kappan* 51, no. 6 (1971): 71-83.

13

NCATE: Analysis

of

Standards

University programs that lead to state certification include not only all kinds of teacher education—early childhood, elementary, and the range of secondary specializations—but also preparation for roles such as guidance counselor, principal, superintendent, supervisor, reading specialist, and school psychologist. If the university program leads to or includes the state requirements for any kind of certificate, there are several agencies that assess the quality of the university program:

1. The legally responsible agency of the particular state department of education. These agencies are responsible for issuing certificates to individuals who have completed an approved university program and are recommended for a specific certificate by the university's certifying officer. Over the past two decades, the state checking of individual transcripts for minimum course requirements has been replaced by the approved program approach. In practice, state department certification officers have been more open than they are usually given credit for. They tend to approve any reasonable change; in cases where a university suggestion is not reasonable, they are likely to approve it as an experimental program for a specific time period. The National Association of State Directors of Teacher Education and Certification, which is their professional association, publishes thoughtful guidelines and suggestions that universities would be well advised to consider.

2. Regional groups. The North Central Association, for example, reviews the basic university programs as a form of prerequisite. High-quality professional education is assumed to be possible only in schools that offer sound general and liberal education as an integral part of the teacher education program. The NCATE accepts regional accreditation as assurance of high overall quality of instruction, faculty, and student personnel program.

3. Groups in particular specialties, such as music, art, English, foreign language, science, social studies, and mathematics. Unlike the state departments and the regional accrediting associations, professional guidelines from these groups are merely advisory. These groups are often too narrow, since they overemphasize their own subject matter at the expense of both general and professional components in the program. Generally, however, such guidelines do specify higher standards than are now practiced, and most institutions could improve their programs if they were aware of the suggestions of these learned societies.

4. The National Council for the Accreditation of Teacher Education (NCATE). Every ten years each institution offering certification programs is accredited on a thorough set of carefully developed standards. NCATE standards are evaluated and revised by the American Association of Colleges for Teacher Education (AACTE), using representatives of universities and organizations concerned with teacher education and classroom teachers. This form of professional self-regulation is comparable in many ways to that exercised in other professions.

This chapter is devoted to helping doctoral students and experienced faculty more fully understand the bases of professional self-regulation. The word-by-word analysis is not an attempt to be overly precise. It is an effort to reveal the complex and interrelated nature of the assumptions that undergird the standards.

At times the standards are verbose and distorted by jargon; in other places they are deceptively simple. In the main, however, they are obviously the work of professionals who know the problems, and they are a marked improvement over the original guidelines of the early 1960s. Although the NCATE offers them as "minimum standards," they are a higher horizons project for the colleges and universities that will use them to prepare self-reports. The next ten years will undoubtedly see much-improved teacher education as institutions refer to these guidelines in changing their programs.

PART I. BASIC PROGRAMS

NCATE Standards	Interpretation and Analysis
1. Curricula for Basic Programs	
1.1 *Design of Curricula* Standard: Teacher Education curricula are based on objectives	Objectives that supposedly reflect the professional role for which the program is designed (e.g., primary teacher) *and* the behavioral outcomes sought (e.g., "Graduates effectively teach word attack skills.").

reflecting the institution's conception of the teacher's role,

"Institution's conception" means that it "reflects the judgment of appropriate members of the faculty and staff, of students, of graduates, and the profession as a whole."[1]

This is, of course, an ideal. It is not startling information that few programs are planned by involving all these constituencies. It is assumed to be desirable to involve these varied groups. The issue of whose voice is finally heard is ignored. The university faculty may courteously seek advice regarding "their" program. However, little can change the reality of whose program it is.

The concept of "the teacher's role" is another ideal. The NCATE is not trying to lay down a single, definitive role but to nudge institutions into defining their own. It would help our profession if we used this term in the plural and added the hope that these roles may be practiced in a future form of schooling rather than merely filling existing job slots in present schools.

and are organized to include general studies,

The key word is *include,* which can mean any amount of any institution's definition of general education.

content for the teaching specialty,

This is neat for the future teacher of English who majors in English. How about the kindergarten teacher who chooses to do forty credits in German? Is there a place for in-depth study not completely applicable to the student's future teaching?

humanistic and behavioral studies,

The amount, nature, scope, interrelatedness, liberal or professional slant, required or elective quality, are all open to the discretion of the institution.

teaching and learning theory

Again this is an ideal; there are no "theories" of teaching.

with laboratory and clinical experience and practicum.

"Laboratory exercises illuminate and demonstrate principles, clinical experience confronts students with individual cases or problems, the diagnosis of which involve the application of principles and theory.[2] Practicum refers to a period of experience in professional practice."[3]

1.1.1 What information shows that each basic teacher education program is designed to achieve objectives reflecting the institution's analysis of the teacher's role?

The catalogue contains this information. Programs of teacher education do not attempt to connect a required program with any carefully conceived concept of the teacher's future role any more than lower schools attempt to connect the teaching of geography, reading, etc. (i.e., the program), with some preconceived overview of the citizen's future role. Ideally, of course, this connection is necessary for evaluation to proceed rationally and systematically.

In truth, we do it backwards, hoping that what professors feel like teaching can somehow be rationalized later as adding up to a total program.

1.1.2 What information shows that each curriculum in teacher education includes the elements identified in the standard?

Again, the word *includes* provides the opportunity to have any amounts of almost anything on a required or elective basis.

Summary: In 1.1 *the teacher's role* might be changed to *teachers' roles.* In 1.1.1, what information indicates that all constituencies, not just faculty, are involved? What information indicates that the institution develops any conception first and the faculty loads to implement them? In 1.1.2, what information indicates that the amount and nature of prescribed study in general studies and content has been intentionally planned to lead to the institution's conceptions of its purposes?

1.2 *The General Studies Component* Standard: There is a planned general studies component requiring that at least one-third of each curriculum

In the preceding standard, amounts were avoided to emphasize that it depended on the institution's conception of the teacher's role. Here, the concept of a minimum standard (one-third) appears.

for prospective teachers consist of studies in the symbolics of information,

This could mean computer science or calculus. More likely it refers to linguistics and the nature of knowledge.

natural and behavioral sciences and humanities.

1.2.1 What courses, seminars and readings

And if there's no course, perhaps a faculty member has some items on his bibliography?

are offered in each area of general studies identified in the standard?

College catalogue has "answers."

1.2.2 What are the arrangements for ensuring

What can be an "arrangement for ensuring" other than requiring?

that courses, seminars and readings are distributed among the areas of general studies as specified in the standard?

College catalogue has "answers."

1.2.3 What evidence shows that the program of study of each student

"Each" is a positive attribution that the institution cares enough about individuals to have differences in programs.

meets the institution's requirements in general studies?

Students' programs of *courses* are checked before admission to school of education, student teaching, and graduation.

1.2.4 What evidence (such as state and regional accreditation reports and/or student achievement data) reflects the quality of the general studies component?

This is answered by telling an assistant to "Dig out the correspondence from the last regional accreditation."

1.2.5 What information shows that some initial assessment is made of the level and quality of the general education backgrounds of each student and each program of study is accordingly individualized?

This standard is an attempt to encourage a mass system to individualize. The problem is the ease with which the standard can be met by finding a stray freshman given credit for an advanced placement course in high school, or someone from Germany who is told to take French, or a student given an exam and permitted to begin in sophomore level music. To put teeth into this standard the *each* would become *every* and the *some* would be dropped; i.e., "Initial assessment of every student in every program."

1.2.6 How does the institution ensure that the selection of content for the general studies component embodies the judgment of both the academic staff and the teacher education faculty?

The easiest way to "cooperate" is for schools of education to require only what the colleges of arts and science already require. In many cases this will be a lowering of standards. Another form of cooperation is for the schools of education to require a particular course that is limited to only future teachers. Most arts and science faculties are pleased to add the staff to teach such required courses since they can fill out the load of these faculty with advanced or graduate work. Problems arise from dropping general education courses from the required list. Cooperation is, therefore, "close" when we provide captive audiences and "strained" when we permit students freer choices in their general education.

Summary: The change from advising institutions to develop general education to meet their "conception of the teacher's role" (previous standard), has been sharpened in this standard to a specific minimum of one-third of the curriculum. The actual substandards can be satisfied by papers (i.e., catalogue copy, regional accreditation, and *any* number of students who are not following the exact program but can be passed off as "individualized"). There is also a confusion between the use of the terms *evidence* and *information.* "How does the institution ensure cooperation" conjures up a vision of political horsetrading for requiring some courses. The standard is not as questionable as the substandards that are intended to implement it.

1.3 *The General Studies Component*
Standard: The professional studies component for each curriculum for prospective teachers includes the study of the content to be taught to pupils;

This is a great breakthrough since it represents professionalized content. The issue in former decades was that liberal arts students got the "real" Biology I, or whatever, and the teacher education students got a watered-down version. We now know the difference between subject matter presented as the first course to future experts in the discipline and the same subject matter as general education for all. It is actually a question of upgrading when we expect a course to develop understanding of key concepts; to provide basic language, the particular research methodology of the subject; and most of all, to relate the study to other disciplines as they can be applied to life problems.

The immediate problem in this standard is for preparing teachers of middle school, elementary, and early childhood, since all (any) content can be appropriate and does not come neatly packaged in college forms of specialization. When four-year-olds engage in water play, has the teacher been prepared by a course in physics or in physical education? When twelve-year-olds take apart an old lie detector, has the teacher been prepared in biology, psychology, or metal shop? To take this part of the standard literally would be to perpetrate the artificial divisions between subjects common in college on the lower schools.

Do we really want a teacher of children who expects to use his college specialization directly? If so, the logical extension of this expectation would be a departmentalized first grade with as many classes as necessary to offer the discrete disciplines replicating the college curriculum.

Lower schools are now in the position of selecting practitioners who can integrate and apply. Relevance of content to individual pupils can make interdisciplinary and general education courses more important for future teachers.

and the supplementary knowledge, from the subject matter of the teaching specialty and from allied fields,

This is an attempt to recognize areas of concentration and other means employed by colleges to break the disparateness of an education offered by totally isolated departments. It also indicates that in working with children and youth the teacher needs a total view of subject matter. Children identify interests and problems (e.g., how to grind lenses) before they become embroiled in whether this is a math or astronomy lesson.

that is needed by the teacher for perspective and flexibility in teaching.

This implies that pupil interest and applications are as important as the more formal forms of content.

1.3.1a What evidence shows that the program of study of each prospective researcher includes both types of content for the teaching specialty identified in the standard?

Here again, the college catalogue and other versions of the programs, on paper, will answer this. The real issue is how much of these forms of knowledge are needed; even more, does the actual coursework offered achieve this noble aim?

1.3.1b What information shows that the selection of course and other learning experiences required for the teaching specialty in each curriculum

embodies the judgment of members of the faculty in the teaching specialty concerned

and members of the teacher education faculty?

This is a (too) gentle reminder that the college may offer things other than courses to achieve learning goals.

Too few are ever "concerned." The reward system of the university does not support the scientist who strays into teacher education.

What ever happened to the involvement of graduates, students, members of the profession (teachers), etc.? Note how easy it is when we get to the "real decisions" (i.e., which courses to require) to involve only the people that count: the faculty in education. Operationally, this standard will be met by hauling out the notes of an annual meeting when some joint committee reviews requirements.

1.3.1c What are the provisions for *ensuring*

that a systematic effort is made to keep the content of the respective teaching specialties current with developments in the appropriate disciplines as they relate to teaching?

requiring

Summary: Is it the basic stance of teacher educators to support the content of lower schools as they have existed in the past or change it to make knowledge more integrated, more applicable to life, and more amenable to the interests of children and youth? Portions of these standards recognize the latter need; however, most will be effective at fixing the lower schools even more firmly in the hands of teachers "educated" in the traditional, chopped-up ways.

1.3.2 *Humanistic and Behavioral Studies*
Standard: The professional studies component of each curriculum for prospective teachers includes instruction in

the humanistic studies

Any amount of almost anything can answer a standard that says "includes."

"It is assumed that problems concerning the nature and aims of education, the curriculum, the organization and administration of a school system and the process of teaching and learning can be traced with respect to their historical development and the philosophical issues to which they are related. These studies will hereafter be referred to as humanistic studies."[4]

and the behavioral studies.

1.3.2a What humanistic and behavioral studies are part of the professional component of each curriculum, and what is the supporting rationale for including them?

This will be answered with catalogue copy.

1.3.2b What information shows that these studies are oriented toward the problems of education, such as the nature and aims of education, curriculum, organization, administration, teaching and learning?

This will be answered with syllabi. Note the words *oriented toward*. How can any syllabi fail to provide such information?

1.3.2c What information shows that the instruction in the humanistic and behavioral studies incorporates the findings of research and scholarly writings and provides experiences for students in their interpretation and use?

This is a solid standard, if actually applied. Some form of student or faculty evaluation of the actual teaching in these areas would seem to be required, since the standard deals with instruction. In addition, it asks for "experiences" in "interpretation and use" of studies. Ideally, this would mean actual experience; in this case it may be a term paper. This standard appears to be a genuine attempt at improving content and instruction.

1.3.2d What data shows that the programs of study of all prospective teachers include the humanistic and behavioral studies prescribed by the institution?

More catalogue copy. Note the word *prescribed*. As more colleges require fewer specific courses in response to the trend toward wider student choice, this standard will become less useful. The assumption, of course, is that teachers should be as broadly educated as all college graduates. The problem arises from the trend of colleges to "prescribe" less and less for anyone.

1.3.3 *Teaching and Learning Theory with Laboratory and Clinical Experience*

This means some form of behavioral system for describing teachers' verbal and nonverbal behavior. But why not

Standard: The professional studies component of each curriculum includes the systematic study of teaching

and learning theory

with appropriate laboratory and clinical experience.

1.3.3a In what courses, seminars and readings are provisions made for the study of teaching and learning theory?

1.3.3b What practices or procedures show that the study of teaching and learning theory requires and is accompanied by laboratory experiences (observation, demonstration, problem-solving, tutoring, microteaching, and/or other direct experiential activities)?

1.3.3c What are the provisions for clinical experiences (diagnosing and treating individual cases, practices or problems)?

1.3.3d What information shows that the instruction in the study of teaching and learning theory incorporates the findings of research and other scholarly writings, and provides experiences for students in their interpretation and use?

1.3.3e What data indicate that all prospective teachers have labora-

studies? Surely they are not advocating one expert's system but a range of alternative approaches; the last time we looked there were 400 such systems.

Why not *theories?* Do they really mean a choice between Skinner, Maslow, Rogers, etc.?

The problem here is that these complementary elements are usually taught in separate courses, as if learning to inhale and to exhale could be taught separately.

This standard is the essence of professional education and what distinguishes it from general education.

There is no way to answer this question incorrectly, provided there is some form of clinical experience. Since clinical is defined as dealing with learning to diagnose and treat individuals, this standard may help guide some institutions where learning to be a "schoolteacher" is still conceived as a matter of learning to manage groups.

Any attempt to evaluate instruction is laudable. However, this question must be answered with active behavior (i.e., what the instructor does in his teaching), not by simply interviewing the instructor or looking at his exams and bibliography.

Someday we may be in a position to change *experienced* teacher to *com-*

tory and clinical experiences under the guidance of an experienced teacher?

petent. This standard will usually be interpreted to mean that any classroom teacher on tenure is qualified to supervise a student teacher. Perhaps an intermediate step for teacher educators would be to define *experienced* as "effective in previous experiences with student teachers and interns." There are countless horror stories of excellent teachers of children and youth who cannot work with adults. *Experienced* should really refer to competence with both pupils and adults learning to teach.

1.3.3f What evidence shows that the programs of study of all prospective teachers include the systematic study of teaching and learning theory with appropriate laboratory and clinical experience?

The key word here is *evidence.* The following is an actual response to this standard from a well-known school of education. "Students in each methods course are expected to visit and observe a class in the Lawrence Schools once every week. Students in PE 194 observe elementary school classes and those in PE 195 review current educational methods and discuss their general implications for physical education. Usually, women's classes also make two field trips to nearby schools."[5] This is not cited merely to criticize but also to exemplify a typical response. When faced with a fundamental and necessary standard of professional education, many institutions can only come up with a skimpy itemization of traditional but highly questionable visiting procedure.

From the positive point of view, this is an area in which the NCATE standards might really help to educate and change practices.

Summary: There are multiple approaches to the study of teaching and a variety of sound learning theories. Once again, distinctions need to be made between what constitutes *information, data,* and *evidence.* Also, the term *provision for* is loose enough to be a meaningless minimum. The attempt to define *laboratory* and *clinical* may prove genuinely helpful in raising practices beyond uncontrolled observation and nonsystematic direct experiences.

1.3.4 *Practicum*
Standard: The professional studies component of each curriculum for prospective teachers includes direct, substantial

An important but vague attempt to upgrade whole states where 180 hours is the definition of "substantial."

participation in teaching

This changes the old goal of "fully responsible for total class" (which makes traditional teacher educators emphasize management at the expense of individual pupil needs), into one of involving the student teacher in the acts of teaching.

over an extended period of time

An important but indecisive attempt to stop summer student teaching and other quick and dirty forms of "getting certified up."

under the supervision of qualified personnel from the institution and the cooperating school.

And means that the college cannot dump this responsibility on cooperating teachers to save the salaries of the college supervisors. This is the most important conjunction in the standards.

1.3.4a What evidence shows that every prospective teacher assumes substantial responsibility

That what the pupils learn in a given unit of content, or what the pupils get from participating in an important activity, is primarily dependent on the instruction, or leadership, of the student teacher or intern.

over an extended period of time

In order that he teach more than a spelling list or lead a trip to the museum.

for the range of teaching duties

Whole class, small group, and individuals; one period to full load; advanced, average, and slow students; immediate, short-term, and long-range objectives.

in the professional role for which he is being prepared?

This relates back to the first standard, in which the "institution's concept of the teacher's role" was called for. It is precisely at this point that the institution's concept should be the yardstick. Unfortunately, institutional goal statements are usually too broad to be helpful.

1.3.4b What information shows that relationships between profes-

This seems to be jargon for asking college supervisors and cooperating

sional personnel in the institution and in the cooperating schools contribute positively to students' experience in practicum?

teachers not to fight, using the student teachers and interns as middlemen. The information that seems most plausible for answering the standard is that college and public school personnel meet regularly to settle differences. But how does this cooperative relationship "contribute positively" to students? (To students it simply means that if they survive the practicum experience and emerge with good references from both school and college personnel, they have been "contributed [to] positively.")

What this standard is trying to get at is the notion that schools and colleges often leave students in poor practicum situations because of administrative convenience and rationalize this malpractice by telling students, "At least you're learning what should *not* be done."

1.3.4c What evidence confirms that the supervision of students in practicum is organized

Organized supervision can mean that it is regularly scheduled, that it focuses on specific aspects of teaching, or that it follows a particular system of rating observations.

and executed under the direction of qualified personnel from the institution?

Direction is the key word; it permits a college administrator to hire graduate assistants, part-timers and other nonregular faculty to do the actual supervision. If the standard really intends institutional commitment, it should change the term *qualified personnel* to *faculty*.

1.3.4d What evidence confirms that the supervising teachers in the cooperating schools are superior teachers,

Superior is a comparative term; superior to whom? On what basis? This suggests a direct evaluation of their classroom instruction, which is rarely done by the schools themselves, let alone by universities assigning hordes of student teachers. This standard makes it an unethical act for colleges simply to turn over the designation of these cooperating teachers to building principals. Principals are notorious for assuming the purpose of student teaching is to provide the

are trained in supervision

school with extra service (e.g., tutors) or to stimulate their poorest teachers.

This is an excellent ideal that, while advocated for half a century, is still not widely practiced. Working with college youth is not considered to require special training by the university faculty; to require special training of cooperating teachers would demand that we put our own house in order.

and are committed to the task of educating teachers?

It is difficult to give "information" of commitment, unless the information is that the cooperating teachers are willing to work without honoraria or stipends.

1.3.4e What systematic methods are used to record or describe the teaching performance of students

This will be easy to answer until the term *systematic* is defined. Even a personal reference can be "systematic" if it uses the same format or is filed at a given time.

and how is the resulting data used by students and supervisors

If *supervisors* also means the cooperating teacher, this is a very difficult standard to implement. Much criticism of students is implicit criticism of the cooperating teachers and is usually shared only by the student and the college supervisor.

to analyze teaching behavior?

1.3.4f How is the supervision of students in practicum translated into an index of faculty load?

How do (most) institutions justify different loads for early childhood, elementary, secondary, exceptional areas?

For how many students in practicum does each teacher education faculty have responsibility?

If *each* implies that every faculty member "should," it is patent nonsense. It might be helpful here if the standard indicated some range (e.g., 15-18 full-time student teachers) as a full load for a regular, full-time faculty member.

Summary: These are very high standards when one considers usual practices. At the same time, they will become more useful in guiding practice when specifications (in some cases numerical ones) are attached to *extended period, faculty load,* etc. There should be a shift from merely asking for numbers, to suggesting ranges and minimum standards.

1.4 *Use of Guidelines Developed by National Learned Societies and Professional Associations*
Standard: In planning and developing curricula for teacher education, the institution gives due consideration to guidelines for teacher preparation developed by national learned societies and professional associations.

This is a critical component in any real profession; it recognizes the need to build on the previous and accumulated knowledge of the community of scholars whose wisdom is the basis of the particular specialization. On the other hand, it is difficult to deal with the overly narrow and the established. Suppose, for example, the best art education for children was partly fine art, partly literature, partly music, partly dance, and partly drama. Which scholarly organization would prepare such guidelines? Interdisciplinary and core efforts are completely out. A second problem is that these specialties represent the practitioners, not those committed to general education. The best example is in music, where the association changes three credit courses to two and then one credit, but still ends up recommending sixty credits of music as a college major. Such groups are not devoted to either professional or liberal studies; they sometimes get fixated in their own areas.

1.4.1 What guidelines has the institution considered in developing the following elements of the professional studies component:

a. The content for each teaching specialty offered?

These standards become incredibly high for early childhood and elementary in some institutions. A secondary teacher of French may have half the requirement of an elementary "specialist."

b. The humanistic and behavioral studies?

There is no association directly connected to this area. The AERA offers no guidelines for the educational psychology component; the educational philosophers, sociologists, and historians are fractionated in separate organizations.

c. Teaching and learning theory with laboratory and clinical experiences?

An excellent standard! The key word is *with*, since the ideas and principles are typically segregated from the opportunities to practice.

d. Practicum?

There is much literature in this area. (The Association of Teacher Educators). Strange how seldom it is used as a basis for arguing for change in student teaching and intern programs.

1.4.2 What information shows that the guidelines identified in 1.4.1 above have been critically examined in relation to the planning and development of the curricula offered?

Another excellent guideline. If *critically examined* means "used in some way," few institutions could pass. The important point is that this standard sets some sights on the nature of planning and development being more than a faculty committee pooling their ideas (ignorance) and then coming to the truth (voting). There must be more to the collective wisdom of teacher educators than pandering to faculty whim.

Summary: These will prove to be (were we actually to check) the weakest sections of the reports submitted to the NCATE. The democratic ethic of the university traps teacher educators into behaving like other professors who confuse democratic faculty deliberations with the most valid program. Teacher education must be rationally planned, with reference to the cumulative wisdom of all teacher educators, to make the teachers it prepares professional practitioners rather than college graduates.

1.5 *Control of Basic Programs*
Standard: The design, approval, and continuous evaluation and development of teacher education programs are the primary responsibility of an officially designated unit;

Except for a few backward state departments, the day of examining transcripts course by course is over. This means students must complete programs conceived as a totality. Teacher education programs cannot be a conglomeration of courses that students "pick up" in this or that department, and then have the state check against its minimum standards course by course. This standard assumes that once a program is assigned to a department or college, it will be looked at by a "responsible" faculty in its totality.

the majority of the membership of this unit is composed of faculty and/or staff members who are significantly involved in teacher education.

Do professional educators or uninvolved academicians control the program?

1.5.1 What administrative unit within the institution has primary responsibility for the preparation of teachers

In places where experimental, or specially funded, or simply different programs are initiated, it is often done by circumventing usual administrative units. This standard is focused on the traditional academician-educationist split and neglects the change strategy of consciously putting new programs within schools of education into administrative limbo to avoid restrictive administrative controls.

and what is the rationale for determining its membership and responsibilities?

The simple word *rationale* means that university traditions, or professors with political clout, are not reasons for public consumption even though they may be the actual reasons for particular administrative control being vested in funny places.

1.5.2 What evidence shows that the majority of the membership of the official unit is made up of faculty and/or staff members significantly involved in teacher education?

Even if an attack of blatant honesty permitted an institution to answer the previous standard (e.g., "We put the secondary English program into the English department because we believe that subject matter and not pedagogy is what is needed!"), it would still not meet this standard which clearly places the control back with a "majority" of faculty "significantly" involved in teacher education. Who can this be but professional educators?

1.5.3 What activities of the official unit during the past two years demonstrate that it has assumed responsibility for the design,

Operationally, design means add a course, change the number of credits assigned, change prerequisites, and rearrange calendars.

approval

Vote and pass on to the next administrative unit.

and continuous evaluation and development of each teacher education program offered by the institution?

This is a duplication of standard 5. In this context *evaluation* simply means that the faculty hears from, bumps into, or receives spirit messages from graduates and uses these data in advocating (or blocking) proposals for changing the "design" of programs.

1.5.4 What information shows that the teacher education faculty members share in the decision making process in matters related to designing, evaluating and developing teacher education programs?

This merely means that the majority cited in 1.5.2 above has a vote as part of their membership.

Summary: This short but fundamental standard deals with who controls the programs. Its terms are those of the old but durable battle of professional versus academic educators. In its understandable zeal to give the power to the professional educators, the standard makes a mockery of involving anyone outside of university faculty in any real decisions. Students are supposed to be involved (standard 3.4) and cooperating teachers supposedly matter too (standard 1.3.4), yet, it is ultimately the education faculty that this standard supports as "most equal."

If a doctoral dissertation were done on these standards, one hypothesis might deal with the amount of control exercised by AACTE over NCATE standards. Evidence to support or refute this contention could be gathered by reading the assessments of teams related to this standard; it will receive a disproportionate amount of concern, and perhaps it should.

2. Faculty for Basic Programs

2.1 *Competence and Utilization of Faculty*

Standard: An institution engaged in preparing teachers has full-time faculty members in teacher education,

This standard reflects the assumption that commitment can be assessed by using the concept of professional identification: half-time professional educators are not "fully" committed. While this may sound like a foolish point, there are differences in the goals of many faculty, and to some degree these differences are manifested in the way they identify themselves. "I'm a teacher educator," or "I'm in the Department of Curriculum and Instruction," or "I'm an Assistant Professor of English with a joint appointment in Education." If the way we view ourselves does influence how and what we do, then these three forms of identification actually represent three different jobs being accomplished.

each with post masters degree preparation

NCATE is not yet ready to threaten the large number of state college faculty without doctorates. The next revision of these guidelines will probably change this.

and/or demonstrated scholarly competence,

This takes care of the published authors and the recognized artists without advanced degrees.

and each with appropriate specializations. Such specializations make possible competent instruction in the humanistic and behavioral studies, in teaching and learning theory, and in the methods of teaching in each of

This is not an attempt to freeze courses and specializations into narrow or merely traditional lines; it is an effort to stop small institutions, or overextended large ones, with too few faculty from offering too many programs, and thus forcing their fac-

the specialties for which the institution prepares teachers.

There are appropriate specializations to ensure competent supervisors of laboratory, clinical and practicum experiences.

ulty to become (play at) experts in more fields than can reasonably be expected of genuine authorities.

The debate between general versus special supervisors is apparently finally over. There is no longer even an opportunity to venture a rationale on how a music supervisor can or should supervise a chemistry teacher.

The problem with all forms of specialization, however, is that they ensure quality in the sense of more knowledge of content. They also ensure that present forms of organizing the disciplines of knowledge will remain unchanged in college and secondary education. By definition, there is no way to specialize in a broad or interdisciplinary area.

2.1.1 What evidence indicates that there is a full-time faculty for teacher education

with qualifications requisite to competent instruction in each of the areas specified in the standard?

In addition to the individual commitment that full-time identification proves, it also measures institutional willingness to support a program.

2.1.2 What evidence shows that all courses and other learning experiences in each of the areas specified in the standard are actually conducted by faculty members appropriately prepared to do so?

The term *actually conducted* makes this one of the few times that there is an attempt to get at real evidence. Faculty are sometimes listed as teachers of courses actually offered by graduate assistants. *Evidence* in this context might actually refer to faculty participation in class sessions, faculty reading of papers, faculty reading of exams, etc.

2.1.3 If any faculty members have been teaching in fields for which they are not qualified, for how long and for what special reasons has this been permitted?

The fact that the state may require a particular course does not dub any faculty member at random "qualified."

2.1.4 What is done to evaluate the effectiveness of the instruction in each of the areas specified in the standard?

If courses are not required then counting student registration is one good indication. A common practice is to use unsystematic bits of hearsay evidence; these usually come from particular advisees in personal conferences.

The "ideal" evaluation is to observe graduates' subsequent behavior. However, it is difficult to have valid connections between teachers' practices and a particular course taken years beforehand. It is also easier to evaluate methods than foundations, if subsequent practice is the arena of judgment.

Students' ratings and faculty evaluation of peers are the two most common kinds of evaluation. This will be an area of increasing interest in future, possibly even replacing publications and research as the public demands higher quality undergraduate instruction in general.

Summary: One-man departments, or a potpourri of some part-timers, can no longer be passed off as an adequate faculty for teacher education. Institutional and personal commitment is indicated by full-time identification with teacher education.

Specializations must be connected to faculty preparation and competence. Even the field supervisor can no longer be a complete generalist but must be highly qualified in the area in which he supervises. The danger, of course, is that this effort to ensure competence by emphasizing specialization also risks reinforcing the rigidities of graduate study organized in the traditional, discrete disciplines. It is hoped that, by including "demonstrated scholarly competence," the standard permits faculty to develop new forms of specialization throughout their careers.

The final piece of this standard, dealing with the evaluation of instructional competence, is very critical. In future, the public will demand more accountable, systematic evaluation of instruction, and teacher educators will be especially vulnerable. This tacked-on little standard will be one of the most carefully scrutinized.

2.2 *Faculty Involvement with Schools*
Standard: Members of the teacher education faculty have continuing association and involvement with elementary and secondary schools.

"Continuing association and involvement" is a vague, gentle reminder. While it is well-intentioned, it is so open that a semiannual meeting with cooperating teachers in the university dining room can meet it.

2.2.1 In what ways have the faculty for teacher education been associated and involved with activities of elementary and secondary schools?

Again, well-intentioned, but how is it possible to answer this form of question incorrectly? What, for example, constitutes bad or insufficient involvement? Even written correspondence is a "correct" response here.

2.2.2 What information shows that such association and involvement are reflected in the institution's teacher education program?

Here, a listing of changes prompted by field contacts would be necessary. The problem, again, is no indication of how to assess the quality or nature of the institution's responses to inputs from field exposures.

2.2.3 What information indicates that the special competencies of the teacher education faculty are reflected in the services to the schools?

This may be an unfair standard for a teacher education institution to bear alone, since it also requires some public school willingness. Suppose a particular school of education faculty had many researchers and few reading experts. Would it be fair to assess that school on how its influence shows up in the public schools?

Summary: Faculty involvement in public schools is assumed to be a basic good for both the faculty involved and the school served. The standard sidesteps the admittedly difficult issue of how much and what kind of involvement. The attempt to pin such involvement to "improved" practices in the teacher education programs is idealistic but worthwhile.

The idea slipped in at the end—service to schools—is a monumental notion. Does it mean accountability? Rather than being appended, it should be a separate major section. In this time of budgetary pressures, expecting universities to expend resources in lower schools is no puny idea; it deserves more than a 2.2.3 burial.

2.3 *Conditions for Faculty Service*
Standard: The institution provides conditions essential to the effective performance by the teacher education faculty.

The assumption is correct and critical; teacher education faculty have additional and different needs from other college faculty. One good example is summer courses. Schools of education serve whole populations of practitioners who can only meet in summer. If budget cuts are made "equally" across the colleges throughout the university, then the needs of some education students and faculty cannot be met. In order to compete for faculty, many schools of education must be able to promise summer employment to recruit able people. There are numerous other examples ranging from special parking facilities for field supervisors (as opposed to faculty who need only hunt for a spot once a day), to promotion criteria that favor faculty who write over those who "run around."

2.3.1 What is the plan and supporting rationale for taking into account all professional duties and activities of the faculty in determining load?

Again, there can be no inadequate answer to a question phrased in this manner. The assumption is that having a "plan" and a "rationale" will cause some thinking and planning, which will be an improvement on the unconsidered traditions so widely used for determining load.

Teaching load in many traditional training institutions is the number of credits (or the number of credits multiplied by the number enrolled) actually taught. In more "enlightened" universities load credit is also assigned for team teaching, field services, research, specially assigned writing (e.g., new programs, proposals, and program evaluations), time-consuming and vital committee assignments, supervising, offering independent reading, and advising on theses. No single indicator so clearly demonstrates what the university leadership and faculty value as their definition of faculty load.

2.3.2 What is the assigned professional load (all services rendered) for each teacher education faculty member?

This requires mere reporting. The greatest unavowed battle in academe is the difference between the preferences of individual faculty and the needs of the institution to staff the programs it advertises in its catalogues. If the program demands triumph, there is a generally unhappy faculty; if faculty preferences win, there are fractionalized programs. This is a major distinction between former teachers colleges and universities, or between junior and senior faculty in the same institution. Low-level people offer programs; high-level people "do their thing."

2.3.3 If the load of any faculty member exceeds the established institutional policy, for what reasons has this been permitted?

Is faculty greed (designated "overload") permitted?

2.3.4 What program does the institution have for faculty development and what evidence shows that it is operative?

Sabbaticals, fellowships, travel funds, and faculty seminars with paid outside speakers are a few examples. An unfamiliar but sensible method would be to include courses and experiences that faculty take as part of their loads. Again, all these options are regarded as plums, not necessities.

2.3.5 What is the plan for allocating supporting services to the faculty and what evidence shows that such services are provided?

Those who really know are aware that the secretaries and clerks keep the institutions going; there are never a sufficient number of them to serve the students, faculty, and administration. The "plan" is usually to scream for as many as can be obtained and then to assign them to administrators. In one school of education we know intimately, twelve administrators have fifteen secretaries, one hundred faculty share half that number, and four thousand students are not allowed near the offices.

Technical help, graduate assistants, and clerical aides are best obtained with outside funds and grants. No institution can meet its needs in this area on its regular budget, since in a forced choice situation money should go for more faculty (which merely increases the need for more assistance) before it goes for additional supporting personnel.

Summary: Whoever decides what and how much faculty does, decides the essence of program quality. This standard prods, hints, and asks for plans and rationales. At issue here are the very resources that legislators legislate, administrators administer, and faculty like to think of as their time to expend as they see fit. Nowhere are acceptable minimum conditions as conspicuous by their absence as in this standard.

2.4 *Part-time Faculty*
Standard: Part-time faculty meet the requirements

for appointment to the full-time faculty

The doctorate has become the necessary but not sufficient condition that operationally defines *requirements.*

Full-time usually means placement in the tenure track, unless it is a soft line funded by a temporary grant. The individual hired has a fixed time period (usually three to four years) to be moved up or out. He will produce the writing and research, teach, and most of all not rock any of the wrong boats. The recommended proportions (i.e., the best recipe for success) of these ingredients depend on the nature of the institution.

and are employed only when they can make special contributions to the teacher education programs.

This is the disclaimer that makes it possible to wash out much of the foregoing, if the institution is located in a remote area or the dean has a conscious plan to keep down the number of more able faculty. More able faculty inevitably include more boat rockers, radicals, deviants, and people who raise questions about local traditions.

Special contributions has been twisted into meaning a classroom teacher who individualized reading and will teach this process to student teachers; a local Black, Chicano, or Indian militant who will be a consultant on minority affairs; or a local superintendent to teach a course in school finance. In sum, anything offered in a university or in a school of education can be defined as a "special contribution" and, therefore, beyond the need for a doctorate and formal credentials. This loophole permits three forms of distortion of the standard: an overconcentration of power in the hands of deans and department chairmen, nepotism, and discrimination against freethinkers in favor of more pedestrian individuals who are perceived as better able to fit into local cultures.

2.4.1 What are the qualifications of the part-time faculty members in teacher education

Qualifications means formal study, work experience, and achievements recognized by publication, award, promotion, and public showings. Personal references of superiors may or may not be considered "qualifications." In addition of course, there are the less formal qualifications of verbal ability and general sensitivity, which are assessed in interview situations. The issue is, How do the prospective employers assign relative weights to whatever dimensions they actually use?

and what proportion of the instruction in each curriculum is assigned to them?

This is a critical question. In academic disciplines the doctoral seminars are not taught by the graduate assistants. In teacher education, however, the clinical experiences we ballyhoo as the essence of our programs are most often taught by supervisors (i.e., classroom teachers or graduate students) who have the least formal qualifications. We dub them clinical professors or whatever, but they are part-time or associated members of the faculty. The issue is, therefore, not only the proportion or amount of the program taught by part-time people, but also the significance of the courses in the program that are assigned to these people.

2.4.2 What is the load within and without the institution,

This covers joint appointments with public schools as well as those individuals split internally, such as graduate students who work at their own studies and supervise student teachers. This standard is also intended to cover the issue of faculty quality in extension and off-campus courses. The assumption is that full-time faculty should not be kept in-house while part-time faculty cover most of the outside offerings.

for each part-time faculty member in teacher education?

The emphasis achieved through *each* is that there should be a separate rationale in every instance rather than a policy for dealing with part-time faculty. If this *each* is a deliberate one, it surely underscores the view that the onus is on the institution to justify every faculty assignment.

2.4.3 What reasons support the use of each part-time member in teacher education?

A classic example of the whole NCATE approach: to avoid setting minimums or specific requirements in favor of broad guidelines based on clear assumptions that require universities to come up with rational explanations in place of expediencies. Thinking should replace the "quick and dirty."

In this case the assumption is that full-time faculty, who are more likely to have advanced degrees and more college and scholarly experiences and be more accountable to their university employer, will offer higher-quality services than part-time and temporary faculty. To deny this assumption is to question the university system as *the* place to prepare teachers, since full-timers (and everything that full-time implies) are the only ones who will succeed and be retained in the university reward system.

Answers such as "We had X dollars and decided on two part-timers"; "It was too late to get anyone"; "The enrollment caught us by surprise"; "Mrs. X is the wife of a faculty member, and we recruited him by promising her some work"; "We needed a Black, but we couldn't afford that level of full-time salary"; or "We wanted good relations with X district and threw the superintendent a bone, i.e., $1000 for a course," may be the real reasons, but they are not acceptable if we understand rationale to mean an explanation in light of program purposes.

2.4.4 What provisions are made to ensure that part-time faculty members are oriented to the basic purposes of, and kept abreast of, current developments in the institution's teacher education programs?

In most cases the answer to this is few or none. Most part-timers rarely do the committee work that is so important and time- and energy-consuming for full-time faculty.

In fact, the obvious benefit to part-time work is that it frequently becomes less than one-half, or one-quarter, or whatever, by virtue of not having advisement responsibilities, service on NCATE committees, recruitment committees, merit committees, reading comprehensive examinations, theses advisement, and so on.

Almost any responsibility is considered an "overload," or at least an intrusion, by the part-timer.

In any event, what could a possible answer be to this standard? "We send part-time faculty a newsletter?" or "We test them on the catalogue and old committee minutes to bring them up to date on the forty years of program development they missed." Obviously not. The usual practice is to hope that part-timers will go to coffee, lunch, or cocktails and get filled in, or at least will listen to the secretarial and administrative staff who really know the programs.

This guideline is a good example of how a standard can indicate the direction for future development; it has pinpointed an obvious, glaring weakness and asked for a systematic form of involvement for part-time faculty.

Summary: This standard is aimed less at state colleges (former teacher training institutions) than at private schools and major, "great" universities, where we have been guilty of playing fast and loose with preservice teacher education. When there was a shortage of beginning teachers and lots of grant money, the regular faculty did their thing (e.g., consulted, wrote, worked with a few doctoral students, and prepared scholarly papers) and left some underlings and part-timers to offer the regular programs. Now there must be a complete justification. Several options are open: (1) to get out of preservice education (not as bizarre an alternative as it may appear at first glance, what with the shortage of dollars and the growth of state colleges); (2) to involve senior faculty in preservice preparation (not only impossible to accomplish but a poor idea), and (3) to use preservice programs as research and field-testing opportunities that can be offered by graduates and part-time staff, but be planned and evaluated by senior faculty (possible).

3. Students in Basic Programs
3.1 *Admission to Basic Programs*
   Standard: The institution applies specific criteria

Thus far (the first five words), the only ones hurt by this standard will be those institutions desperate for any students (bodies) to pay the bills. Unfortunately, this is a growing number of institutions and no longer merely the private ones; many state colleges were expanded too quickly in the 1960s.

for admission to teacher education programs; these criteria require the use of both objective

and subjective data.

"Objective" data might include tests, grades, the number of college credits completed, English and speech proficiency, and possibly a minimum number of hours in some form of field work.

References, personal statements (e.g., "Why I want to teach . . ."), and interviews are examples of "subjective data." Occasionally, decisions perpetrated on the basis of assumptions of no shortage or lack of funds have included random selection, or "first come, first served." In these cases, students might sign up for student teaching and be tentatively listed several semesters or years in advance of when they needed the course. In such cases, would "first come, first served" (and it really is used in some institutions) be subjective or objective criteria?

Obviously, the standard does not deal with self-selection, even though this is the most important determinant and control of the quality of students and how well they turn out. Suppose an institution moved to a five-year program rather than a four-year one. Would the self-selection that took effect continue to be a valid indication of commitment, or would it be more indicative of financial resources?

3.1.1 What are the requirements for admission to the teacher education programs and what is the supporting rationale?

Grades, chest X rays, particular courses, speech, swimming, non-Communist affidavits? The critical point is, On what grounds has the institution chosen their criteria? Many reasons will have to be abandoned, since we dare not embarrass ourselves by revealing publicly (to NCATE) that we use them (e.g., the chairman of the speech department believes adamantly that people with lateral lisps should be identified and required to take a course, whether such courses help or not. The speech department chairman is an old colleague and friend. We support his vehement belief in spite of no evidence or reason.).

3.1.2 What evidence shows that the admission requirements are being met?

This looks like a clerical scavenger hunt. There should be valid reasons in cases of students who have been admitted without having met standards. The best indicator of "paper" standards is when students are admitted before completing admission "requirements," the obvious implication being that no one who gets around to it could possibly not do well enough to meet the standards of admission.

3.1.3 How many students applied for admission to teacher education during the last two years?

A more difficult (unfair?) question than it appears to be. Many students inquire but do not formally fill out the applications. This is especially true of graduates and adults who often inquire about requirements and then self-select themselves out. The numerous steps frequently required form a clerical barrier that will also cause many "now" oriented people to self-select themselves out.

How many were denied admission?

A good question. A better one would be; "How many students with B or higher averages are turned down for failure to meet any of the other criteria?"

How many who were denied admission were subsequently admitted, and for what reason?

Bravo! The least studied, most critical factor in teacher education is self-selection. Very often, straightforward people, who believe their rejection letters, disappear into the woodwork. More aggressive, persistent people are almost always admitted. They appeal, get admitted on condition, or just keep coming. This standard may give the simple, honest types an equal chance with the pushers. In any event, it may make us less willing to respond to the factor of persistence as the most critical factor in the self-selection process.

3.1.4 What objective data, including test results with national norms,

Creativity tests, dogmatism scales, social values, personality, and I.Q. tests often have national norms. This standard should not limit institutions to the usual ACT (American College Testing), SAT (Scholastic Achievement Test), or Graduate Record Exam.

are used for admitting students to teacher education programs?

The assumption is not that we now have nationally standardized instruments that are accurate predictors of success, but that students transfer and teachers change jobs. Admission to a teacher education program is, in a very real sense, a national passport to the profession.

3.1.5 If the institution admits

If equals *When* here.

students who do not meet its usual admission criteria, what special resources does it devote to the remediation or enrichment necessary to enable some of these students to meet the institutional requirements for admission to teacher education programs?

This is a monumental task. Nowhere is there a standard more critical and more universally ignored. This standard is a straight effort at leading the institutions into doing something. Those who do not see the sweeping character of this standard should consider the following alternatives. If students are admitted to teacher education programs as freshmen, resources are expended on large numbers of students who will not only never enter teaching but also will drop out of the university. The whole issue of open enrollment for freshmen compounds this issue further, if that is possible. If students are admitted as sophomores or juniors, there would have to be help provided beforehand as part of the general education program. The same is true for transfer students. If students are admitted as special or graduates, the "help" usually comes in the form of requiring extra courses that do not count toward the degree or certification.

The sweeping implications of this standard are felt more keenly when we realize how little individualization is offered those admitted to programs on a regular basis. Imagine devoting shrinking resources to helping marginal students rather than promising ones, particularly when the job market for teachers is also decreasing!

This standard may have been conceived as a means of aiding minority group students, but even this trend seems to have ebbed.

3.1.6 What characteristics of the students admitted are revealed by the data obtained through applying objective and subjective admission criteria?

This is a subtle way of asking, "Does anyone ever look at the results of the data gathered? Are any implications drawn?" Our own experience is that most institutions will be hard pressed to find the data in student folders, let alone analyze the material to the point of knowing anything generalizable about their students. We avoid these kinds of data in order to hold onto the generalizations we feel comfortable with (e.g., "Future teachers are vocationally oriented, feminine, and nonactivist, and don't bother me with facts, particularly about students in my own institution"). In the few cases where data are analyzed, the sketch of education students is often informative and sometimes startling.

Summary: Admission is the most critical process in teacher education. In practice, it is accomplished quite frequently by self-selection. Assuming that institutions make the real decisions, these standards present some excellent guidelines for moving institutions toward self-improvement. If the simple first step of presenting a rationale for admission criteria were taken, it would be a quantum leap forward from what we now do. The reciprocity of certification among many states makes the need for more systematic, generalizable knowledge in this area all the more urgent. Entry into the profession is a national issue with lifelong implications, not a simple, one-time mistake of Siwash Tech's admission procedure. We must not only learn what the best admission criteria are but also disseminate the evidence.

3.2 *Retention of Students in Basic Programs*
Standard: The institution applies specific criteria for the retention of candidates in basic programs

Passing the courses is the usual one.

who possess academic competencies and personal characteristics appropriate to the requirements of teaching.

Again, even if there are not generally accepted professional characteristics, the hope is that the particular institution will have systematically considered its own. It is interesting that this standard is stated positively. This demonstrates the expectation of systematic planning. If stated negatively, it would be limited to the rare psychopath about whom we could reach consensus. This way there is a hope, albeit a slim one, that the faculty might agree that students who demonstrate eliciting behaviors be retained. In other words, we need reasons to keep students, as well as to drop them.

3.2.1 What objective means are used to evaluate the achievement of students in each area of the professional studies component of teacher education?

If students are savvy enough to prevent faculty from knowing them well enough to complain about them (usually not too difficult), cumulative grades are such evidence.

3.2.2 What information other than course grades

NCATE predicted how most institutions would answer 3.2.1.

is used to evaluate the achievement of prospective teachers?

The references of college supervisors and cooperating teachers are the usual methods; of course, by then it is too late. The student is about to graduate and we rarely prevent that, especially in institutions where graduation and certification are linked.

3.2.3 What requirements for academic competence must students meet to continue in the teacher education program?

This standard is another example of NCATE prodding institutions into seeking reasons for keeping people rather than dropping them. The assumption is that schools will develop program goals. This standard will lead many faculty and administrators to ask, "You mean there are places that use more than grades?"

3.2.4 On the basis of what personal characteristics does the institution screen out students from the teacher education programs?

("You mean there should be continuous, rather than a one-shot concept of admission?") In public, tax-supported institutions, we are somewhat reluctant to incur law suits. If a student has voluntarily produced three independently signed affidavits from licensed psychiatrists that he is non compos mentis; if he has bitten people repeatedly, in the presence of witnesses who are willing to testify; if he is an active, avowed Communist; if his record of child molesting can be documented; if he is not a member of a minority group, a female, or a homosexual; then there is a possibility that the administrator of the teacher education program might, under certain circumstances, consider the feasibility of making a tentative suggestion that an ad hoc committee might be formed for the purpose of studying the recommendation that this student be asked to voluntarily remove himself from the program, provided, of course, he is guaranteed that nothing negative will appear on his record, that his grades will be good enough to get into graduate school, and that if some time in the future he desires readmission it will be automatic.

The hope that any institution in this day and age will act with professional courage and integrity on the basis of "personal characteristics" must be tempered by the knowledge that the above over-generalization has important bits of truth in it.

3.2.5 Under what circumstances, if any, are students who do not meet the institution's requirements for retention

permitted to continue in the basic programs?

Once again, here is reinforcement for the idea that we need reasons to keep people; that is, continuous evaluation.

One common procedure (cop out?) is to permit questionable students to receive the degree but to withhold certification. There are also exceptions to this; for example, the foreign student who will be returning home often needs to save face, and the faculty knows he will not remain in their particular state.

Summary: These standards embody an important set of concerns, which at present may seem to be pipedreams, but which must be dealt with before teacher education can become a genuine profession. Faculties need to become more willing to state their assessments at the risk of criticism or even lawsuits. Just as no written test data are as valid or reliable as the cumulated (evened-out) responses of a child's teacher, groups and committees of teacher educators have the best knowledge of particular students. Subjective, emotional, and personal reasons have been denigrated, while "objective criteria, such as grades, swimming tests, and attendance, which signal nothing, have been institutionalized. One reason for this situation, in addition to our reluctance to rely on our emotions, is efficiency. If we are operating mass institutions for hordes of students that can never be known to us personally, what is more expedient (cheap) than a computer search of grades.

3.3 *Counseling and Advising for Students in Basic Programs*
Standard: The institution has a well-defined plan for counseling and advising students in teacher education.

3.3.1 What special counseling and advising services are provided for students in teacher education?

3.3.2 What information shows that counselors and advisors for teacher education students know the nature and scope of the teaching profession, the problems of the schools, and the institutional resources available to students?

3.3.3 What information shows that the institution maintains a comprehensive system of records for all prospective teachers which is readily and easily available to faculty members and placement officers for professional purposes?

Reaction: We have not summarized but must react to this standard, because it is the first one with which we are in total disagreement. All professional education should be a personal-professional experience. There is a constant interrelationship between *what* a student is learning and how he *feels* about it. Everything he learns to do for or with others he relates to what it may mean in his own life. One goal of teacher education is to plan and integrate this personal dimension throughout the program.[6]

To draw out and separate the personal dimension is nonsense; then to hold institutions responsible for staffing and expanding such facilities makes a series of bad assumptions. The only justification for these services would be as support for the admission and retention standards discussed previously. But for some curious reason this natural connection is not made.

There is an even stranger link with placement. Instead of providing counseling experts to help select and/or guide students out or employ teacher educators capable of building the personal component into the program, we are being advised to show how an extraneous concept of counseling should somehow be appended to a program and, worst of all, be used for placement purposes.

This whole disastrous standard is probably an unconsidered reflection of our assumption that the cognitive and affective exist as independent domains and that emotional problems can somehow be patched up outside students' real studies and professional and life experiences, in short periods of time as a kind of prerequisite.

3.4 *Student Participation in Program Evaluation and Development*
Standard: The institution has representative student

participation

in the evaluation and development of its teacher education programs.

It is hoped this does not mean the students "voluntarily selected" by faculty from their classes.

They come to committee meetings.

The trend of activism, which was always a disproportionate reaction to a minority activity, has petered out so that now activist types question the sincerity of faculty and will not "participate," i.e., be token students. Youth now are savvy enough to insist on the protagonist role in order to negotiate, rather than make believe they are equal participants and be co-opted.

3.4.1 What evidence shows that students participate in the evaluation and

development of preparation programs offered by the institution?

An annual or monthly gripe session that culminates in coffee rather than real program change has become a tradition on many campuses. Faculty have also become expert at soliciting graduates' criticisms and then not responding as a group with real program changes.

Students sometimes feel they will be discriminated against by faculty they disagree with during meetings; others object to being a minority on these committees. The fact that students are often denied voting privileges does not sharpen their enthusiasm. At the same time, there are some students who simply don't care about long-term program decisions; their own need to get over existing hurdles is the extent of their concern.

Many faculty resent real student involvement. Meeting times are at faculty convenience. There is little inclination to change university rules and enfranchise students.

3.4.2 What are the major concerns which students

Who decides? Some students might answer that jobs and finding personal-professional meaning in life are the concerns that teacher education programs least help them to deal with.

have expressed during the last two years and in what ways have these concerns influenced the development of teacher education programs?

One problem here is that we (i.e., those responsible for the students' previous twelve years of socialization in places called schools), respond to the majority student view, rather than the wisest student leadership. Most students seek direction and are not change oriented. They also lack the real life and professional experiences on which to make valid criticisms of their programs. This leads to a numbers game in which most students are used by the administration-faculty to counteract what fewer, more perceptive students may propose.

Most students want to keep the grading system. (High grades are relatively easy to get in teacher education programs and help students get into graduate school.) Most student teachers regard this experience as the most relevant part of their program. (This is certainly true when relevance is determined by comparison with Geology 6.)

In essence, teacher educators use students in much the same way that lawyers use psychiatrists. We select those who support what we want and keep things pretty much the same or propose limited changes that *we* value on the basis of support from hand-picked students.

Summary: The trends for and against student involvement have been changing with the frequency of women's fashions. The real issue, however, lies at the heart of teacher education as a professional or as a university function. If it is the former, our involvement in self-criticism and development should rest primarily with inservice practitioners; if it is the latter, college students' reactions should be the primary basis for improving college programs.

4. Resources and Facilities in Basic Programs

4.1 *Library*

Standard: The library is adequate to support the instruction, research, and services pertinent to each teacher education program.

The issue revolves around the term *adequate.* Who is to define it? We have no agreed-on list of fundamental or minimum references. Perhaps one should be developed and kept current. Most faculty now arrive as specialists, and the materials they require do *not* necessarily cumulate into a total set of holdings of basic materials. There is also the usual problem of how quickly the library can obtain new volumes and sources.

4.1.1 What evidence shows that the library collection includes: a. Standard and contemporary holdings in education (books, microfilms, microfiche copies, etc.)?

Who determines what is standard? On what criteria?

b. Standard periodicals in education? c. Such additional specialized books, periodicals, and other resources needed to support each teacher education program?

Each is important here, because there may be a limited number of faculty in some programs. Keeping materials current is not often done when this occurs.

4.1.2 What evidence shows that the institution, in maintaining and improving the quality of its library holdings in teacher education, seriously considers the recommendation of:

Seriously considers should mean "purchases what is recommended by."

a. Faculty? b. Appropriate national professional organizations and learned societies? c. A nationally recognized list (or lists) of books and periodicals?

Should the recommendations of classroom teachers, school personnel, and community be considered? How about registered students?

4.1.3 What information indicates that both students and faculty have access to and use the library holdings?

One institution we know keeps the library open twenty-four hours a day, seven days a week. Other "information" might be that rules about access and use of library materials were being made more equitable so that faculty would not be permitted to keep a book for one calendar year while students could use it for only twenty minutes at a time.

Another key word here is *use*. What evidence can be presented to indicate the actual use of materials: number of check-outs?

4.1.4 What is the annual record of library expenditures for the total library

This is necessary since the total setting (general education) is the basis for sound teacher education.

and for teacher education during the last five years?

Should there be a correction factor for inflation, the rising cost of books, etc.?

Summary: Involvement of students and practitioners should be heaviest in this area, because their experience and needs make such participation most sensible. It is curious that such involvement is omitted here.

4.2 *Materials and Instructional Media Center*
Standard: A materials and instructional media center for teacher education is maintained either as a part of the library, or as one or more separate units and is adequate

"Adequate" by what standards?

to support the teacher education programs.

Does one judge the equipment by what an institution can be expected to have or by student use? Should these materials "support" the program or be the major core of the program?
Many of us are starting to believe that direct experiences are less useful than simulated ones. This position is supported by change advocates, who do not want students to fit in and adapt to existing forms of schooling. Another basic issue here is whether it is an all-university facility or a teacher education facility. The standard obviously does not require a separate facility. This is a serious mistake; teacher education has special needs that require distinct university commitments to capital outlay.

4.2.1 What information shows that the center contains materials and equipment that: a. Are utilized

Instead of "are" it might be better to state this as "Could be used . . . ." This simple change might take the emphasis off what is now being done in schools and place a value on

at different grade levels in elementary and secondary schools?

change; that is, what might be done in future.

Instead of "at different grade levels," which is an artificial form of organization, it might be more change oriented if stated as "with children of various ages . . . ."

b. Are utilized for teaching and learning in the teacher education curricula offered by the institution?

c. Are representative of the teaching specialties offered by the institution?

This is an open statement, because *specialties* can be defined by age of youngster taught, by subject taught, or by need (e.g., mentally retarded).

d. Reflect recent developments in the teaching of various subject fields?

In contrast to the preceding statement, this is closed. It assumes only subject matter as a criterion for specialization.

e. Illustrate the wide array of available instructional media (such as films, filmstrips, realia, audiovideo tapes, transparencies, teaching machines, and closed circuit T.V.)?

This is a good beginning attempt to raise institutional sights. It is to be hoped that "illustrate" will become "include."

4.2.2 What evidence shows that the institution, in maintaining and improving the quality of the center, seriously considers the recommendations of: a. Faculty and staff members? b. Appropriate national professional organizations?

How about students? Practitioners? Private technology? The developments in and out of professional education also need to be considered.

4.2.3 What information shows that the center is directed by personnel who are knowledgeable about instructional media and materials?

This is laudable: it is the first place where the standards have asked for such a competency check. Would a vita, a personal interview, personal references, etc., be "evidence?" This seems to indicate that more than the usual (i.e., written professional credentials) are required. While this is desirable, it is not consistent, because the same standard can be raised throughout. Why do we need this extra competency check on the individual who runs the media center when there is no such check on the admissions officer, the certification officer, etc.?

4.2.4 What information shows that the center is available to and used by a. Students? b. Teacher education faculty members?

Practitioners? Other faculty? Community?

Summary: This is one of the most neglected areas of teacher education. Students generally graduate without the ability to use instructional materials and technology and, even worse, without even realizing they are handicapped. The response that "Schools they will serve in don't have any equipment," does not mitigate the need to teach the latest technological advances in their teacher education programs and to instruct them in the means for devising their own instructional materials. Other frequently used explanations for neglecting this area include lack of funding, lack of faculty preparation and experience, faculty prejudice against technology, the tradition of emphasizing direct experience to the exclusion of almost everything else, and the pressures of vocal students who use media for entertainment rather than for instructional purposes.

These standards are a good stride in the right direction. Their only major weaknesses are the unclear administrative control (which should be vested in the School of Education) and the lack of practitioner involvement (inservice education is a major responsibility for the school of education).

4.3 *Physical Facilities and Other Resources*
Standard: The institution provides physical facilities and other resources essential to the instructional and research activities of each basic program.

This standard relies on teacher education programs really being unable to specify their objectives. If we examine the NCATE explanation of this standard we find the following: "Assuming that the other aspects of an institution's teacher education programs are acceptable, the adequacy of the physical facilities, equipment and special resources is judged in terms of the operational requirements of the basic programs offered. It is assumed that such facilities and resources are readily accessible so that faculty and students may effectively pursue instructional objectives."[7] Suppose, however, that an institution were to say, "We believe teaching is good lecturing on the traditional liberal arts. Therefore, we prepare our teachers to orate to large groups in an intelligent, logical, interesting manner." In such a case, no physical facilities and equipment would be necessary. While NCATE is saying that they evaluate on the institution's goals, therefore, we can now see that NCATE knows very well that no institution will make a clear, highly specific statement on its objectives and thereby avoid this standard.

4.3.1 What facts

Here "evidence" has been hardened to "facts" because of the measurable nature of factors like space.

indicate that for each basic teacher education program offered, faculty and students have office space, instructional space, and other space necessary to carry out their responsibilities?

Is the assumption made that students need office space? What does *other space* mean?

4.3.2 What information indicates that the institution draws on the full range

Full range is merely jargon for "lots."

of its resources to support its basic programs?

Are public, private, and community schools "its resources"?

4.3.3 What information indicates that the institution has given serious consideration

"Serious consideration" means an honest hearing. How can this be assessed? It would require knowing whether decisions are really open to those involved in meetings, or the meetings are merely the trappings of participation.

to the recommendations of faculty members

Should practitioners and/or students be involved?

for improving physical facilities and other supporting resources?

Supporting resources is a vague term that might include parking spaces. College supervisors, cooperating teachers, students, and community people, often do not come to university committee meetings because they have no convenient parking.

Summary: This is a more critical standard than it might seem to the inexperienced eye. Space represents university money and commitment; it reflects status and emotional needs. In operation, space requirements are unimportant, provided the faculty feels there are sufficient arrangements. If there are insufficient provisions, there is a real problem. Meeting areas, private conference areas, large group meeting facilities, flexible areas, production areas, and dining and coffee sites, will actually control and limit the content and quality of the program. Given some minimal conditions, the real issue is to get teacher educators to use their space in ways that connect what we do about flexibility with what we advocate. Teaching about "open education" in lecture halls is one example of the present gap between what we say and what we do.

5. Evaluation, Program Review and Planning

5.1 *Evaluation of Graduates*
Standard: The institution conducts a well-defined plan for evaluating the teachers it prepares.

"Maintenance of acceptable teacher education programs demands a continuous process of evaluation of the graduates of existing programs, modification of existing programs, and long-range planning. It is assumed that faculty and administrators in teacher education evaluate the result of their programs and relate the findings of this evaluation to program development. This requires the continuous review of the institution's objectives for its teacher education programs. It is also assumed that, in its plans for total institutional development, the institution projects plans for the long-range development of teacher education.

Criteria for admission and retention provide some assurance that students of promise and ability enter and continue in teacher education programs. Such criteria do not ensure that students of promise and ability will complete the programs, nor that they will enter the teaching profession, nor that they will perform satisfactorily after becoming teachers. The ultimate criterion for judging a teacher education program is whether it produces competent graduates who enter the profession and perform effectively. An institution committed to the preparation of teachers engages in systematic efforts to evaluate the quality of its graduates and those persons recommended for professional certification. The institution evaluates the teachers it produces at two critical points: when they complete their programs of study, and after they enter the teaching profession.

It is recognized that the means now available for making such evaluations are not fully adequate. Nevertheless, the standard assumes that an institution evaluates the teachers it prepares with the best means now available, and that it attempts to develop improved means for making such evaluations. As progress is made toward more adequate evaluation procedures, this standard will become increasingly important.

Any effort to assess the quality of graduates requires that evaluations be made in relation to the objectives sought. Therefore, institutions use the stated objectives of their education programs as a basis for evaluating the teachers they prepare."[8]

5.1.1 What information shows that the stated objectives

for the teacher education programs are used as a basis for evaluating the teachers prepared by the institution?

Few institutions have stated objectives for each program.

One of our problems is that institutional program statements are too general to serve an evaluative function. How do we use a general statement such as, "Prepare teachers who can help youngsters survive in a world of change, chance, and choice," as a basis for assessing graduates? How might the graduates' knowledge, skills, emotions, or actual acts of teaching support or refute the institution's goal? The problem is one of connecting two disparate levels of generalization.

5.1.2 What means are used to collect data about teachers prepared in the various programs (graduates and persons recommended for certification): a. At the point when programs of study are completed?

Written tests, self-evaluation and assessments by simulation are examples of such means.

b. After they enter the teaching profession?

The preceding means, plus expert observation, supervisory records, pupils' reactions and achievement, parents' opinions, and peer evaluation are examples of these. Obviously, the different means vary in cost, personnel and time required, and feasibility in reaching the population of practitioners to be followed up.

5.1.3 What information shows that the institution is keeping abreast of new developments in the

Assuming there are new developments in this field (and there are precious few), which teacher education

evaluation of teacher education graduates

faculty can reasonably be expected to make this their area of expertise? Clearly, there are few such specialists. When outside studies are supported, lay people (e.g., Conant and Silberman) are used as experts.

At the other extreme, anyone who has any contact with a program is considered "a teacher educator." What are the credentials of a bona fide expert? Perhaps an expert is one who can answer this standard with a thorough knowledge of the literature and current practices.

and is engaged in efforts to improve its plan for making such evaluations?

A committee is one, fairly low-level vehicle. Giving a specific staff member the direct responsibility is another. Developing a systematic plan is an important first step.

5.1.4 What percent of the teachers prepared by the institution during the last two years actually entered the teaching profession?

This standard was developed during a period of teacher shortage. The clear indication is that a university program could be assessed not only on its relevancy and ability to prepare teachers for the real world, but also on its ability to instill in students the confidence to meet the challenge. When there is a shortage of jobs, this standard loses its usefulness.

5.1.5 What characteristics of teachers prepared by the institution have been revealed through evaluation of graduates?

This standard goes beyond asking for a plan or means of assessment and pushes the institution to reach some generalizations about the nature of its graduates. In a sense it fosters a research attitude without pinning down the form any study should take.

Summary: This standard is a critically different and significant advance over the standard used in the early 1960s. It is pushing toward accountability in teacher education and asking that universities expend resources, from their regular budgets and on a continuing basis, in order to evaluate themselves. This will sound like common sense to the uninitiated. To the experienced denizen of academe it is a radical departure to move from selling college credits to large numbers of students to becoming responsible for what those people do subsequently and to pay for this self-developed system of accountability!

There are other basic assumptions: faculty have the ability to evaluate practitioners and to relate the evaluations to their previous preparation; schools will permit the kinds of evaluation necessary; teachers (i.e., the graduates) will permit this kind of evaluation; the teachers associations and unions will permit this kind of evaluation; and there will be a sufficient number of representative graduates who gain employment to make this form of evaluation valid.

If the above were insufficient, there is also a fundamental assumption that makes them seem minor: that schools of education *should* prepare teachers who will succeed in the present school systems rather than people who will seek to innovate, change, sabotage, or establish competing forms of alternative schools. The essence of this evaluation standard is that schools of education will generally support the present system of public education and seek to improve it from within. It is an understandable position, since no publicly supported school of education would dare to do otherwise. The evaluation problem arises with individual faculty who do not support the institutional purposes and who have an academic (freedom) right to prepare students to change schools from without or through nonparticipation. How might an NCATE standard possibly get at this disparity between individual faculty and student values and the more conservative institutional position of the school of education?

5.2 *Use of Evaluation Results to Improve Basic Programs*
Standard: The institution uses the evaluation results in the study,

"We formed a committee . . ." should not be good enough.

development,

"We proposed a course change . . ." should not be good enough.

and improvement of its teacher education programs.

"We approved the course change . . ." should not be good enough.

5.2.1 What strengths and weaknesses in the teacher education programs are revealed as a result of evaluating teachers prepared by the institution?

Drawing potentially damaging implications such as these will not be done by those faculty directly responsible for offering the program. Defensiveness and the need to shape one's job in future are natural and predictable needs. Such needs, however, should not be permitted to interfere with real analysis. Outside consultants are a definite necessity.

5.2.2 What does the institution do to ensure that the results obtained from evaluating the teachers it prepares are translated into appropriate program modifications?

This is a noble hope; its vagueness makes it easily answerable and not very thought-provoking. Any new policy or diddling modification can be presented as evidence of responsiveness. The long-term answer here should be a process: some organizational vehicle that would become a self-policing agency with power to approve and disapprove programs. Neither NCATE nor the state departments can serve this function. Perhaps if every certification program were automatically terminated after three years, there would be a real need to create a university agency with outside evaluators to ensure that this standard was met.

Summary: Unless evaluative data are used to change and improve programs there is clearly no need to evaluate. Given valid feedback, the issue is what program components should be changed? The forces arrayed to resist change are all those who have been and will be most directly involved, because they may very well value what they are doing. How to create a knowledgeable, yet more objective, vehicle within the university is the challenge of implementing this standard.

5.3 *Long-Range Planning*
Standard: The institution has plans for the long-range development of teacher education; these plans are part of a design for total institutional development.

It would really be terrific if this standard had the following exclusion: "Architectural designs for new schools of education are not to be included."

5.3.1 What evidence indicates that the institution has, or is engaged in, studies and/or research to improve its teacher education programs?

The committees started to answer 5.1 above might be a good example here.

5.3.2 What information shows that the faculty for teacher education participates in the formulation of the institution's long-range plans for teacher education?

This seemed like a sound standard until we observed the dean of a leading institution declare the planning committee "competely open! Anyone who wants to come to this committee [128 faculty, 4,000 students] is welcome!" Under the ruse of openness and democracy any person knowledgeable in group dynamics can turn involvement into a force for inaction. Planning is thus turned into a sounding board or ego trip for anyone who feels the urge. This standard would be better if it specified the membership of planning committees, e.g., "duly elected representatives of the faculty and six or fewer students."

5.3.3 What is the institution's plan for future development of basic teacher education programs and what rationale supports significant changes that are proposed?

This plan should include a process for transmitting it to agencies throughout and outside the university. Within a state system the plan should be coordinated with other branches of the university; outside the system it should involve public and alternative schools, industry, state agencies, teachers' groups, parents, and students.

Summary: Long-range planning cannot be confined to the traditional arena of teacher education. We react to problems such as declining job market and state budget and national crises; we have not been an initiating force for social or even university-wide change. This standard addresses itself to the planning function to promote an orderly, conceived-in-advance, justifiable plan for the future.

This effort requires broad involvement within and outside the university. Granted that plans will be changed in response to unforeseen conditions, the effort is nevertheless worthwhile, since the process of setting directions requires a rationale based on philosophical purposes and research evidence rather than on the unreflective response to pressure that has and does characterize teacher education developments.

GRADUATE AND ADVANCED PROGRAMS

G1. Curricula for Advanced Programs

G1.1 *Design of Curricula*

Standard: Curricula for advanced programs are based on objectives reflecting the institution's conception of the professional roles for which the preparation programs are designed.

It is not uncommon to find advanced programs that do not have a professional role in mind. This is true because of the subject matter (e.g., a masters degree in social and philosophical foundations) or because there may be a conscious effort to prepare for roles that do not yet and may never exist (e.g., a doctorate in urban education). It is important to remind ourselves that NCATE is concerned primarily with programs that lead to some form of certification and that graduate programs frequently go beyond, or at least are not precisely congruent with, all forms of certification.

G1.1.1 For what professional school positions does each advanced program prepare personnel (school superintendent, principal, supervisor, specialist, teacher, and/or other positions)?

And/or other permits the preparation of people for new kinds of jobs, assuming that the particular state department will certify them in the new role.

G1.1.2 What evidence indicates that specific objectives for the curriculum of each advanced program have been defined

We must stop assuming that experts (i.e., college people) know and agree on the purposes of programs for preparing guidance counselors, administrators, school psychologists, etc.

This standard is a prod to get on with the job of specifying both purposes and rationale for our training programs.

and that these objectives reflect the institution's analysis

This is a serious problem. The specialists in various departments maintain control of programs for specialists. For example, should the program for preparing psychometrists reflect the school of education's view (i.e., "institution's analysis") of what psychometrists should do, or should it implement goals set by the experts in psychometry? Traditionally, the latter has been the approach. If this is not a mistake, this standard is seeking a radical reform.

of the professional school position for which the candidate is being prepared?

G1.2 *Content of Curricula*
Standard: The curriculum of each advanced program includes a. content for the specialty, b. humanistic and behavioral studies, c. theory relevant to the specialty with direct and simulated experiences in professional practice, all appropriate to the roles for which candidates are being prepared and all differentiated by degree or certificate level.

G1.2.1 What information shows that the curriculum for each advanced program includes: a. Appropriate content for the specialty?

This is relatively easy, since it is all that many departments offer.

b. Humanistic and behavioral studies?

If such study were "required" (and it is not) outside the school of education, it would not be feasible, because most graduate departments require prerequisites for graduate study that large numbers of graduate students in education do not have. In undergraduate and preservice programs it is relatively easy to get the psychology department, or whatever, to offer a special or new course for teachers. This is not so readily accomplished on the graduate level. This standard will most frequently be answered, therefore, by referring to educational psychologists, sociologists, historians, and philosophers within the school of education who offer such course work.

c. Theory relevant to the specialty?

For the reason stated above, this program component is also accomplished most frequently by having experts within the school of education. Guidance, school psychology, reading, etc., all tend to view learning theory as this "theory." Administrators and supervisors study principles of organization, leadership, and change as their "theory," and those in exceptional education tend to get physiology.

G1.2.2 What information shows that the curriculum of each advanced program includes direct

This is one of the most difficult standards for the graduate programs to meet. Graduate students are often employed full-time and attend school in the evenings and summers. They are not eager or financially able to take off for direct fieldwork, practicum, and laboratory experiences. In addition, graduate faculty regard themselves as scholars and professors, not as supervisors of anyone's fieldwork.

and simulated experiences

Stop-action films, with questions, and videotapes are examples. It is significant to note, however, that the wording is *direct* and *simulated experiences*. If NCATE is serious and this is not a poor choice of conjunctions, it means that graduate professors will have to get off their duffs and into the field. If past performance is any predictor, we will get teaching assistants to do this supervision.

professional in practice which relate significantly to the school position for which the preparation program is designed?

This means that large graduate schools with many people preparing to be administrators, supervisors, guidance people, etc., are not meeting the standard unless they get out of the traditional course-work syndrome and into organized, supervised fieldwork.

G1.2.3 How are the studies and experiences in professional practice that are prescribed for the curriculum of each advanced program differentiated by degree or certificate level?

This is merely rubbing salt in the wound. In the general absence of direct experiences and fieldwork, it becomes academic to stress their sequence and organization.

G1.2.4 What evidence indicates that candidates for degrees or certificates in each advanced program during the last two years

This time dimension is wise; it helps us get some perspective on how the institution is developing or changing at all.

have completed the studies and practice experiences identified in the standard?

This may sound like an unimportant point to the uninitiated. Actually, there is such loose control in the administration of many masters level programs that it is a difficult standard to meet. The assumption is that knowing how many and who completes the program will indicate whether the program is viewed as a totality rather than a lot of discrete courses. If student progress is known to the faculty, then there are staff being held responsible for a program beyond "their" courses. This may not be a bad assumption.

G1.3 *Research in Advanced Curricula*
Standard: Each advanced curriculum includes the study of research methods and findings;

And findings is important; it means not only the results of research but also the practice required to become an intelligent consumer.

each doctoral curriculum includes the designing and conducting of research.

This is difficult or easy depending on the particular institution's definition of *research*. In some places there is a hard-nosed approach, in others there are opportunities for exploratory, historical, and case studies as well.

G1.3.1 What provisions are made for including the research com-

A course requirement is the usual way; a required study or thesis is

ponent in the curriculum of each advanced program?

another. Proficiency examinations at the end of independent study are frequently talked about but seldom implemented.

G1.3.2 What information shows that the requirements for research

This probably means "to complete the research requirement" and does not refer to the prerequisites needed to take some courses.

are relevant to the professional role for which the student is preparing?

While this is relatively easy in doctoral programs, it is difficult in masters and specialists' programs, which require fundamental concepts and special field study of the various functions. It is difficult for experts with much experience to do research that is genuinely useful and relevant to a particular professional role; what is the likelihood that a masters student will do so? The suggestion in this standard is intended to strike a realistic balance; for example, if X is going to be a reading specialist, what research skills will enable him to continue to learn on the job?

G1.3.3 What data

Information, which was used in the standards for basic programs, has been changed to *data*. Is this simply a choice of words, or do they really mean a more rigorous form of evidence?

show that the requirements for research are met in each student's program of study?

Grades in courses that have blurbs similar to the standard will be the usual answers here. *Each student* means that sample programs may actually be checked.

G1.4 *Individualization of Programs of Study*
Standard: Each advanced standard provides for the individualization of students' programs of study.

The common practice is to permit students various electives. Such choices are then used synonomously with the term *individualization*. Genuine individualization also occurs within courses. One means for accomplishing this is to differentiate assignments.

Institutions are handicapped in this area. Syllabi are not asked of graduate faculty, and close supervision of their texts, assignments, or examinations is not likely. After a program has been initiated there is little opportunity to check on how it is actually offered without eliciting cries of "academic freedom." The university tradition is that undergraduate courses can be supervised but graduate work is a personal relationship with an outstanding scholar. The stronger this tradition is in a particular institution, the more difficult it will be to deal with programmatic evaluation on the graduate level.

G1.4.1 What data are used to ascertain the professional needs and interests of each candidate at the time of admission

Initial requirements should be tailored to previous education and work experience. Should an individual who has served as an assistant principal, guidance counselor, or whatever, have precisely the same requirements as a beginner? Should an individual with an advanced degree in sociology or some other related field be required to take the same course work?

and subsequently as necessary?

This may appear to be a tacked-on phrase. Actually, in many (most?) institutions individual students' programs are not assessed for their relevance to students' needs and changed accordingly. The usual reasons for change are that a required course is not offered in the right semester or at a convenient hour.

G1.4.2 What evidence shows that the programs of study have been planned to meet individual professional needs and interests?

The use of previous transcripts in planning students' programs is the usual way. The real issue is the conflict between what experts (faculty) believe the student should learn in order to become a particular kind of practitioner and what the student believes is necessary. Unfortunately, many of our students are full-time teachers seeking a new role, and they lapse into a search for convenience. The faculty opts for teaching what it specializes in. As a result, both groups sometimes neglect genuine needs and interests.

Direct experiences for the aspiring

supervisor, school psychologist, etc., are good examples of learning experiences that meet neither student interests (since they are working full-time) nor faculty proclivities (since the university rewards writing rather than supervision).

G1.5 *Use of Guidelines Developed by National Learned Societies and Professional Associations*
Standard: In planning and developing curricula for its advanced programs, the institution gives due consideration to guidelines developed by national learned societies for the preparation of teachers and other professional school personnel.

Here the list of associations used in the undergraduate (basic) section is usually hauled out and repeated. The problem at this point is that learned societies and professional associations do not usually think of professional roles involving state certification.

G1.5.1 What guidelines has the institution considered in developing the curricula of its various advanced programs?

G1.5.2 What information shows that the guidelines in 1.5.1 have been critically examined

That anybody has read them.

in relation to the planning and development of the advanced programs offered by the institution?

That those who may have read the guidelines were involved in making any decisions that demonstrate their implementation.

G1.6 *Quality Controls*
G1.6.1 *Graduate Credit*
Standard: Institutional policies preclude the granting of graduate credit for study which is remedial or which is designed to remove deficiencies in meeting requirements for admission to advanced programs.

While most institutions have this policy, many faculty circumvent it on a case-by-case basis. (This situation is recognized in 1.6.1b below.)

G1.6.1a What regulations govern the granting of graduate credit in the advanced programs?

Common responses here will deal with policies related to faculty quality, total hours of instructional class time, how much time has elapsed since student's completion of course, transfers from other graduate schools, availability of library, what constitutes a full load, etc.

G1.6.1b What evidence shows that the institution's regulations for granting graduate credit are enforced?

"Evidence" here might be the number or percent of students not admitted to graduate school and denied graduate credit for particular experiences. An examination of the department chairman and dean's files would reveal criteria for these rejections.

G1.6.2 *Graduate Level Courses*
Standard: At least one-half of the requirements of curricula leading to a master's degree and to a sixth-year certificate or degree are met by courses, seminars, and other learning experiences offered only to graduate students; at least two-thirds of the requirements of curricula leading to the doctorate are met by courses, seminars, and other learning experiences offered only to graduate students.

The assumptions of this standard are that (1) students learn from each other, (2) there is a body of educational knowledge that can be characterized as "elementary" leading to "advanced," (3) classes are not really individualized but do much group work and have many group discussions, and (4) faculty should be different for various levels.

G1.6.2a What is the institution's policy with regard to the proportion of undergraduate work that may be counted toward degrees or the proportion of graduate study that must be included in degree programs at each level (master's, sixth-year, doctoral)?

The preceeding standard gives one-half as a minimum. This is one of the few places where the NCATE standards are this specific.

G1.6.3 *Residence Study*
Standard: Some period of full-time residence study, or provision for comparable experiences, is required for candidates pursuing advanced degrees other than the doctorate; at least one academic year of full-time continuous residence study is required for candidates pursuing the doctorate.

The proximity of on-campus students to the library is not the rationale for residence. Only total immersion will lead to the informal contact with faculty and other students that is the heart of graduate education. Quality courses are a minimum but far from sufficient condition for this real education.

G1.6.3a What are the institution's requirements for full-time residence study for each degree (or certificate) program? What are the precise definitions of "full-time" and "residence?"

This standard would be improved if it asked for the rationale supporting the various time limits that have been established.

G1.6.3b What evidence shows that the residence study requirement was met by those candidates who received the masters degree and the sixth-year certificate or degree during the past two years?

This is a good point. Transcripts might indicate only that a full load was carried. The issues of whether a student was on campus and of the nature of the work he did simultaneously cannot be answered by an examination of transcripts. This standard might require some student interviews.

G1.6.3c What evidence shows that the one-year, full-time residence study requirement was met by each candidate who received the doctorate during the past two years?

What is the rationale for making one academic year the standard? It might be the result of dealing with people who could take only one year's leave or a sabbatical to finance their studies. Perhaps in the future, with no shortage of Ph.D.'s and with advances in knowledge, this will be lengthened to three years. One reason there are now so many ABD's (All But Dissertation) is that these students assumed they could complete their work in close to one full-time year. If programs really required three or four full-time years we ought to change the requirement to meet the de facto situation.

G1.7 *Control of Advanced Programs* Standard: The primary responsibility for initiation, development, and implementation of advanced programs lies with the education faculty.

This is to ensure that schools and departments of education are not merely service operations for other divisions of the university.

G1.7.1 What is the administrative structure for controlling the advanced programs and what is the supporting rationale?

This might be a committee or an administrative officer. It should include both, with some voting students on the committee.

G1.7.2 How are advanced programs initiated?

Recent trends might make a standard, such as "How are programs discontinued?" more appropriate. Why do we never consider the mechanisms of closing down as well as expanding?

What bodies approve changes and new programs?

How would it be possible to answer this in any manner that might be deemed unsatisfactory?

G1.7.3 What activities of the education faculty demonstrate that they have assumed responsibility for the initiation, development, and approval of all advanced programs?

G1.7.4 What information shows that the faculty controls the quality of all courses, seminars, and workshops offered primarily at the conveniences of school personnel in the field (such as at off-campus locations and at "irregular" hours) and counted as credit toward graduate degrees or certificates?

Again, any answer to a question in this form is correct. The usual response would involve a description of rights and responsibilities of the school or department of education.

This is the best single standard for showing the ambivalence of situating professional education in a graduate university. On one hand, quality means on-campus residency, prestigeous senior faculty, and courses limited to advanced students. On the other hand, professional education is supposed to affect real practices in the schools. This means reading out the practitioners who work with children and youth, whether or not they have the scholarly credentials to be admitted or to complete graduate programs. We frequently try to brush over this difference with special credit and special programs. The real choice is often a forced one between genuine graduate work and real efforts to change school practices. It is difficult to have both. All in all, the standard seems to prefer scholarship to more immediate considerations.

Summary: To what extent should graduate programs "fill slots" as opposed to creating new roles? The standards seem to emphasize the former.

To what extent should the liberal studies become transformed into educational psychology, sociology, and history in graduate programs? The standards seem to say this should happen.

To what extent should direct experiences and internships become a major concern of graduate preparation programs? The standards appear to say to a great extent.

Are graduate education and all the quality standards of admission, residency, and research on this level actually compatible with the inservice needs of practitioners? The standards say we had better retain the quality standards in sound graduate education.

All this leads to the issue of whether graduate schools of all professions should become more like each other or mimic the traditions of graduate schools of arts and sciences.

G2. Faculty for Advanced Programs
G2.1 *Preparation of Faculty*
Standard: Faculty members teaching at the master's level in

It is easy to demonstrate competence in lieu of a formal doctorate if one has administered an early childhood

advanced programs hold the doctorate with advanced study in each field of specialization in which they are teaching or have demonstrated competence in such fields; those teaching at the sixth year and doctoral levels hold the doctorate with study in each field of specialization in which they are teaching and conducting research. Faculty members who conduct the advanced programs at all degree levels are engaged in scholarly activity that supports their fields of specialization and have experience which relates directly to their respective fields.

G2.1.1 What evidence shows that each faculty member teaching at the master's level holds the doctorate from a regionally accredited institution or a recognized foreign university with advanced study in each field of specialization in which he teaches, or has demonstrated competence in his field of specialization?

G2.1.2 What evidence shows that each faculty member teaching at the sixth year and/or doctoral level holds the doctorate from a regionally accredited institution or a recognized foreign university with study in each field of specialization in which he teaches or conducts research?

G2.1.3 What information shows that each faculty member who teaches and/or conducts research in the advanced programs has had field experiences during the past five years which support his teaching and research assignments?

center and shown leadership in the training of aides, the development of curriculum, and the involvement of community. How does one demonstrate competence in the specialization of black studies?

Conducting research is a double-edged sword. It may ensure competence, but also may lead to graduates who replicate what their advisors do. A new doctorate, such as one in urban education, must be an interdisciplinary study and offer in-depth study of the change process, but no present faculty could yet have his specialization in this area!

A vita is the usual response to this.

Why is there a need to control the kinds of people who choose to do research?

Field experience is fairly easy to identify in narrow areas such as school psychology or remedial reading, although faculty rarely practice in these roles once they "arrive" in graduate school. Senior faculty in these areas are frequently long absent from direct work and substitute other activities (e.g., consulting) as evidence that they have kept in touch. The five-year stipulation is meaningless for another reason; more and more experts are new doctorates with no experience in administration who have specialized in organizational science on a theoretical level. The same lack of experience is true of many physiologists in exceptional education, clinicians in guidance, and curriculum people who educate for the role of curriculum director.

On the other hand, many faculty would be most willing to take every fifth year in some real role but have no opportunity. How many districts will permit a professor to update himself as director of research, special education, principal, or whatever? The standard assumes a possibility for fieldwork that is not present without outside funding or sabbatical and a great spirit of cooperation by public schools.

G2.1.4 What data show that each faculty member who teaches in the advanced programs has been engaged during the past two years in writing, research, and/or consultation, and that these activities support his teaching assignment?

Vitas and load reports are the usual responses here. This approach should be replaced by some assessment of the quality of the research, writing, and consultation. Itemizing what faculty do should give way to evaluating their production. Also, *support* is a poor word; who decides what "supports?"

G2.2 *Composition of Faculty for Doctoral Degree Programs*
Standard: The faculty for each advanced program leading to the doctorate includes at least one full-time person who holds the doctorate with specialization in the field in which the degree is offered, and at least three persons who hold the doctorate in fields which directly support each program.

This is a critical standard; the numbers are forced out of NCATE because of the need to prevent every little college department from getting into the doctorate business.

G2.2.1 What evidence shows that there is at least one full-time person who holds the doctorate with appropriate specialization for each advanced program in which the doctor's degree is offered?

G2.2.2 What data confirm that there are at least three specialists who hold doctorates in fields which directly support each degree program offered?

There is a need for doctoral faculty to serve as a community of scholars who are themselves learning; this is one of the reasons for requiring some number to collaborate. A valuable side effect of this standard is that university commitment is best measured by expenditures. If the university is not willing to support full faculty positions, how much institutional support can there be for assistantships, scholarships, small seminars, and the other costly accoutrements that are really required for a sound doctoral program?

G2.3 *Conditions for Faculty Service* Standard: The institution provides conditions essential to the effective performance by the faculty in the advanced programs.

"The institution provides time and some financial support to enable faculty members to engage in research. ... To maintain and to improve the quality of its faculty, the institution has a plan for faculty development which provides such opportunities as inservice education, sabbatical leave, travel support, summer leaves, intra- and inter-institutional visitation, and fellowships. ... provision is made for supporting services (such as those provided by instructional media technicians, instructional assistants, research assistants, project assistants, secretaries and clerks) that permit faculty members to fulfill their instructional, research and other responsibilities."[9]

G2.3.1 What is the plan for taking into account all professional duties and activities of the faculty in determining load?

The only real answer here is whether the system for reporting this load is connected with the merit and promotion system. When the rhetoric has subsided, genuine recognition of faculty service is given by very specific processes: promotion, salary, load credit, or providing the faculty member power to determine his assignment.

G2.3.2 What has been the total load assigned to each faculty member in the advanced program over all terms during the last two years and what are the duties (such as teaching courses, advising students, supervising experiences in professional practice, supervising or chairing dissertations, research, committee assignments, professional development, and others) that make up each load?

This standard is merely asking for a report, which is useful because it requires a system of accounting. Few institutions presently have carefully conceived ways of accounting for all these activities in load, and this rehearsal of all the activities faculty commonly engage in is a helpful drill.

G2.3.3 What is the institution's policy regarding the provision of time for faculty to engage in research, and what evidence shows that this policy is being implemented?

G2.3.4 What evidence indicates that the institution provides financial support to encourage research activities by faculty in the advanced programs?

This is a very important dimension. The usual reply would be that if a particular faculty member got a grant he would be released. The real answer would require built-in load time paid for by the institution as part of the regular assignment. This is a vitally important standard. It will pressure faculty to continue to do research or to stop advising doctoral students, and it will pressure the institution to support research activities, whether or not those activities are federally funded. This will be an even more important standard in future since regular budgets will be shrinking.

G2.3.5 What is the institution's plan for the continuous professional development of faculty in the advanced programs and what evidence shows that it is operative?

This kind of standard can be useful even without a minimum standard, because few places have a carefully conceived plan for faculty growth.

G2.3.6 What is the plan for allocating supporting services to faculty in the advanced programs and what evidence shows that such services are provided?

Again, this will be more important in the coming age of more careful fiscal controls.

G2.4 *Part-Time Faculty*
Standard: Part-time faculty meet the requirements for appointment to the full-time faculty and are employed only when they can make special contributions to advanced programs.

There should be an academic reason (not shortage of funds) for using part-time, "specialized" instruction. The local superintendent who comes for a weekly class cannot really be justified as this kind of need.

G2.4.1 What proportion of each advanced program is assigned to part-time faculty?

This is an old enough problem for the standard to do more than push thinking; there should be a stated minimum.

G2.4.2 What evidence shows that each part-time faculty member meets the requirements for appointment to the full-time graduate faculty?

Vitas again. The issue, of course, is assessing the quality of the service, writing and research that is itemized.

G2.4.3 What reasons support the utilization of each part-time faculty member in the advanced programs?

Asking for a rationale here should get the faculty to reflect on what is regarded as an absolutely essential specialization.

Summary: Advanced study, particularly on the doctoral level, is expensive. The university is forced not only to make an extensive commitment, but also to do so at the expense of other programs, because it can no longer expand everything simultaneously.

Undoubtedly, many institutions have overextended themselves into advanced programs. This standard should help well-established institutions limit and improve their programs and, at the same time, encourage the phasing out of marginal programs. The changing job market and financial prospects should help programs move toward concerns with higher quality.

The biggest weaknesses in the content of these standards are: (1) no clear indication of how to use resources other than traditional faculty; and (2) no guidelines for developing graduates in new forms of specializations, with new skills, for new roles. Quality is too closely linked to what senior faculty already know; what is gained in traditional forms of scholarship is lost in preparing with old skills for an unknown but changing future.

G3. Students in Advanced Programs

G3.1 *Admission to Advanced Programs*

Standard: The institution applies specific criteria for admission to each advanced program at each level; these criteria require the use of both objective and subjective data.

What weight is given to objective data (e.g., the candidate is fifty-three years old, scored xxx on the GRE, etc.) versus subjective data (e.g., personal references, a faculty interview, etc.)? Every institution collects both kinds of data, but which are really used to make the determination?

G3.1.1 What are the admission requirements for each advanced program and at each level (master's, sixth-year, doctoral)?

This could be improved by stating it differently. For example, "What would prevent the admission of a student with a 3.5 gpa and GRE's in the 600s?" (Stated conversely, "What criteria could counterbalance the record of a student with low gpa and GRE's and get him into the program?") This one question will cut through the rhetoric and indicate whether the institution has any operative criteria beyond the traditional ones.

G3.1.2 What evidence indicates that the institution's requirements for admission to advanced programs are being met?

Another way to get at this would be "In what percent of the cases are the standards met? What rationale and criteria are used for exceptions?"

G3.1.3 What objective data, including test results with national norms, are used for admitting students to advanced programs?

Better questions would be "What level is set as acceptable? What is the rationale for this?"

G3.1.4 What characteristics of the students admitted to advanced programs are revealed by the data obtained through applying objective and subjective criteria?

Excellent. This requires systematic self-study over a period of time.

G3.2 *Retention of Students*
Standard: The institution applies specific criteria for retention of candidates in advanced programs who possess academic competencies and personal characteristics appropriate to the requirements of the professional roles for which they are being prepared.

"Because the failing grade in graduate courses is rarely given, 'satisfactory progress' frequently has to be judged by subjective criteria. However, subjective judgments are inadequate unless the institution first has ways of formally collecting and evaluating these judgments, and then of translating them into a decision on the student's status."[10]

G3.2.1 What is the plan and its supporting rationale for ensuring that only qualified candidates are permitted to continue in each advanced program and at each program level (master's, sixth-year, doctoral)?

Asking for a plan when we know none probably exists is an excellent means for spurring an institution to self-analysis.

G3.2.2 How many students have been permitted to continue in each advanced program during the past two years and for what reasons?

This is a shift in emphasis from student to institutional responsibility. Most frequently students screen themselves out, and institutions help *them* to do it.

Under what circumstances, if any, may such students reenter the advanced programs?

This is usually answered by a university procedure, (e.g., an appeals committee) rather than a set of criteria. This standard is helpful in indicating that there should be a plan for the many students who disappear and reappear.

G3.2.3 What is the average and the range for the length of time required which students took to complete master's programs during the past two years? Sixth-year programs? Doctoral programs?

Why is this important information?

G3.3 *Planning and Supervision of Students' Programs of Study*
Standard: The program for each student in the advanced program is jointly planned by the student and a member of the faculty;

This is to provide individualized attention to each program. It assumes both student and faculty voluntarily select each other; otherwise "caring" is not built into a one-to-one relationship.

the program of study for each doctoral candidate is approved by a faculty committee;

This is to guard against the tyranny of one professor and to represent a collective, broad scholarship.

the sponsorship of each thesis, dissertation, or field study is the responsibility of a member of the faculty with specialization in the area of the thesis, dissertation, or field study.

This is to locate responsibility. Ultimately, the student is or is not supported by his advisor.

G3.3.1 What provisions ensure that each graduate student's program of study is jointly planned by the student and an official faculty advisor?

Signatures on planned programs are important because of faculty who die, change jobs, or simply change their minds.

G3.3.2 What evidence indicates that each doctoral candidate's program of study is approved by a faculty committee?

Signatures. It would be helpful if these committees also included some doctoral students. Suppose the standard said "a committee chosen by student and advisor?" It is too open in its present form.

G3.3.3 What evidence shows that the sponsorship of each thesis, dissertation, or field study, (master's, sixth-year, doctoral) is assigned to a qualified member of the faculty?

Who would make this assignment? The assumption must be that all faculty who are approved to have advisees on a particular level of study would not be so unprofessional as to undertake to support a thesis in an area in which they are weak. This standard highlights the dilemma of trying to safeguard with committees a system that ultimately depends so heavily (and wisely?) on the individual advisor.

G3.4 *Student Participation in Program Evaluation and Development*
Standard: The institution has representative student participation in the evaluation and development of its advanced programs.

This is another reason why residence is so important to doctoral and all graduate study; "Ask not what the institution can do for you, but what you can do for the institution."

G3.4.1 What evidence shows that graduate students participate in the evaluation and development of advanced programs?

Somehow the concept of student representation must be dealt with more directly. Do students vote? If not, why not? If yes, then how is the minority voice heard?

G3.4.2 What are the major concerns which students have expressed during the last two years and in what ways have these concerns influenced the development of advanced programs?

Excellent. This would systematize both student whining and faculty defensiveness; hopefully, as it gets into writing to answer the standard, both groups will become more constructive.

Summary: Who gets in? Who gets out? What criteria determine these processes? The standards of admission and advisement will require a rethinking of present policies and assumptions. The standards on retention of students and student involvement will require a whole new set of responses.

There should be something in this section that specifically relates to the number of advanced students an advisor may take on. Doctoral advisors might be limited to a given number of students working on their dissertations and in residency in any given year. If some number is not set, all the standards on individualization, quality of scholarship, etc., are rhetoric. If fifteen to eighteen undergraduate student teachers are a full load in many institutions, then a similar number seems to be a minimal level at which to set a full load for advanced graduate students. The number of classes a faculty member taught could be halved or divided into thirds or quarters.

G4. Resources and Facilities for Advanced Programs
G4.1 *Library*
Standard: The library provides resources that are adequate to support instruction, independent study, and research required for each advanced program.

It would be interesting to learn how many institutions really assess the quality of their own libraries before launching an advanced program.

G4.1.1 What evidence indicates that the library collection includes

Duplicates of current materials is one form of evidence.

standard and contemporary holdings (books, microfilms, microfiche copies, periodicals) to support each advanced program?

G4.1.2 What information shows that the institution is maintaining and improving the quality of its library holdings, gives serious consideration to the recommendations of:
a. Faculty members?
b. Appropriate national professional organizations and learned societies?
c. A nationally recognized list (or lists) of books and periodicals?

G4.1.3 What information indicates that students in advanced programs have access to, and use, the library holdings?

G4.1.4 What is the annual record of expenditures for the total library and for the advanced programs during the past five years?

Summary: These standards are essentially the same as those in the basic section; the major difference is that the basic program standards emphasized media, while these emphasize size. "The operation of advanced programs require library resources substantially larger than those required for basic programs."[11]

G4.2 *Physical Facilities and Other Resources*
Standard: The institution provides physical facilities and other resources essential to the instructional and research activities of each advanced program.

G4.2.1 What information confirms that faculty and students have instructional, research, and office space necessary to carry out their responsibilities?

It would not be unreasonable to state that "advanced students require mail boxes, telephones, and desk space."

G4.2.2 What evidence shows that specialized equipment (such as

Many advanced students in many places would be happy with access to

open and closed television, computers) and laboratories

typewriters, Ditto machines and Xerox copiers. This is a good, but an ideal standard.

necessary to support each advanced program are available and that they are used by faculty and students?

Faculty define *use* as giving students assignments that require the "use" of facilities.

G4.2.3 What information shows that the institution has given serious consideration to the recommendations of faculty members for improving physical facilities and other supporting resources?

Summary: These standards are among those that can and should be made more specific. Certainly there are relationships between the size and diversity of an institution and the space required. The number of faculty, students, and programs could all be weighted, and some specific guidelines in terms of equipment, office space, etc., might be indicated. The simple truth is that graduate study is not an "open school" or a camping situation, and we have very clear ideas of needs in this area. If we do not, how have we been justifying all the schools of education that have been built?

G5. Evaluation, Program Review, and Planning

G5.1 *Evaluation of Graduates*
Standard: The institution conducts a well-defined plan for evaluating the teachers and other professional school personnel it prepares on the graduate level.

"The institution evaluates its graduates at two critical points: when they complete their programs of study, and after they enter the professional roles for which they have prepared. It is recognized that the means now available for making such evaluations are not fully adequate. Nevertheless, the standard assumes that an institution evaluates the school personnel it prepares with the best means now available, and that it attempts to develop improved means for making such evaluations."[12]

G5.1.1 What information shows that the stated objectives for each advanced program are used as a basis for evaluating the graduates of its respective programs?

As we have already seen, program goals are usually much broader than usable evaluation criteria.

G5.1.2 What means are used to collect data about teachers and other professional personnel pre-

This will require a form of behavioral objective, whether institutions like it or not.

pared in the advanced programs:
a. At the point of program completion?

b. After they enter the professional roles for which they are prepared?

This will require trying to find out where graduates go. Right now only the alumni office does this.

G5.1.3 What information shows that the institution is keeping abreast of new developments in the evaluation of graduates and is engaged in efforts to improve its plan for making such evaluations?

An hour with the ERIC and a half-hour with the *Dissertation Abstracts* is all that is required to "keep abreast" of this literature.

G5.1.4 What percent of the teachers and other professional school personnel prepared at the graduate level during the last two years actually entered the professional roles for which they prepared?

This is a hangover from an over-supply of jobs. Right now and in the future, it will be no basis for assessing institutional relevance.

G5.1.5 What characteristics of school personnel prepared in the advanced program have been revealed through evaluation of graduates?

This is fine; it requires continuous institutional research.

G5.2 *Use of Evaluation Results to Improve Advanced Programs*
Standard: The institution uses the evaluation results in the study, development, and improvement of its advanced programs.

This should be more than dropping or adding a course. It might deal with changing the objectives of a program, the selection of students, or the field work involved.

G5.2.1 What strengths and weaknesses in the advanced programs have been revealed through evaluation of graduates?

Students who quit should be involved; too often the "successful" student is the only feedback. Shouldn't this standard also seek reactions and data from employers and clients?

G5.2.2 What does the institution do to ensure that the results obtained from evaluating its graduates are translated into appropriate program modifications?

The best way is to have the study conducted by an objective group outside the university or, at least, use faculty to look at other programs than their own.

G5.3 *Long-Range Planning*
Standard: The institution has plans for the long-range development of its advanced programs; these plans are part of a design for total institutional development.

This will be even more important as time passes. With less money there must be priority setting. More programs will be dropped and decreased in size than in the past.

G5.3.1 What evidence indicates that the institution has, or is, engaged in studies and/or institutional research to improve its advanced programs?

A council meeting of deans, directors, and department chairmen will not be equal to this task; they have neither the data nor the ability to deal with the issues apart from representing their particular faculty constituencies.

G5.3.2 What information shows that the faculty members conducting the advanced programs participate in the formulation of the institution's plans for the long-range development of these programs?

The key word here is *participate.* If it means that faculty will not be the only voice but will also be involved with graduate students, employers of their graduates, clients of their graduates, the public, disinterested faculty, etc., there is a chance the planning will be genuine. If *participation* means faculty domination, the concept of real planning is irretrievably lost.

G5.3.3 What is the institution's plan for future development of advanced programs and what rationale supports significant changes that are proposed?

Lack of funds is not a rationale. This standard is stated in an unappealing manner that assumes that change should be justified. The programs that go unchanged in a society that is four feet off the ground and whirling in random directions should be justified. What is the rationale for *not* changing programs when the needs of the schools, the knowledges required, the purposes of public education, and the social setting itself are undergoing genuine growing pains?

Summary: Who should be involved in evaluation and planning? Successful and unsuccessful students, faculty, and other constituencies need clearer guidelines of the ways in which they should be involved, with how much power, and in which decisions.

Generally these standards are a marked improvement over the days of unbridled expansion when there was no need to set goals and priorities. The shortage of jobs and funds will have a salutary effect in fostering planning, but these circumstances are not in themselves the criteria or rationale for program development.

Planning standards could be significantly improved if specific mention were made of the faculties throughout the university, public school officials, all forms of professional personnel, the public, students, and youth. It is perfectly possible, and unfortunate, that even if these standards are met, teacher education may remain buried in the university, where everyone is an innovator regarding the world outside and a preserver regarding academe.

The NCATE standards are quite clearly the most comprehensive guides ever developed for assessing educational training. They provide a sound basis for judging present programs, as well as systematic guidance for institutions engaging in self-study and self-improvement.

The glaring shortcoming of these standards—their frequent lack of specificity—may in the final analysis be their greatest strength. Driven by budgetary necessities, professional pressures, and public scrutiny, institutions may very well establish higher minimum standards and expectations than those set at a national level.

The particular standards analyzed here will be in use through the 1970s. They were developed and put into the field just as the job market for teachers and other personnel shifted from shortage to oversupply; beginning faculty with doctorates became plentiful; state legislatures began to cut university budgets; trustees and regents began to look at faculty work loads; federal grants to schools of education started to fade; the appropriateness of the university's direct involvement in social action (Head Start, community development, alternative schools, etc.) came under serious reconsideration; and the view that education as a social institution could be "the" vehicle for equalizing economic and social opportunity in America was recognized as a fantasy.

The next decade, in which universities will be pushed and pulled in random and contradictory directions simultaneously, will be a severe test of whether these standards have identified some persistent truths about teacher education or were merely "children" of their time, that is, the best guides we could conceive, given the social setting of the late 1960s. Our feeling is that these standards will become as effective and as high as the national faculty of teacher educators make them. Will teacher educators become "professionals" or remain disassociated individuals who happen to work in universities?

Notes

1. National Council for the Accreditation of Teacher Education, *Standards for the Accreditation of Teacher Education* (Washington, D.C.: The Council, January 1970), p. 3.

2. Ibid., p. 5.

3. Ibid., p. 6.

4. Ibid., p. 5.

5. *A Report of The School of Education, University of Kansas to The NCATE* (Lawrence, Kan.: Spring 1971), p. 34.

6. Seymour B. Sarason, Kenneth Davidson, and Burton Blatt, *The Preparation of Teachers* (New York: John Wiley & Sons, 1962).

7. NCATE, *Standards,* p. 12.

8. NCATE, *Standards,* p. 12.

9. NCATE, *Standards,* p. 18.

10. NCATE, *Standards,* p. 20.

11. NCATE, *Standards,* p. 21.

12. NCATE, *Standards,* p. 22.

14

Implications for the Future of Teacher Education

When analyzing bureaucracies, the obvious trends are the most misleading. The shortage of teaching jobs and the financial cuts being forced on schools of education seem to indicate clear directions. It must be remembered, however, that the universities controlling teacher education are more complex organizations than is generally supposed, and therefore all commonsense truisms are inevitably inaccurate. If the history of bureaucratic functioning is a valid basis for predicting the future of schools of education, they will continue to expand in the next decade in spite of sporadic setbacks. Similarly, the numbers of students being prepared to teach will not be reduced but continue to grow.

The reasons for this apparently unreasonable growth are natural and not difficult discover. Since schools of education budgets, like all other college budgets, are related to the numbers of students who are enrolled in courses and programs, even the most modestly endowed administrator soon discerns that it is to his disadvantage to cut back on students in his courses. If a cut is forced on him by an overly specific state legislature or board of regents, he can expand elsewhere. For example, if a ceiling were placed on the preservice preparation of secondary social studies teachers, the administrator affected would quickly become sensitive to a new "need" for courses and workshops for inservice teachers of the social studies. Administrators can become quite creative at maintaining and even expanding the numbers of students they serve, since these figures form the basis for justifying their operating budgets. The school of education administrator is frequently protected by the general administration of the university, which also has a need to keep enrollments up. In a few cases, some central administrators see this as an opportunity to cut down on education students and "beef up" other colleges, but these kinds of administrators are both ill-advised and nonresponsive to students.

From the students' point of view, there will be an uninterrupted growth of their need for relevance as they perceive it. The shortage of jobs is more likely to fan interest in nonschool forms of alternative education than to cause students to self-select out of preservice programs and abandon their interests in teaching altogether. Other social service professions will not fire the imagination of these students, and the cutback in less humanely oriented occupations may actually increase the number of preservice students. The likelihood that this latter population of students may be less socially conscious and less action oriented than education, social science, and arts types, does not change the fact that they will be added to the ranks of future preparation programs.

The implications of present trends for teacher education are, therefore, relatively straightforward. Our entire system of higher education is moving toward increased access. We seem to have accepted the notion that equal opportunity means that everyone who chooses should have at least a chance to try some form of higher education. As this trend develops, it will change our values in three stages. The right to open access or open enrollment will become the right to self-select or participate in any university program, and ultimately this will become the right to universal, successful completion. For teacher education, these general university trends will culminate in a continuous increase in self-selected, certified graduates. Therefore, the important question is not, Will teacher education expand or contract? but, In what directions will teacher education programs develop in the future?

Intensification of the College-Public School Schism

The growing group identity and organizational power among teachers will lead to an increasing estrangement between classroom practitioners and teacher educators on college faculty, if it is possible to rupture this "partnership" any further. The intensification of this cleavage will be not only the most likely but also the most significant future trend in education. An example of this trend, if one were needed, can be seen in the problem of finding support for *The Journal of Teacher Education.* Although this is the only journal in the field of teacher education and an outstanding publication when compared to other professional journals, the National Education Association will discontinue its support. The association will rhetorically ask the question, Why should an association that represents classroom teachers support a journal for college professors, graduate students, and others interested in teacher education? The fact that this seems to be a reasonable question for teachers to ask in the first place is evidence of the schism between the practitioners and the teacher educators; the fact that it will be answered behaviorally by the NEA's withdrawal of support for activities in teacher education, testifies to the intensification of the existing breakdown of communication.

The general lack of concern among teacher educators about teachers' contract negotiations and strikes and the attempt to impose accountability measures on them, is another symptom of this growing divergence. In truth, many college faculty have been in the forefront of the accountability movement and in the education of and consultation with school administrators engaged in negotiations with teachers. Other college faculty regard these problems as worthy of a new lecture or another article, but they are increasingly less likely to take an activist part in the teacher movement. As college teachers, professional educators are more likely to demonstrate for peace or academic freedom than to express their activism in relation to issues that also concern classroom teachers, such as salary, individualized instruction, open education, year-round schools, teacher aides, and new media.

The most legitimate reason for mutual relations in the past was that colleges needed placements for student teachers. This partnership was never an expression of felt need by the main body of either teacher educators or classroom practitioners. The "cooperation" was between college administrators and public school administrators, or more specifically between college directors of student teaching who sought student teaching placements and school administrators who needed new teachers and wanted to attract large numbers of students and interns from whom to recruit their beginners. Now that teaching positions are scarce, even that much cooperation must inevitably wither, because it is no longer necessary to public schools.

Decrease of Teacher Involvement in College Program Accreditation

The foregoing predictions might give the impression that the growing schism between college faculty and practicing teachers is the responsibility of the associations representing them. This is not the case. Another group that must share the responsibility is the college administrators, i.e., deans, who control the accreditation procedures used by the National Council for the Accreditation of Teacher Education Programs (NCATE).

Classroom teachers have traditionally been part of the visitation teams that NCATE sends to colleges and universities for the on-site gathering of data on which to base its accreditation decisions. In recent years some teams did not include classroom teachers, and the NEA is now quite likely to withdraw its annual support to the NCATE, because it feels that classroom teachers are being slighted in the composition of visitation teams. Whether there are enough classroom teachers on these teams is actually a less important question than whether classroom teachers are genuinely involved in teacher education decision making on a real rather than token basis. Some of the justifiable questions being raised include: "To what extent were any classroom teachers initially involved in planning these 'college' programs in the first place?"; "To what extent has the advice of any classroom teachers been implemented as a force for significantly changing any program of teacher education?"; and "Why should the NEA, whose primary constituency is the classroom and school practitioner, support an accreditation bureaucracy that serves only to legitimize and justify school of education administrators with their central administrations and regents?" While many of us think we can successfully answer these questions, we can easily predict that the members of NEA (i.e., organized teachers) will withdraw their support for the NCATE and for all other teacher education activities if they are expected merely to rubber-stamp the college-dominated system of teacher education.

It seems to many teachers that the deans of the schools of education, more than any other constituency, need to be successfully accredited and superficially "involve" faculty, students, graduates, and practitioners as they deem necessary. It is difficult for the deans to deny this charge when their own association literature points out the threats and dangers of too much involvement by classroom teachers in any real and powerful decision-making process. One bulletin distributed at the 1972 convention of the American Association of Colleges for Teacher Education (AACTE) fairly whined about the balance of classroom teachers to college faculty and administrators on a proposed commission to control state certification and oversee licensure practices. "Bad balance" means more teachers than college people and "control" means sharing the power now exercised informally and discreetly (inhouse) by state department officials and college deans. It is not difficult, therefore, to foresee a decrease in organized teacher involvement in teacher education (recognizing that it was always token involvement anyhow), when the NEA is pulling back, and the AACTE is cooperating by responding very defensively to any honest teachers' proposal to become involved in teacher education with real power to resist and initiate in place of the token power to recommend and rubber-stamp.

Increased Direct Competition for State Funds

The trend toward more support for public education from state funds and less from local property taxes is already well established. It is inevitable that state legislators will view funds for education as coming from one basic source and therefore, to be dispensed in one package. In place of the old issues, such as which campus of the state university should get a new dormitory, future decisions are more likely to pit one level of education against another and then set priorities; for example, Should kindergarten attendance be made compulsory? or Should a new community college be built? "After all, it's all state money to be expended in the best interests of all the people."

Another example of this competition for the same funds between public schools and institutions of higher education is exemplified in the recommendation of some school superintendents to drop the fourth, or senior, year of high school and make secondary education a basic three-year program. Obviously, this puts a greater financial burden on postsecondary facilities. In effect, most public school schemes to save money achieve this "saving" at the expense of other state-supported institutions. Similarly, many college-initiated proposals for improving educational opportunities would increase the cost of high schools and other postsecondary schools that are also state supported.

Against this background of increasingly open competition for the same state funds will come an even more lethal form of combat. Salaries for the faculty in state colleges and even in state universities will inevitably be compared with those of faculty in technical schools, junior colleges, community colleges, and high schools. Since the overwhelming expense item in supporting schools is teacher salaries, and since the state will assume a larger share of such local school support, it takes little imagination to see that comparisons will be readily made among teachers in all forms of publicly supported schools, regardless of their level.

The drive, led by college regents, to reemphasize the values and importance of undergraduate instruction will also further such teacher comparisons. As college faculty are rewarded for teaching, rather than for writing and research, and moved out of merit systems into set salary schedules, comparisons between teachers on all levels will be simplified. Obviously, it is easier to compare the work of a high school teacher with that of a college teacher if the latter is expected to devote all his time to instruction.

Theoretically, competition is desirable because it improves effort and product. In the case of teachers and other functionaries in large bureaucracies, it is more likely to increase stress than output. In any event, for the purposes of this analysis it is sufficient to close the argument at this point. New directions in state funding will place classroom teachers and college faculty on a collision course over salaries. This confrontation will be one major cause of the widening schism discussed in the previous two sections.

Clarification and Intensification of Differences in Teacher Education Approaches

Curriculum controversies have always been present in schools in an oversimplified form. At various times these issues have been dichotomized as statements of purpose: the subject matter or the child; cognitive versus affective development; basic skills versus thinking processes; and most recently, open education versus behavioral objectives. The distinctive feature of the present controversies is not that they are really new but that they are finally exerting a real force on teacher education. New preparation programs are being developed and old ones revised in ways that support open education or that prepare teachers to function behaviorally. The former is characterized by an emphasis on students' self-determination of what they think they need to learn to be teachers, i.e., wide student-selected electives; student-controlled grading; student evaluation of faculty; and student-controlled professional laboratory experiences. (The Institute in Education at UWM is an outstanding example of open teacher education.) The latter is characterized by microteaching and other forms of demonstrated student competence in skills defined by experts as minimum essentials for all teachers. (The Wilkits and program developed at Weber State in Utah are a good example of this approach.) The trend toward greater instructional control, behaviorism, and accountability is certainly the more dominant trend. This accurately reflects the conditions in public schools, where, while open education is receiving some scattered trials and much more rhetoric, the real force is for greater clarity and narrowness of learning and teaching objectives, more careful assessment, and more teacher and school accountability for its "products."

More Federal Support for Practitioner Controlled Teacher Education

The Office of Education, during the tenure of Sidney Marland, and congress, under the educational leadership of Edith Green, have made it quite clear that they regard the extensive federal expenditures to schools of education as not having changed anything important about teacher education: particularly its nonrelevance to school problems. When one views the problems faced by urban school teachers and assesses the responsiveness and applicability of the special programs offered by universities, it is indeed a dismal picture. Colleges and universities have generally accepted support for extra or special programs without altering their basic programs. As a result, when federal support is terminated the programs are discontinued with little permanent imprint on teacher education. Schools of education would be hard pressed to specify any important differences in their present programs that have resulted from NDEA Institutes, Teacher Corps, Headstart Leadership Training, aides programs, or the numerous teacher grant programs.

Since federal and private foundation officials are unanimous in their view that schools of education will neither change themselves radically nor bring about significant change in other educational institutions, the future is not hard to anticipate. Renewal centers controlled by classroom teachers, or other organizational vehicles that are practitioner dominated, will be more likely to receive major federal support than programs in schools of education. The real issue will be the extent to which classroom teachers and their organizations are willing to take over programs and assume real responsibility for teacher education. In the past the basic funding went to colleges and universities, provided they could demonstrate "cooperation" with local school administrations. (In behavioral terms, *cooperation* means a signature on a proposal.) In future, more funding for teacher education is likely to go to teachers' groups, who will then involve college faculty and anyone else they choose as individual resources.

The dangerous result of making teachers second-class citizens in teacher education is that they have learned this role perhaps too well. The issue to be resolved in future is whether teachers' groups can meet the challenge of being genuinely powerful in determining new forms of teacher education. The money and opportunity will be available, provided teachers rise to the challenge. Many classroom teachers feel that they have more immediate functions than preparing beginners for nonexistent jobs. Others see that this involvement can make teachers' groups more powerful in both teacher education and as political organizations. Which of these two factions prevails in the determination of teacher organization policy will determine the nature of teacher education for decades to come.